CW00393522

Heidegger's *Being and Time*

Continuum Reader's Guides

Aristotle's Nicomachean Ethics – Christopher Warne
Hobbes' Leviathan – Laurie Bagby
Hume's Enquiry Concerning Human Understanding – Alan Bailey
and Dan O'Brien
Hume's Dialogues Concerning Natural Religion – Andrew Pyle
Nietzsche's Genealogy of Morals – Daniel Conway
Plato's Republic – Luke Purshouse
Wittgenstein's Tractatus Logico Philosophicus – Roger M. White

Heidegger's *Being and Time*

A Reader's Guide

WILLIAM BLATTNER

continuum

CONTINUUM INTERNATIONAL PUBLISHING GROUP
The Tower Building   80 Maiden Lane
11 York Road   Suite 704
London SE1 7NX   New York, NY10038

© William Blattner 2006
First published 2006
Reprinted 2007, 2008 (twice), 2009

All rights reserved. No part of this publication may be reproduced or
transmitted in any form or by any means, electronic or mechanical,
including photocopying, recording or any information storage or retrieval
system, without prior permission from the publishers.

William Blattner has asserted his right under the Copyright, Designs and
Patents Act, 1988, to be identified as Author of this work

British Library Cataloguing-in-Publication Data
A catalogue record for this book is available from the British Library.

Library of Congress Cataloging-in-Publication Data
A catalog record for this book is available from the Library of Congress.

ISBN 978-0-8264-8608-0 (hardback) 978-0-8264-8609-7 (paperback)

Typeset by RefineCatch Limited, Bungay, Suffolk
Printed and bound in the U.S.A. by Versa Press, Inc

For Alisa

CONTENTS

ACKNOWLEDGEMENTS

I would not have been able to write this book without the inspiration, assistance and support of many people. Just more than a quarter century ago I was fortunate to take courses on Husserl and Heidegger at UC/ Berkeley with Bert Dreyfus. Bert's approach to *Being and Time* remains to this day an inspiration for my own reading. After leaving Berkeley, my study of *Being and Time* continued under the supervision of my doctoral advisor, John Haugeland, who modelled for me a commitment to never letting the text become stale, to remaining open to surprise. Over the past eight years I have received considerable assistance not only from Bert and John, but also Taylor Carman, Steve Crowell, Charlie Guignon, Mark Okrent, Iain Thompson, Mark Wrathall, as well the participants in the annual meetings of the International Society for Phenomenological Studies in Asilomar, Ca., where I presented elements of the interpretation I offer in this Reader's Guide. I would also like to thank Mark Wrathall and the Philosophy Dept., College of Humanities, and Center for the Study of Europe at Brigham Young University, who sponsored the "Colloquium on Contemporary European Philosophy" (2005) at which I presented some of this material; Stephen Käufer and his Spring 2006 *Being and Time* course, and the Dept. of Philosophy at Franklin and Marshall College; as well as Chris Williams and the Dept. of Philosophy at the University of Nevada, Reno, for the September 2004 "Symposium on Phenomenology." All of my courses on *Being and Time* over my sixteen years at Georgetown University have been laboratories for presenting, discussing, and modifying my approach to *Being and Time*, and I am grateful to my students for their enthusiasm and engagement. I am grateful to my chair, Wayne Davis, who allowed me to teach those many courses on *Being and Time*, as well as for his unrelenting support of my research. I received funding for a critical summer of work on this book from the Graduate School of Arts and Sciences at Georgetown. Finally, my family, Alisa, Willie, and Sam, have put up with a lot of distraction over the past two years, but have also encouraged me to follow my passion.

CHAPTER I

CONTEXT

Being and Time was published in 1927 and rapidly became one of the most significant and controversial philosophical texts of the twentieth century.[1] It sits at the confluence of several important streams of thought in the early twentieth century, including phenomenology, existentialism, neo-Scholasticism, and hermeneutics. It also stands at the "parting of ways" between so-called analytic and Continental philosophy, as one scholar has called it.[2] It is, in short, a focal point of many of the most interesting and contentious philosophical debates of the last century.

Martin Heidegger's journey on the way to *Being and Time* is improbable. It was a journey that led him from his childhood in Meßkirch, a small town in rural Baden not far from Lake Constance (or the *Bodensee*, as Germans call it) where he was born in 1889, to Freiburg, one of the more outward-looking cities in Germany. Heidegger was raised Catholic, and his education was supported by the Church. After beginning his education in state schools, he was able to attend college preparatory secondary schools in Konstanz and Freiburg as a "scholarship boy" preparing for the priesthood. His early ambition in life was to be Jesuit priest. After completing his secondary education in Freiburg in 1909, Heidegger briefly sought to join the Jesuit Order, then subsequently to become a diocesan priest, but in both cases he was judged physically unfit due to a heart ailment. (The same ailment kept him off the battlefront during the First World War.)

Heidegger studied at Freiburg University, spending his first two years in theology as preparation for the priesthood, then his third and fourth years in mathematics with the aim of becoming a secondary school math teacher. While "majoring" in theology and then math, Heidegger also studied philosophy, and four years after enter-ing the University he submitted a doctoral dissertation on the phil-osophy of logic and was awarded a PhD. In Germany still to this day, after earning a doctorate one must write a second dissertation, the *Habilitation*, in order to earn the right to teach at a university. Between 1913 and 1915 Heidegger wrote his *Habilitation* on "The Theory of Categories and Meaning in Duns Scotus," while being supported by a grant from the Church in Freiburg.[3]

Heidegger's intellectual focus during this time period was already indicative of his future course: in both his doctoral dissertation and his *Habilitation*, Heidegger explored issues in the foundation of meaning, logic, and intentionality (the mind's capacity to represent the world around it) by means of phenomenological method. Phe-nomenology was the name that Edmund Husserl (1859–1938) gave to his philosophical methodology. It is way of studying intentionality by disentangling the mind's representation from both the objects it represents and from the psychological states that do the represent-ing. By means of phenomenology, Husserl aimed to free philosophy both from insecure foundations in what people happen to or even must think, and from distracting metaphysical questions about the "true" nature of the world.

Heidegger appropriated phenomenological method to address questions that Husserl thought he had put out of play, questions of metaphysics and ontology. In doing so he was deeply influenced by Immanuel Kant's (1724–1804) transcendental philosophy. Kant argued that we are not able to know the constitution of the world as it is in itself; we are restricted to examining the world as it appears to us. We are able to learn *a priori* the structure and rules that govern this world of appearance, and so some *a priori* knowledge is available to philosophical reflection. Put this simply, Kant's position sounds like a form of skepticism, but Kant added a twist that blunts its skeptical implications. Kant argued that space and time and every-thing within them are merely appearances, so that in learning the structure and rules of appearance, we are knowing the structure of nature itself. In rejecting knowledge of the world as it is in itself, Kant merely blocks claims to know an unintelligible supersensible or supernatural realm.

Heidegger develops a synthesis of Husserlian phenomenology, Kantian transcendental philosophy, and traditional ontology. Trad-itional ontology, beginning with Aristotle and reaching an apex in the High Middle Ages, sought to develop a theory of the basic categories of things that are (entities), an inventory of the furniture of the universe. Detailed questions, such as whether there are both cats and dogs or whether duck-billed platypuses are mammals, should be left to scientific research. Philosophers concern themselves only with the highest order genera of entities, such as souls, physical things, numbers, etc., and with the categorial structure of entities, such as the distinction between essence and accident. During the late nineteenth century, neo-Scholasticism became a strong force in the Catholic intellectual world, and among the aspects of the Scholasticism of the Middle Ages it revived were these ontological questions. Heidegger reports reading Franz Brentano's *On the Manifold Senses of Being in Aristotle* in 1907 (at the age of eighteen),[4] finding himself drawn to neo-Scholastic ontological questions.

Whereas traditional ontology and neo-Scholasticism thought of ontological questions as "hard" metaphysical questions about the nature of the world as it is in itself – what else could "being" be? – Heidegger applied Kant's transcendental turn to ontology and converted it into a study of the structure and rules of our *understanding* of being. Kant declined to refer to transcendental reflection on the structure of understanding as a form of "ontology": "The proud name of ontology must give way to the modest one of a mere analytic of pure understanding."[5] After all, if transcendental reflection cannot study the world as it is in itself, then it is not a form of ontology. Heidegger responds that the very distinction between the world as we understand it and the world as it is in itself is ill-formed, so that to investigate the limits and requirements of our understanding of being is to investigate the only thing we can mean by "being." Ontology, as the science of the meaning of being, *is* the "analytic of pure understanding." Phenomenology, as the study of intentionality, will be the method of Heidegger's inquiries.

Two other major streams of nineteenth and early twentieth century thought feed into Heidegger's philosophical project as well. In his youth Heidegger was a deeply religious man. After abandoning his aspirations to the priesthood, he set his sights on a chair in Catholic philosophy, and the Church supported him with grants for his *Habilitation* research on Scholastic philosophy. After completing his *Habilitation* (and also failing to receive an appointment as a professor of Catholic philosophy) Heidegger's religious convictions began to change. At the same time he also met and courted his future wife, Elfride, who was a Protestant. By 1919 Heidegger was ready to break formal ties with the Catholic Church, and in a letter to his friend Father Engelbert Krebs he avowed that "Epistemological insights extending to a theory of historical knowledge have made the *system* of Catholicism problematic and unacceptable to me, but not Christianity and metaphysics – these, though, in a new sense."[6] Heidegger continued to lecture on the philosophy of religion, but increasingly his philosophical perspective on religion reflected existentialist and historical concerns.[7]

"Existentialism" is not a precisely defined term. It refers not to a movement or school of thought, but rather to a sensibility and a set of issues. It is, moreover, as much a literary sensibility as it is a set of philosophical ideas. Heidegger was deeply influenced by two existentialist philosophers, Søren Kierkegaard (1813–1855) and Friedrich Nietzsche (1844–1900). Kierkegaard and Nietzsche are in many respects deeply opposed in their ways of thinking, yet they share a reaction to the philosophical tradition that precedes them. They regard it as overly focused on the achievements of cognition and as offering very little insight that can touch the *lives* of individuals. It is also characteristic of existentialism to regard everyday human life as something of a sham, as a distortion of a more distressing underlying truth. This truth, once exposed, can serve as a springboard for personal liberation, however, and that makes confronting it worthwhile.

This interest in the everyday and the meanings it both embodies and covers up calls for some way of approaching human practice and mining its significance. It calls for a method of interpreting meaningful behavior. Wilhelm Dilthey (1833–1911) had developed just such a methodology with his theory of hermeneutics. Dilthey argued that the techniques we must use in order to understand meaningful human behavior, symbols, and linguistic expressions differ from those techniques used in the natural sciences. The natural sciences seek to "explain" natural events by subsuming them under general laws that are applicable everywhere and at all times, whereas the human studies aim to "understand" meaningful human expressions by putting them into their concrete social and historical contexts. The natural sciences aim for generality, whereas the human studies aim for context-sensitivity. In *Being and Time* Heidegger argues that meaningful human activity, language, and the artifacts and paraphernalia of our world not only make sense in terms of their concrete social and cultural context, but also only *are* what they are in terms of that context. In other words, Heidegger converts Dilthey's methodological theses into an ontology. As we shall see below, existentialism and hermeneutics have as significant an influence on *Being and Time* as do phenomenology, ontology, and transcendental philosophy.

During the time of his assistantship with Husserl, Heidegger began working on what he hoped would be his first significant piece of scholarship, a phenomenological interpretation of Aristotle. On the basis of a draft of this work, as well as Husserl's recommendation, Heidegger secured appointment as an "extraordinary" or associate professor at the University of Marburg in 1923. During his time at Marburg (1923–1928) Heidegger focused on Aristotle and Kant, and he wrote *Being and Time*. He also engaged in a notorious affair with his then student, Hannah Arendt, which has been the focus of much prurient interest and fodder for intellectual gossip. He maintained a close friendship with Karl Jaspers (1883–1969), a leading existentialist philosopher who taught in Heidelberg, and the correspondence between Heidegger and Jaspers makes for fascinating reading. Heidegger conceived of himself and Jaspers as philosophical revolutionaries aiming to overturn the abstractions and ossifications of the philosophical research of the previous generations.[8] Heidegger's lectures from this time have also proven to be of lasting interest for scholars, especially his *History of the Concept of Time, Logic, Basic Problems of Phenomenology*, and *Metaphysical Foundations of Logic*. This was a very creative period in Heidegger's life, and it was the time when he drafted and then published the extant portions of *Being and Time*.

In 1926, while he was working on *Being and Time*, the philosophical faculty at Marburg recommended Heidegger for promotion to a vacant chair in philosophy, but the promotion request was denied higher up the food chain on the grounds that Heidegger had not published any significant work in ten years. The draft of division I of *Being and Time* was not sufficient. Heidegger kept hard at work, and divisions I and II were published in Husserl's journal of phenomenology – the *Yearbook for Philosophy and Phenomenological Research* (vol. 8, 1927). The reception of *Being and Time* was strong enough to secure Heidegger Husserl's chair in philosophy at the University of Freiburg upon Husserl's retirement in 1928.

He had, however, drifted rather far from his mentor's guiding ideas, as became clear to everyone quite rapidly. Heidegger's "inaugural address" as professor of philosophy at Freiburg was his "What is Metaphysics?" In this lecture Heidegger argues for two theses that are antithetical to Husserl's thought: that philosophy must break the "dominion of logic" and that the experience of anxiety is indispensable for carrying out intellectual research. "What is Metaphysics?" was a pivot point in Heidegger's intellectual development. By 1929 he was beginning to see that the philosophical project on which he had been at work did not hang together, and this led him to abandon it and turn in a new direction altogether. By 1936 or so, the complexion of Heidegger's writing had changed dramatically. Gone were the systematic metaphysics and ontology of his earlier years. Gone was the explicit devotion to phenomenology. Gone were the repeated forays into Aristotle, the Scholastics, and Kant (although of course he never abandoned these authors entirely). Nietzsche supplanted the earlier authors as the prime focus of Heidegger's interest, and Heidegger (like Nietzsche) began to experiment with a philosophical form of cultural criticism (e.g., "The Question Concerning Technology"). Further, poetry supplanted logic as the originary bearer of our understanding of being. This transformation of Heidegger's thought is generally called his "turn."

This is the Heidegger to whom so many English-speaking academic philosophers have reacted so negatively. In "breaking the dominion of logic" Heidegger looks to some as someone who would disregard the controlling influence of consistency and clear thought. He looks like an irrationalist. This is a misimpression, but it is true that in his later period Heidegger rejects the standard concerns of academic philosophy – logic, theory of knowledge, philosophy of language, metaphysics. Like Nietzsche, Kierkegaard, and others, Heidegger's later thought takes on a style that places it on the outskirts of philosophy. This alone would be sufficient to alienate many academic philosophers, who are committed to the traditional problems and methods. It was not the sole factor in Heidegger's exile, however.

In 1933 Heidegger became *Rektor* (president) of Freiburg University, joined the Nazi party, and implemented some of the Nazi program of *Gleichschaltung* or realignment. Heidegger's flirtation with extreme right-wing thought had been growing for a number of years. His presidency lasted only about a year, after which he returned to his regular teaching duties until the end of the War in

1945. He broke off or destroyed many friendships during this period, including with Jaspers (whose wife was Jewish). Although the evidence for Heidegger's anti-Semitism is equivocal,[9] it is impossible to imagine anyone joining the Nazi party without sympathy for anti-Semitism. Heidegger's subsequent self-exculpation, that he had joined the party and become rector of the university in order to protect it from Nazi encroachment, has been conclusively refuted. When he tried to enlist Jaspers in his defense during his de-Nazification trial, Jaspers rebuffed him and submitted a damning letter recommending that Heidegger lose his right to teach. The de-Nazification commission indeed did strip him of his right to teach, a right he regained some years later along with the title of professor emeritus.

One of the more vexing problems studied by scholars of Heidegger's work over the past twenty years has been the question whether there is any connection between Heidegger's political engagement with Nazism and his philosophy.[10] One can find thematic associations between *Being and Time* and the revolutionary conservatism of the Nazi movement. One can also find some of the anti-urban rhetoric (under the heading of "the public") that was characteristic of attacks on urban Jewish life. Attempts to construct a direct connection between *Being and Time* and Nazism have failed, however. Nevertheless, Heidegger's cooperation with the Nazi regime, and some of his speeches and actions during this period, forever and understandably alienated many of his contemporaries, who have passed their antipathy on to their students. Without trying to exculpate the man Martin Heidegger for his disgraceful behavior, nor soft-pedal the wreckage caused by the rectorship of Martin Heidegger the academic politician, we can read *Being and Time* with a wary eye on Heidegger's politics, but an open mind for his philosophical innovations. Such a reading is worth pursuing, both because the ideas advanced in *Being and Time* are so powerful, as well as because of the immense influence that this treatise had on the further development of European philosophy from the 1930s on (of which more in chapter 4 below).

During the 1950s and '60s Heidegger lectured extensively, held seminars, and continued to think about the issues that had come to organize his reflection: the history of being (the way in which our understanding of being, along with the being of entities itself, changes); the modern understanding of being, which he called "technology"; the "truth of being" as the most basic experience of intelligibility, one which he came to associate with the thematics of medieval mysticism; and the role of language in human experience. His later works have no *magnum opus*, as *Being and Time* is for his early period, and his reflections appear to wander this way and that, groping for an adequate way to talk about the phenomena in which he is interested. Heidegger gave a "parting" interview to *Der Spiegel* magazine, in which he covered a lot of ground, including the dire threats to human life that he saw in the modern era, as well touching in an unsatisfactory way on his involvement with Nazism. He asked that the interview not be published until his death.[11] It was published shortly after Heidegger died in 1976 at the age of eighty-six.

CHAPTER 2

OVERVIEW OF THEMES

Being and Time is a phenomenology of everyday human life and an exploration of the transformations of self that can take place in encounters with the most extreme existential challenges that we confront. Officially, however, the extant portion of the treatise is the first step on the path to a general ontology, an examination of the most rarified of philosophical questions, the "question of being." Heidegger conceived *Being and Time* as an ambitious two-part work, each part with three divisions. Part One of the treatise was to be a systematic development of a phenomenological ontology and Part Two a critical evaluation of the history of Western philosophy. Of this formidable plan, Heidegger only wrote two-thirds of Part One, what we know today as divisions I and II of *Being and Time*. Division I is the phenomenology of everyday life, division II the exploration of existential themes.

The main thrust of division I of *Being and Time* is that the philosophical tradition has misunderstood human experience by imposing a subject–object schema upon it. The individual human being has traditionally been understood as a rational animal, that is, an animal with cognitive powers, in particular the power to represent the world around it. The relationship between the cognitive powers of mind and the physical seat of the mind in the brain is, of course, a vexed issue (the so-called Mind–Body Problem), but whatever position one takes on that issue, the notion that human beings are persons and that persons are centers of subjective experience has been broadly accepted. If left rather vague there is no harm in such a way of talking about our experience. Where the tradition has gone wrong is that it has interpreted subjectivity in a specific way, by means of concepts of "inner" and "outer," "representation" and "object."

The language of internal and external, inner and outer, and so on, dominates modern philosophy, from Descartes through Kant to Husserl. Descartes tells us, for example, that the idea of the sun *is* the sun, albeit as it normally exists "in" the mind.[1] Even after Descartes's medieval way of talking about ideas was replaced by more antiseptic language, such as talk of ideas having "content," the notion persisted that ideas are "in" the mind and that when they are true, they correspond to a world "outside" the mind. Philosophers, Descartes first among them, are quick to remind us that ideas are not literally inside us, at least not in the way in which neurons are, but rather are in us in some other, unspecified way. This way of talking about ideas derives ultimately from Aristotle's theory of mind, which in turn was embedded in his physical theory and metaphysics. Even though the Scientific Revolution left Aristotle's account of the world in the rearview mirror, philosophers continued to rely on its metaphorical economy, talking about objects that exist "in" ideas, ideas that have "content." Divorced from their Aristotelian context, however, these metaphors have lost all meaning.

And no matter how this inner sphere may get interpreted, if one does no more than ask how cognition makes its way "out of" it and achieves "transcendence," it becomes evident that the cognition which presents such enigmas will remain problematical unless one has previously clarified how it is and what it is. (87/60)

It is charming to think of ideas as having content, just as it is charming to think of stars as revolving on crystalline spheres, but none of this means anything after the Scientific Revolution.

Heidegger's worry here cannot merely be that the language of inner and outer, subject and object, is metaphorical. Heidegger himself relies extensively on metaphors throughout *Being and Time*. In §28 he tries to clarify the concepts of disclosedness and being-in by way of the metaphor of a clearing, a clearing in a forest, an open space in which things can make their appearance. He contrasts this metaphor of clearing with the traditional metaphor of light (as in the light of nature), thereby recommending replacing one metaphor with another. Heidegger's worry is, rather, twofold. First, philosophers use the language of inner and outer, idea and content, without doing anything to ground the language in a new theory of mind. Philosophers do often give very detailed analyses of the semantics of content and the logical structure of ideas or language; Husserl's own theory of intentionality was certainly the most formidable such theory ever offered, but humbler (and more plausible) contemporary theories of content do the same thing. Still, we are never told what the basic building blocks of intentionality and linguistic meaning are. These building blocks have names, like "reference," but we do not know what reference *is*. Since Heidegger wrote *Being and Time* some theories that would address this worry have been offered, notably causal theories of reference. Even though the causal theory of reference is generally thought not to work, we would not want to rest Heidegger's case entirely on his identification of a deficiency in existing theories of mind.

His principal charge against the language of subject and object, inner and outer, is that it leads us to offer distorted descriptions of our experience. That is, his objection is *phenomenological*. The language of inner and outer suggests a division or gulf between me, the subject, and it, the object. This gulf is then one that needs to be overcome or transcended by means of a cognitive achievement. Phenomenologically, however, this way of thinking about our position in the world, if it fits any of our experience, fits only modes of experience that Heidegger describes as "deficient."

> If cognition is to be possible as a way of determining the nature of the present-at-hand by observing it, then there must first be a *deficiency* in our having-to-do with the world concernfully. When concern holds itself back from any kind of producing, manipulating, and the like, it puts itself into what is now the sole remaining mode of being-in, the mode of just tarrying amidst. . . . (88/61)

Being in touch with an independent or transcendent object, as an achievement, makes sense as a goal in a situation in which my normal familiarity with the world has become problematic. I type at my keyboard, drink from my coffee mug, and swivel in my chair. When one of these things defies or obstructs my ordinary familiarity, then its nature becomes problematic, and understanding it shows up as an achievement for which to strive. When I spill my coffee, I stare at the mug and ask myself whether it has a leak. I can then try to figure out whether it does, and when I succeed at this, I have overcome a gulf between myself and the object. With this situation in mind, I can begin to ask whether I really ever do overcome this gap, or whether

I am not trapped in some form of isolation. The language of inner and outer captures this isolation well. Heidegger's point is, then, that such isolation is not very common, that it is an unusual way of being in the world. Typically, I am familiar with the world, and its things present no trouble for me. The language of inner and outer does not capture this sort of experience very well at all.

Similarly, normally our interactions with others present no difficulties for us. We smoothly and easily work with others, talk with them, enjoy them, fight with them, and we do not have to ask ourselves what they mean. We do not have to infer the existence of "other minds" from evidence, nor "reconstruct" others' experience in order to understand them. Certainly sometimes we do run into trouble understanding others; in such circumstances expressions such as "a penny for your thoughts" make sense. Such situations, however, are exceptional, rather than normal. Heidegger formulates the issue in terms of empathy: " 'Empathy' does not first constitute being-with; only on the basis of being-with does 'empathy' become possible: it gets its motivation from the unsociability of the dominant modes of being-with" (162/125). Empathy makes sense as a corrective response to indifference or callousness. It does not underlie our understanding one another, however. This point can be extended to other forms of inter-subjective re-construction, such as Donald Davidson's "radical interpretation."[2] If we really were field linguists sojourning with an utterly foreign tribe, we would have to reconstruct the meaning of behavior. This is the sort of thing exploited in the British comedy show "Trigger Happy TV," where Dom Joly and his crew carry out gags like putting a toilet in an elevator and having someone relax on it with a newspaper. Having to interpret someone's behavior by inferring what they are doing from evidence is highly exceptional. Normally we do not have to do this.

Heidegger offers an alternative description of experience. He argues that our fundamental experience of the world is one of *familiarity*. We do not normally experience ourselves as subjects standing over against an object, but rather as at home in a world we already understand. We act in a world in which we are immersed. We are not just absorbed in the world, but our sense of identity, of who we are, cannot be disentangled from the world around us. We are what matters to us in our living; we are implicated in the world. The bulk of division I of *Being and Time* is devoted to spelling out the phenomenology of this familiarity, which Heidegger also calls "disclosedness" and "being-in." That we are primordially familiar with the world and cannot be disentangled from it leads Heidegger to one of his lasting terms of art, *being-in-the-world*, which is (one of) his name(s) for our being.

After devoting chapters 1–5 of division I to the phenomenology of familiarity, Heidegger turns to some philosophical implications of his account, implications of a largely negative nature: he argues that epistemological skepticism, questions about idealism and realism, and the traditional Correspondence Theory of Truth are all unmotivated, because they all rest on the subject–object model of experience. In the case of truth Heidegger replaces the Correspondence Theory not with another theory, but rather with a phenomenology of truth that brings into view the dependence of ordinary truth (the truth of judgments and assertions) on something more basic that he calls "primordial truth." Primordial truth is the world-disclosive function of our basic familiarity.

After working through his phenomenology of everyday life, Heidegger turns to the "existentialist" facet of his thought. He argues that we are susceptible to an extreme condition of experience, in which the mood of anxiety (which I will interpret as closer to our contemporary conception of depression) catapults us into a condition in which we cannot understand ourselves (existential "death") and have nothing to say ("conscience"). This extreme condition of existence brings us face to face with the most elemental aspect of our being, that we are, as Heidegger says, "being-possible." Confronting our being-possible enables us to see more clearly what *sort* of entity we are, that is to say, to see our *being*, and this in turn opens possibilities of liberation and self-ownership that Heidegger explores in division II. Heidegger constructs a "factical ideal" of human life, which he called "ownedness" or "resoluteness," which we will explore below in sections (xiii)–(xvii) of chapter 3.

After revising his phenomenology of everydayness to accommodate the extreme condition of existence and the possibility of self-ownership, Heidegger turns to more abstract themes, including time and what he calls "the Temporality of being." This stage of Heidegger's inquiry in *Being and Time* develops his introductory ontological themes. He opens *Being and Time* with an introduction to the problem of being. As we saw in the previous chapter, his ultimate aim during this early phase of his thought was to develop a general ontology, an account of the meaning of being, and to do so by analyzing the understanding of being phenomenologically. In the first chapter of the introduction to *Being and Time* Heidegger indicates that he will show how the understanding of being is essentially temporal, that is, that being is always understood in terms of time, and that this feature of the understanding of being is to be explained by its temporal structure. Heidegger returns to this theme in the second half of division II. Both because it is unusual for students to venture that deep into *Being and Time* on their first reading, and because the account Heidegger offers is both highly obscure and almost certainly unsuccessful, I will not wade into chapters 4–6 of division II.[3] I will conclude my discussion in this Reader's Guide with Heidegger's account of self-ownership in division II.

We must, however, begin with Heidegger's broad reflections on ontology, for that is where *Being and Time* begins.

A NOTE ON THE TEXT AND TRANSLATION

The standard translation of Heidegger's *Sein und Zeit* is Macquarrie and Robinson's *Being and Time*, published by Harper's in 1962. It is overall an excellent translation, both readable and clear.[4] The texts I quote from *Being and Time* are from this translation. In citations I will use dual pagination, so: (171/132). The number before the stroke refers to the English translation, the number after to the original German. Those readers of this Guide who are using the original German or a different translation can use the German pagination to locate passages cited. Also, as is standard in books on *Being and Time*, I will refer to the chapters of the text thus: I.1, where the Roman numeral refers to the division, the Arabic numeral to the chapter.

Although Macquarrie and Robinson is overall an excellent translation, it is not without its mistakes. I will generally flag such errors as we go, but there are a couple that are worth noting in advance. (Whenever there is an asterisk after the page number, this means that I have altered or corrected the translation beyond merely substituting technical terms as outlined below.)

Being: Macquarrie and Robinson insist on capitalizing the word "being." The capitalization does nothing but add an odd sense of mystery and obscurity to Heidegger's language, something that it certainly does not need. Thus, I will throughout write "being" with a lower-case "b."

Being-alongside: Macquarrie and Robinson render Heidegger's term "*Sein-bei*" as "being-alongside," which is very misleading. *Sein-bei* is our basic familiarity with the entities we encounter in our engaged activity in the world. We are not "alongside" them at all. I will translate "*Sein-bei*" as "being-amidst."[5]

Discover/uncover: Heidegger uses one word, "*entdecken*," where Macquarrie and Robinson use two, "discover" and "uncover." There is no good reason for this confusing of Heidegger's already challenging language, and so I will use "uncover" throughout, mostly because the English word "discover" does not suggest quite the right thing.

The "They": Macquarrie and Robinson use this odd term to translate Heidegger's neologism "*das Man.*" *Das Man* is a noun constructed from the third person, indefinite pronoun "*man*," which means "one," as in "one should not step on the highest rung of the ladder." German uses "*man*" more consistently than English uses "one," for which one largely substitutes "you" these days. Heidegger is quite clear in his descriptions of *das Man* that it is not "them," others from whom I am to be distinguished, but rather something more like everyone and no one. I will interpret *das Man* as the phenomenon of social normativity, and in order to avoid the incorrect suggestions of the phrase "the 'They'," I will use "the Anyone."[6]

State-of-mind: The phenomenon that Heidegger calls "*die Befindlichkeit*" is our always being attuned to the way things matter to us, primarily by way of our moods. I will discuss this term in more detail below, but I should flag now that I will render "*die Befindlichkeit*" as "disposedness."[7]

Authenticity/authentic: The condition of existence that Heidegger calls "*die Eigentlichkeit*" is the counter-possibility to what he calls "being lost in the Anyone." "Authenticity" is a plausible translation of this term, but I will render it as "ownedness," because the phenomenon Heidegger is trying to capture with this language is not a matter of being true to anything, but rather of owning who and how one is.

CHAPTER 3

READING THE TEXT

I. ONTOLOGY

What is being? The word "being" is one of those philosopher's words that makes non-philosophers a bit uncomfortable. It feels like it should mean something important, but it is hard to say what that is. Macquarrie and Robinson, the translators of *Being and Time*, compound that obscure feeling of weightiness by capitalizing the word "being." We can begin with the most basic observation about the word "being": it is a gerund, that is, a noun that refers to the activity or condition described by its associated verb, "to be." What is the "condition" of being?

> In the question which we are to work out, *what is asked about* is being – that which determines entities as entities, that in terms of which entities are already understood, however we may discuss them in detail. (25–26/6*)

Being "determines entities as entities." The verb "to determine" here does *not* mean to produce or cause; Heidegger is not suggesting that being produces entities. Entities produce or cause one another; it may be that God produces or causes everything that is. To suggest that being produces entities, or put a little differently, that God is being, is a fundamental conceptual error, one that lies at the heart of what Heidegger comes to call "ontotheology."[1]

> The being of entities "is" not itself an entity. If we are to understand the problem of being, our first philosophical step consists ... in not "telling a story" – that is to say, in not defining entities

as entities by tracing them back in their origin to some other entities, as if being had the character of some possible entity. (26/6)

Being determines entities as entities, not by making entities into entities, but in some other sense. In the passage from pages 25–26 above, Heidegger offers two formulations in apposition with each other: "that which determines entities as entities" and "that in terms of which entities are already understood." The second formulation is elliptical for "that in terms of which entities are already understood *as entities*." We understand entities *as entities* in terms of what makes an entity an entity (*not* what makes entities). Let us begin with an analogy. What makes a scarlet tanager a scarlet tanager? To be a scarlet tanager, an item must be an insect-eating passerine bird that has a scarlet body with black wings. This is how we laypeople (non-ornithologists) understand what it is to be a scarlet tanager. Suppose we see a flash of red in the trees and start looking for a scarlet tanager. If we see a red bird without black wings, we will conclude that we did not see a scarlet tanager. Thus, our notion of what it is to be a scarlet tanager sets *standards* for what can count as a scarlet tanager.

Similarly, we make discriminations all the time as to whether things exist. I think I see a man in my backyard and do a double-take. On the second look, I realize that there is no man in my backyard. Is it possible that there was a man in the backyard, but that he existed for just a split-second and vanished? No, that is not possible, because our conception of being a physical thing requires that the thing endure through time and obey very basic principles of regularity. Because the momentary man in the backyard violates these standards, he cannot have been. Heidegger's point is that we "already understand" what it is to be, in so far as we already employ a set of standards that determine whether something exists. These standards are the meaning of being.

The phrase "the meaning of being" immediately suggests that Heidegger seeks to know the meaning of the *word* "being." While a linguistic exploration of the semantics of "being" is not irrelevant to Heidegger's concerns, neither does it exhaust them. As we shall see in section (x), Heidegger does not regard meaning as primarily a linguistic phenomenon. Rather, meaning (*Sinn*) is that in terms of which we understand something. In Heidegger's use of the verb "to understand," we do not just understand ideas, concepts, and words, but rather (mostly) understand things or phenomena. If you are having trouble with someone in your office, you might say something like, "I don't know how to get through to him," or "I don't get him." A co-worker might reply, "Let me talk to him. I know what makes him tick." "Knowing what makes him tick" does not mean having a psychological theory about him or even being able to say how you will get through to him. Rather, it means *knowing how* to talk to him, being *able* to work with him. Understanding in this case is ability or know-how, competence. We have other colloquial phrases which refer to this sort of pre-theoretical ability: "I have a feeling for Mac computers"; "I know my way around the subway system"; "I have a sense for how to behave in a snooty restaurant."

This distinction between "having a feel" for something and having a theory of it is Heidegger's distinction between pre-ontology and ontology. Ontology is a "theoretical inquiry which is explicitly devoted to the meaning of entities" (32/12). An ontology (the result of such an inquiry, e.g., *Being and Time* itself) is an explicit and conceptually articulated account of the meaning of being. The very premise of *Being and Time* is that we do not possess a successful ontology of this sort. Indeed, the introductory page of the text states that Heidegger aims to "raise anew *the question of the meaning of being*," and that this requires that he "first of all must reawaken an understanding for the meaning of this question" (19/1). Philosophy hardly even understands any longer what it is to ask about the meaning of being, much less has an ontology to offer us. Nonetheless, we do understand being, albeit not in an explicit, conceptually articulated way. We understand being in much the same way that we "have a sense for" things or "get" them, without being able to spell out what we understand. Understanding like this is an *ability to do something*, rather than a cognitive grasp of a theme.

What are we able to do, in so far as we understand being? We are constantly discriminating between things that do exist and things that do not. We also regularly discriminate among *kinds* of entity. Heidegger distinguishes between persons, things, and the paraphernalia of human life, and he argues that in our pre-reflective practice, we respect and employ this three-way distinction, even if we neither *talk* nor *think* about matters this way. For example, we instinctively treat the paraphernalia or gear of human life, what Heidegger calls "equipment" or "the ready-to-hand," as having a function or purpose that defines it. Hammers are for driving nails, pens are for writing. This understanding of equipment is most obvious, when someone *mis*uses equipment. If someone scratches his foot with a ball-point pen, his behavior stands out, because he is misusing the pen. This shows how we understand paraphernalia as defined by its functional role in human life.

If we saw someone treat another person as a piece of equipment, such behavior would stand out, in fact, shock us. (We experience shock, rather than bemusement, in virtue of the moral contours of such behavior.) According to Heidegger, people are (at least partly) self-determining entities: we take a stand on who we are by how we lead our lives. Equipment does not. We do not wait for the hammer to "decide" whether it is a hammer, but we do wait for people to decide whether they are going to be parents, employees, friends. So, if Jones treated Smith as a piece of equipment, not merely take advantage of him or mislead him, but rather pick him up and put him at the corner of a door, as if Smith just *were* a door-stop, this would shock us. It would represent a misunderstanding of *what sort of entity Smith is.*

Our feeling for being is mostly inarticulate. Sometimes our pre-ontological understanding does come to the fore and receives explicit treatment, for example, in fundamental scientific revolutions, as Thomas Kuhn calls them.[2] Evolutionary theory, quantum mechanics, relativity – these revolutions in scientific thought not only altered the internal dynamics of biology and physics, but fundamentally shifted scientists' understanding of what it is to be an animal and what it is to be material. Heidegger anticipates Kuhn's notion of a scientific revolution, when he refers to the "real movement of the sciences" (29/9). A scientific revolution contrasts with the typical progress of scientific inquiry, which Kuhn calls "normal science." Heidegger argues that normal science proceeds on the basis of pre-ontological assumptions about the being of the domain of research under study.

> Basic concepts determine the way in which we get an understanding beforehand of the area of subject-matter underlying all the objects a science takes as its theme, and all positive investigation is guided by this understanding. (30/10)

Scientific revolutions take place when these basic concepts change, when scientific research bleeds into ontology. Kuhn's conception of scientific revolutions helps us to understand the philosophical dimension of science, as Heidegger sees it. It does not, however, underwrite Heidegger's next move.

Heidegger maintains that ontology is an *a priori* discipline, thus that shifts in our understanding of being explain, but are not justified by, changes in scientific theory. Ontological research, he avers, "must run ahead of the positive sciences, and it *can*." It

> leaps ahead, as it were, into some area of being, discloses it for the first time in the constitution of its being, and, after thus arriving at the structures within it, makes these available to the positive sciences as transparent assignments for their inquiry. (30–31/10)

Ontological reflection lays the foundations for empirical science. For this reason, Heidegger writes further, "Ontological inquiry is indeed more primordial, as over against the ontical inquiry of the positive sciences" (31/11). Because ontology explores the standards in terms which we distinguish what is from what is not, as well as among the various fundamental sorts of entities that are, Heidegger concludes that science presupposes ontology. The priority of ontology over the empirical sciences is especially important in *Being and Time*, because Heidegger offers a novel ontology of human life. He believes that much empirical research in the social sciences is compromised by an inadequate ontology of human life. In I.1 he argues that anthropology and psychology must take their guiding clues from *Being and Time*'s analysis of human being.

Heidegger is not the first philosopher, of course, to assert the priority of metaphysics or ontology over the empirical sciences. Heidegger's approach is governed, however, by the Kantian transcendental turn that we discussed in chapter 1 above: ontology is an exploration of our *understanding* of being. We have a pre-ontological understanding of being, and our job as philosophers is to make that pre-ontology explicit in an ontological theory. Thus, ontology is interpretive or "hermeneutic." Because our pre-ontological understanding is embedded in our conduct and pre-reflective ways of going about our lives, ontology is an attempt to put our practical understanding of being into words. Ontology does not require any special epistemic capacity, such as innate ideas or the rational intuition of Platonic forms. Rather, ontology requires careful attention to the contours of our engagement with entities and precise attempts to express those contours in language. Because ontology is not based on any special epistemic capacity, it cannot claim any peculiar certainty on its behalf. Indeed, our first attempts to put our understanding of being into words invariably go astray.

> Yet that which remains *hidden* in an egregious sense, or which relapses and gets *covered up* again, or which shows itself only "*in disguise*," is not just this entity or that, but rather the *being* of entities, as our previous observations have shown. (59/35)

Our first attempts at ontology typically rely on common sense or the philosophical tradition, which embody a distorted expression of our understanding of being. Heidegger offers two different accounts of *why* common sense and the tradition have gone astray. According to one account, a clear-sighted interpretation of our own being would expose some deeply unsettling aspects of our existence, such as that we have no core self and that we are constantly threatened by anxiety. We cover up the unsettling truth about our being by interpreting ourselves on the model of a non-human thing. This is the theme of "fleeing" that runs throughout *Being and Time*.

Heidegger offers the rudiments of second account in *The Basic Problems of Phenomenology*. In §11 Heidegger argues that the ancient Greek philosophical conception of being was formed as an expression of the experience of production. In artisanal production, the artisan envisages the product she is seeking to produce and is guided by that image. "The *eidos* as the look, anticipated in imagination, of what is to be formed gives the thing with regard to what this thing already was and is before all actualization" (*Basic Problems*, 107). If we think of all of reality as a creation of God, and we think of God as a super-artisan, we will think of all entities, including ourselves, as having an ideal form, an *eidos*, an essence. The "ontotheological" tradition transfers the model of artisanal creation to all entities and misinterprets being as being-created.

This latter account (and others like it)[3] are examples of the "destruction of the history of ontology," as Heidegger calls it (63/39). This "destruction" is a disassembly of the conceptual history of ontology, in which one analyzes the experiences that gave rise to the earliest philosophical attempts to say what being means. The examples in the previous paragraph sketch such an attempt: ancient Greek ontology arose (according to Heidegger) out of the experience of production. Seeing this should loosen up our attachment to the received ontology by showing how it arose from a distinctive and limited range of experience. Heidegger believes that through his own phenomenological analyses he can dig deeper and wider in experience and reveal the full range of modes of being that we confront.

As we expand our ontological horizons, we need some sort of benchmark for what might count as a mode of being. This need generates something of a methodological circle, for how are we to know what counts as a mode of being, unless we already have an ontology to-hand? We cannot have an ontology to-hand, however, before we have explored candidate modes of being and evaluated their suitability for this distinguished honor. Heidegger affirms this conundrum, when he writes:

> *Basically, all ontology, no matter how rich and firmly compacted a system of categories it has at its disposal, remains blind and perverted from its ownmost aim, if it has not first adequately clarified the meaning of being, and conceived this clarification as its fundamental task.* (31/11)

Circularity is not necessarily a problem, because ontology proceeds hermeneutically and hermeneutics is essentially circular in method. As Heidegger writes in §32, "What is decisive is not to get out of the circle but to come into it in the right way" (195/153). Just as in reading a book we move back and forth between an understanding of the part of the book we are reading and our understanding of the whole book, so in doing ontology we move back and forth between articulating some specific mode of being and our vision of the whole field of being. In the course of ontological inquiry a map or structure of the field of being in general will come into focus.

Heidegger argues that the structural articulation of the field of being in general follows the contours of the phenomenon of time: ". . . we shall show that whenever Dasein tacitly understands and interprets something like being, it does so with *time* as its standpoint" (39/17). I will not develop this theme in this Reader's Guide, because it is too obscure and convoluted for a compact treatment. The basic idea, however, is this. Our understanding is structured by certain deep temporal characteristics. As a first approximation, think of this structure as a grammar of understanding, much like Kant's "categories of pure understanding" in *The Critique of Pure Reason*. According to Kant, we take a thing as objective (as opposed to an illusion or misunderstanding) when it exhibits regularity through time. Things do not pop in and out of existence; to exist involves *enduring through time* (in specific ways). We conceive nature as a domain of law-like regularities. The requirement that nature be law-governed is laid down by the grammar of understanding; it is a requirement imposed on the business of making sense of nature, an element of the ontology of nature.

Heidegger extends the spirit of this analysis to other kinds of entity, principally human beings and the paraphernalia of human life. They too exhibit temporal characteristics in their ontological structure, and the aim of a general ontology is to spell these temporal characteristics out and systematize them. The result of a successful general ontology would be a detailed conception and articulation of the temporal structure of being in general, what Heidegger calls "Temporality."[4] Time thus becomes the final horizon for ontological understanding:

> The series, mentioned earlier, of projections as it were inserted one before the other – understanding of entities, projection upon being, understanding of being, projection upon time – has its end at the horizon of the ecstatic unity of temporality. (*Basic Problems*, 308)

Although we will not explore this theme here, the reader should bear in mind that some of Heidegger's formulations reflect this commitment to time as the underlying structure of being.

The official project of *Being and Time* is to develop an explicit ontology, an account of being. Ontological inquiry proceeds hermeneutically, by expressing in conceptually articulate form our pre-ontological understanding of being. To do this, we must dig down into our pre-reflective, practical forms of engagement with the world and express what is afoot in them. Doing this well will require a grasp of the nature of our pre-reflective, practical understanding. Thus, Heidegger sets as a preliminary goal developing an ontology of human being. Securing the "point of access" to the object of our study is a recurring theme in *Being and Time*. In the first chapter of the introduction, he refers to this point of access as "that which is interrogated" (24/5). To secure the point of access to our understanding of being, we must first develop a careful account of our understanding, and this in turn requires that we work out an ontology of human life. This, then, is the preliminary goal of *Being and Time*.

Before closing this section, let me list some of Heidegger's technical terms from the first chapter of the introduction to *Being and Time* for future reference:

Ontological: of or pertaining to being.
Ontic: of or pertaining to entities.
Dasein: we (we will discuss this more thoroughly in section iii).
Existence: our being.
Existential: of or pertaining to our being.
Existentiell: of or pertaining to some ontic aspect of us.
An *existentiale*: a feature of existence, i.e., of our being (pl. *existentialia*).
Presence-at-hand: see p. 64
Present-at-hand: (adj.) see p. 64
A category: a feature of non-human being.

Study Question

How do you think Heidegger might respond to the objection that the meaning of the word "being" is purely logical or grammatical, essentially that from "*x* is a dog" one may infer "there is a dog" and that from "there is a dog," one may infer that "*x* is a dog?" (If you are familiar with elementary logic, think of the objection like this: the existential quantifier exhausts the meaning of "being.")

II. PHENOMENOLOGY

How do we go about investigating being? How do we *do* ontology? Although Heidegger's ontological aspirations may be traditional, his method for achieving them is not: phenomenology. Ontology traditionally uses an array of methods, including conceptual and linguistic analysis, theoretical generalization (e.g., from the results of science), and intuition-massaging. Heidegger eschews these techniques in favor of phenomenology, which at first seems peculiarly ill-suited to ontology. In order to understand how Heidegger intends to use phenomenology to carry out ontological inquiry, we must first take a brief look at Husserl's conception of phenomenology.

Phenomenology in Husserl

Phenomenology is the product of the confluence of two philo-sophical concerns prominent toward the end of the nineteenth cen-tury. First, philosophy as an academic discipline found itself in a methodological crisis. The idea of philosophy as a separate discip-line, distinct from physics, theology, and psychology, for example, is a relatively new innovation. The writings of the major philosophers from the time of ancient Greece up until the nineteenth century covered a wide range of topics that would not be considered as philosophical today. Indeed, natural science was called "natural philosophy" until the end of the eighteenth century. As the sciences slowly separated themselves from philosophy, it became increasingly unclear what philosophy was meant to study. Philosophy had been left with a handful of themes: ethics, logic, metaphysics, aesthetics, and theory of knowledge. Are these areas of reflection unified by any common concern, object, or method? One feature stands out in common among the various topics of philosophy: the objects of philosophy are not natural phenomena. Ethics explores what we ought to do, not what we in fact do; logic analyzes correct thought, not actual thought; and metaphysics provides theories of the super-sensible and ultimate nature of reality, not simply nature as it is studied by natural science.

A second concern dovetails with this first one. During the nine-teenth century philosophers sought to distinguish the meaning of a thought both from the psychological state in which it is realized and from the object that it means. When you and I both think "Mt. Everest is high," we are "thinking the same thought," but our minds and acts of thinking that bear this thought are distinct. Our distinct acts of thinking share the same meaning, which implies that this meaning is neither identical with nor contained within these acts. Perhaps, then, to think something is to stand in relation to that object: in thinking of Mt. Everest, we both stand in relation to the mountain. The problem with this suggestion is that we can think of non-existent things, such as Mordor, but we cannot stand in relation to them, precisely because they do not exist. Mordor may be to the east of Anduin, but it is not in any direction from my house. Thus, the meaning or content of my thought of Mordor is neither my *thinking* of this thought nor the place Mordor itself (the *object* of my thought). Meaning is something highly unusual, neither psychological nor "real." Meaning is non-natural, like the other objects of philosophical inquiry.

Consider, then, the proposal that we divide the totality of what is into the real and the non-real or ideal. Ethical norms, political rights, logical laws, and epistemological standards are all ideal, as are meanings. None of these items are really existing objects (for they do not exist in any place or at any time), yet they are all *about* objects (whether or not those objects themselves are real or imaginary). Brentano christened the relation of aboutness that defines these non-real items *intentionality*.[5] He analyzed it thus: when we consider our experience, we can note that all mental acts have an object. Hatred is about what is hated, desire what is desired, contemplation what is contemplated, etc. Mental acts have an object, even when what one is thinking about does not exist, as when I imagine Mordor. Thus, the object of thought is not a "transcendent object," a real thing existing in the world. Rather, it is an "immanent object," something that subsists simply in so far as I think about or intend it. Once we begin talking about "immanent objects," however, it is easy to slide into thinking about meaning as a special sort of thing, something that belongs to the furniture of the universe. Sometimes Brentano even falls prey to this temptation to reify the immanent object of thought. It was Husserl's great achievement to find a way to resist this temptation systematically.

Husserl's technique for resisting reification is the phenomenological reduction.[6] The phenomenological reduction "reduces" our experience by "suspending" or "putting out of play" any interest we might have in either the transcendent object of our thought or ourselves as thinkers. I must learn to ignore the question whether the objects of my thinking really exist and, if they do, whether they exist as I experience them. I must also learn to ignore questions about the reality and nature of the psychological acts in which I experience those objects. Instead, I focus on the object just as it presents itself, the object *as I mean it*, or as Husserl also called it, the "object *qua* object."

Brentano conceived of the study of intentionality as a branch of psychology, what he called "descriptive" psychology. Husserl argued that the study of meaning was not a form of psychology, at least if we conceive psychology as an empirical investigation into a real thing, namely, the human mind. The term "descriptive psychology" is highly misleading, since it suggests that we are describing our experience, as we might do when we introspectively reflect on our thoughts and feelings (say, in the context of psychotherapy). In studying meaning, we are not investigating an empirical object; rather, we are investigating how any object of human experience, whether it be an external physical thing or an internal psychological state, presents itself to us. Phenomenology does not study minds. It studies *meaning* or *intentionality*.

In focusing on the object just as it presents itself, one does not simply "narrate" one's experience. Phenomenology seeks to understand the grammar or structure of meaning. For example, it is a merely idiosyncratic fact about my experience that the computer at which I am gazing now is located in Maryland. It is not idiosyncratic, however, that it has location. Location belongs to the very structure of the presentation of physical objects. A physical object presents itself as having a backside I cannot see, which sets up an expectation that if I were to turn it around (or walk around it), I would see that backside. These are structural features of physical objects as they present themselves. Whether transcendent physical objects themselves have backsides, or perhaps, as in a skeptical worry, are all only two-dimensional facades cleverly arranged in order to fool me, is a question about which phenomenology has nothing to say. Phenomenology can tell us *what we mean* by the distinction between a full object and a facade, but it cannot answer the question whether this object is a full object or a facade.

Phenomenology in *Being and Time*

Heidegger proposes to use phenomenological method in ontology. This should elicit an immediate objection, however: if phenomenology is the study of objects *as they present themselves*, it cannot be used in ontology, for ontology is the study of objects *as they really are*. The phenomenological observation that physical objects typically present themselves as being single or unitary objects that have parts, rather than as being many things loosely associated with one another, does not settle the metaphysical question about whether physical objects really are one thing or many. Whereas ontology is the study of reality, phenomenology is the study of appearances, and thus surely phenomenology cannot be the method of ontology. Part of the burden of §7 of *Being and Time* is to rebut this objection.

Phenomenology studies phenomena, objects as they present themselves. It is misleading to characterize these phenomena as *appearances*, however. Heidegger defines a phenomenon as "*that which shows itself in itself,* the manifest" (51/28). An appearance is something that is indicated by way of something else that shows itself in its place. Heidegger's example is a disease appearing by way of its symptoms. When I see my son flushed for no obvious reason, I begin to worry that he has a fever. The flushed complexion shows itself, and in doing so it indicates the presence of a fever. The fever, however, does not show itself directly. (In a further variant, a "mere appearance" is an appearance that indicates something that cannot show itself.) To interpret phenomena as appearances is to assume a doctrine sometimes called Indirect Representationalism.

According to Indirect Representationalism, objects announce themselves (or are announced to us) by internal surrogates, ideas or representations. Transcendent objects affect the mind by causing representations of them to become present to consciousness. In a normal visual experience of a coffee mug the coffee mug interacts causally with our sensory apparatus, and this interaction produces a sensory experience of the coffee mug. We are only directly aware of the representation and must infer the existence of the coffee mug itself. Indirect Representationalism gives rise quickly to skeptical worries. The internal representations of which we are aware might well not correspond with any transcendent objects in the world beyond the mind. For this reason philosophers working in this tradition have felt forced to choose among several unpalatable options: acquiescing in a sort of skepticism about the external world (as Hume does), seeking some sort of rational guarantee for the veracity of our representations (as Descartes does), or trying to "reduce" external objects to constructions out of our representations (as Berkeley and other phenomenalists do).

The worry that phenomena are appearances and hence unsuited for use in ontology rests on the covert assumption of Indirect Representationalism, because only if we are thinking of phenomena as a surrogate for a transcendent reality will we be inclined to exclude phenomenology as a method for ontology. To charge phenomenology with studying appearances, rather than reality, is to load the concept of a phenomenon with representationalist baggage that neither Husserl nor Heidegger accepts. "[O]ne has not," Heidegger says, "thereby defined the concept of a phenomenon: one has rather *presupposed* it" (53/29–30). A phenomenon is simply something that shows itself, not an appearance. An appearance is a special kind of phenomenon, one that indicates something beyond itself that does not show itself. The concept of a phenomenon in general is an epistemically and metaphysically neutral concept. This defense of phenomenology points to a reformulation of the basic worry, however: surely ontology, unlike phenomenology, is not metaphysically neutral, for it studies being. In order to rebut this worry, we must dig a little deeper into what phenomenology is.

Before proceeding, we must wade through the usual bevy of technical terms that Heidegger throws in. Apart from *appearance* (something that indicates itself by way of a surrogate phenomenon) and *phenomenon* (what shows itself), Heidegger also defines the *phenomenon in the ordinary sense* (that which shows itself to our senses, objects of perception), the *formal conception of the phenomenon* (the concept of a phenomenon, but in which we do not specify anything about what shows itself), and the *phenomenological conception of the phenomenon* (that which is latent in what shows itself and thereby enables what shows itself to show itself). It is, of course, the latter that is most interesting to us, since it characterizes what phenomenology studies in studying phenomena. What is the phenomenological conception of the phenomenon?

All his life Heidegger maintained that the piece of Husserl's writings that had the deepest influence on him was the sixth of Husserl's *Logical Investigations*.[7] The Sixth Investigation explores, among other things, what Husserl calls "categorial intuition." Categorial intuition is Husserl's term for the way in which modal or logical aspects of an object present themselves. For example, I take in visually that the book in front of me is black, thick, rectangular, and so on. In taking it *as* a book that is black, thick, and rectangular, I am taking it as a *unity*. Its unity is not, however, a feature of the book in any ordinary sense. It is a categorial structure of the book as it presents itself, not a sensible feature. In Kant's terminology, the unity of the book is not a "real predicate" of the book.[8] In order to see the book, one must experience its unity, but the experience of its unity is not a sensory experience. It is an aspect of experience latent in and enabling of the ordinary experience.[9]

Like the unity of the book, its being is a categorial, rather than real, aspect of how the book presents itself. To take a physical object to exist is not to have identified some definite property of it, but rather a structure in the object's presentation. To take a physical object to be a cat, rather than a dog, by contrast, is to have identified a distinctive set of properties. Cats and dogs are distinct *species* of physical object, differentiated by real predicates, whereas existing and non-existing physical objects are objects that exhibit distinct *formal structures*. As we saw in the last section, Heidegger believes that the formal structures that are central to ontology are temporal structures. Thus for Heidegger doing phenomenological ontology will be a matter of exposing the temporal structure of phenomena, that is, of entities as they show themselves.

Heidegger does not just offer phenomenology as *a* way to do ontology; he insists that it is *the only* way: "*Only as phenomenology, is ontology possible*" (60/35). Why? Being is not an entity or domain of entities, and thus it cannot be the object of one of the "special" or "positive" sciences, such as biology or literary theory. Each of these disciplines takes a domain of entities as its object and studies it empirically. Being is not such a domain, but rather a structure of anything that is. Being is not a feature or property of what is manifest, but rather a meaning-structure that is latent in any experience of anything, even experiences of imaginary things (which do not exist, but present themselves as if they did). We must, therefore, study being as we study the meaning of phenomena, namely, phenomenologically.

The being of a phenomenon is latent in experience, Heidegger has told us, and thus must be drawn out. That is, the phenomenological ontology is interpretation, or as Heidegger puts it, hermeneutic: "Our investigation itself will show that the meaning of phenomenological description as a method lies in *interpretation*" (61/37). We do not just describe phenomena exactly as we experience them; rather, we extract from them something that is not apparent at first, a latent structure, ". . . something that proximally and for the most part does *not* show itself at all: it is something that lies *hidden*, in contrast with that which proximally and for the most part does show itself . . ." (59/35). Despite this, Heidegger insists that phenomenology is purely descriptive: "the expression 'descriptive phenomenology' . . . is at bottom tautological" (ibid.). How can Heidegger reconcile these two claims?

". . . [T]he term [*description*] has rather the sense of a prohibition – the avoidance of characterizing anything without . . . exhibiting it directly and demonstrating it directly" (ibid.). To say that phenomenology is descriptive is to say that it eschews constructive theorizing. The goal of phenomenology is not to posit "deep" structures that lie behind meanings and explain them. But why not? Consider an alternative approach to meaning, contemporary philosophical semantics, in particular the thesis that meanings are combinatory. Meanings are hierarchical, with more complex meanings constructed out of more basic meanings according to some identifiable set of combinatory operators.[10] Combinatory theories of meaning are appealing, because they promise to explain how the mind can generate an indefinite set of meanings by means of finite materials and capacities. With a finite set of basic meanings and a finite set of combinatory operators, the mind can generate an indefinitely large set of complex meanings, as long as the combinatory operators can be applied recursively. This is quite an attractive feature of combinatory theories of meaning. Notice, however, that this motivation treats meaning as something that is produced by the mind. It *explains* the structure of meaning in terms of the nature of mental activity. It thus involves a metaphysical assumption that meaning is produced by mental activity. To treat meaning in this way is to conceive it as a real thing governed by causal laws and systems of production. This assumption is at the very heart of what Husserl rejects as "psychologism."[11] If meaning is an aspect of the object as it manifests itself, and not a real feature of either the world or the mind, then it cannot be explained causally. Meaning is not a real thing in competition with tables and chairs, inscriptions on paper, sound waves, or psychological states. There is nothing to do with them *but* describe them.

So, to say that phenomenology is descriptive is simply to exclude constructive theorizing guided by assumptions about meaning implied by a metaphysics or psychology of mind. This does not mean, however, that phenomenology is not also interpretive. Indeed, Heidegger regards all description as interpretive.

An interpretation is never a presuppositionless apprehending of something presented to us. If, when one is engaged in a particular concrete kind of interpretation, in the sense of exact textual interpretation, one likes to appeal to what "stands there" [on the page], then one finds that what "stands there" [on the page] in the first instance is nothing other than the obvious undiscussed assumption of the person who does the interpreting. (191–192/150*)

All description, Heidegger argues, requires guidance from a set of what he here characterizes as "assumptions," but which on the previous page he somewhat more carefully described as "a definite way of conceiving" what is described (191/150). Whenever we understand anything, we do so by grasping it in terms of our "pre-understanding," our advance feel for the object, including its being.

This view of description implies that we already "pre-understand" the being of an object we are seeking to describe. We saw in section (i) above that the discipline of ontology seeks to articulate our pre-ontological sense of being, and this makes ontology interpretive or hermeneutic. Just as a sociological commentator might try to articulate what is at stake in the suburban way of life in contemporary America,[12] so an ontologist will try to articulate what our sense of being is. In doing this, the ontologist tries to develop a set of ontological concepts that is rich enough to capture what we mean by being. Phenomenological ontology is interpretive in the same way in which some social science is.

When we put our pre-ontological understanding into conceptually articulate form, we bring out features of our experience that are, at first, not salient. This is to say that we bring something otherwise unapparent into focus *by* describing it. As an analogy, think of what it is like to try to get someone to see a painting as you do. You might well appreciate or enjoy *The Removal of St. Mark's Body from the Funeral Pyre*, by Tintoretto, but not be able to articulate aspects of the painting that a critic can draw out. For example, ". . . the rapidly receding vista, the inexplicable disjunctions of scale, the oppressively dark sky, and the strange, wraith-like figures of the Muslims fleeing from the storm into the arcade on the left, all contribute to a mood of eeriness and disquiet. . . ."[13] Here the critic articulates something you had not, and in doing so he brings into relief aspects of the painting that you might well have felt, but did not see. Similarly, when Heidegger writes, "the peculiarity of [equipment] is that, in its readiness-to-hand, it must, as it were, withdraw in order to be ready-to-hand quite authentically" (99/69), he is drawing out something we probably had not noticed. This is a form of description, albeit not a completely straightforward description of something apparent "right before our eyes." Rather, it is description by articulation, which seems to be what Heidegger means by hermeneutic description.

Heidegger's goal in *Being and Time* is to offer an articulation of how we understand being. To articulate what we mean by being, he will describe phenomena in such a way as to draw out those structural features in virtue of which they show up for us as entities. As we saw in section (i), Heidegger proposes to begin his ontological inquiries with a study of the being of Dasein, human beings. His ambition was to develop a general ontology of all forms of being and to link them into a systematic whole by exposing the temporal features that structure being. He never got that far, however. He left us only with divisions I and II, most of which are devoted to the being of Dasein. Let us turn now to Heidegger's ontology of human being.

Study Question

What kinds of philosophical inquiries can, and what cannot, be carried out phenomenologically?

III. EXISTENCE

Heidegger opens §9 with a densely packed paragraph that lays out the fundamental outlines of his ontology of human life:

> We are ourselves the entities to be analysed. The being of any such entity is *in each case mine*. These entities, in their being, comport themselves towards their being. As entities with such being, they are delivered over to their own being. *Being* is that which is an issue for every such entity. (67/41–42)

He identifies four ontological traits of Dasein:

(1) Dasein's being is in each case mine.
(2) Dasein comports itself towards its being.
(3) Dasein is delivered over to its being.
(4) Being is at issue for Dasein.

Let us begin with (1).

We can restate (1) in a phrase: Dasein is a person. Heidegger does not call Dasein a person, however, or use the related language of subjects and subjectivity in analyzing it. Why? The language of persons and subjectivity is freighted with objectionable historical baggage. Heidegger's discussion of this baggage is somewhat abbreviated here in I.1, but fortunately he offers us a lengthier treatment in *Basic Problems*, §13b. There he explores Kant's conception of subjectivity and personality, and by implication the German tradition in which Heidegger is working.

A little historical background: modern philosophical reflection on the nature of subjectivity began with Descartes's thesis that one's experiences inhere in one as any property inheres in a substance, as for example shape inheres in a tree. The term "subject" is the logical correlate of the metaphysical term "substance." Just as properties cannot subsist without a substance in which to inhere, so experiences cannot subsist without a subject (or *res cogitans*, thinking thing) to experience them. All one's experiences belong to a single subject, because they all inhere in this substance that thinks, and the persistence of this subject-substance through changes in experience explains one's identity through time.

Kant transforms Descartes's conception of the subject by pulling its metaphysical teeth, as it were. Experience cannot empirically fund the thought of our own unity and identity, as it can for the material objects of experience. Ice melts and turns into water, for example, and chemistry provides a means for talking about this transformation. Melting is a change in the underlying state of a quantity of H_2O. In one's own case, however, one never becomes aware of any underlying material or psychological substance of which one's changing experiences are merely alterations of state. This is one of David Hume's skeptical observations, and Kant endorses it. Kant does not, however, give up on the unity and identity of the subject. Kant affirms that, "The proposition, that in all the manifold of which I am conscious I am identical with myself, is likewise implied in the concepts themselves, and is therefore an analytic proposition."[14] The unity and identity of the subject is a logical requirement of self-consciousness, rather than a metaphysical fact.

What we *mean* by saying of an experience that it is *mine* or *belongs to me* is that I can become aware of it, or in Kant's words, "It must be possible for the 'I think' to accompany all my representations."[15] With this formulation we have arrived at the *core conception of subjectivity in post-Kantian German philosophy*: subjectivity is the self-conscious unity of experience. To be a subject is not to be a *thing* or *substance*. Rather, subjectivity is a form of experiential unity, unity constituted and exhausted by my ability to become aware of my experiences *as mine*.[16] This is Kant's conception of "transcendental personality."

In eschewing the language of subjectivity and personality, Heidegger is rejecting this way of looking at experience. Why? Heidegger believes that you have an experience of yourself that is more basic than your cognitive awareness that all your experiences are *yours*. Heidegger names this more basic experience with his second characterization of Dasein: (2) Dasein comports itself towards its being. This formulation is derived from Kierkegaard and embodies Heidegger's existentialism. Kierkegaard is particularly interested in understanding the non-intellectual life-transformations that occur in the search for a stable sense of self that culminates, in his view, in religion. In Kierkegaard's analysis of these transformations, not only are one's desires, aspirations, convictions, and commitments changed, but the very being of the self is modified. In *The Sickness Unto Death*, Kierkegaard writes,

A human being is spirit. But what is spirit? Spirit is the self. But what is the self? The self is a relation that relates itself to itself or is the relation's relating itself to itself in the relation; the self is not the relation but is the relation's relating itself to itself.[17]

Heidegger's phraseology, "Dasein comports itself towards its being," echoes Kierkegaard's: "comports itself" translates "*verhält sich*," which can more anemically mean "relates itself."

The formulation that the self *is* a relation of itself to itself might seem hopelessly circular. What is the "it" that gets related? Where's the beef? Yet Heidegger embraces precisely this circularity:

The "essence" of this entity lies in its to be [*Zu-sein*]. Its what-being (*essentia*) must, so far as we can speak of it at all, be conceived in terms of its being (*existentia*). . . . The "essence" of Dasein lies in its existence. (67/42*)

In the first sentence Heidegger identifies what it is to be human with our "to be." Macquarrie and Robinson helpfully give us the German equivalent of "to be": "*Zu-sein*" rather than the infinitive "*Sein*," which we are translating consistently as "being." *"Zu-sein"* is a gerundive: just as Dasein may have things to do, it has being to be. Put more colloquially, then, Heidegger is saying that *I am a life to live.* He wants to refocus our understanding of what it is to be a person away from reflection and self-consciousness and towards how we live our lives.

Readers who find standard discussions of personal identity and the nature of self to be sterile will be sympathetic. Many students of philosophy who feel this way turn to discussions of the self in moral philosophy. Moral philosophy, after all, is concerned with who we are in so far as we are practically engaged with the world. Heidegger does not think that turning to moral philosophy in this way is sufficient to address the failures of the tradition, and his dissatisfaction goes a long way toward explaining why moral philosophy is so peculiarly absent in *Being and Time*.

After he discusses the transcendental unity of apperception in *Basic Problems*, Heidegger turns to Kant's conception of "moral personality." Moral personality is a notion of subjectivity that goes beyond self-consciousness and is resolutely practical. Moral personality is structurally similar to transcendental personality: it involves a logical unity, rather than a metaphysical unity of substance. The logical unity of the moral personality is not the unity of self-consciousness, but rather the unity of the agent that is constituted through one's awareness of her moral accountability. I am aware that my perceptual experience of this coffee mug belongs to me, because I can be aware of myself as experiencing the coffee mug. I am aware that my action of drinking this coffee belongs to me, because I can impute the action to myself by taking responsibility for it. Just as, according to Kant, I have a transcendental cognitive awareness of my own existence as a thinker, so I have a transcendental awareness of my own existence as an agent that is captured in the feeling of respect for the moral law. The details are not so important here, but merely the basic idea that we are aware of who we are by way of the experience of moral accountability and responsibility. My actions are mine, according to this view, in so far as I experience those actions as imputable to me.

Heidegger wants to identify a form of self-awareness more basic than cognitive apperception *or* moral self-consciousness. His proposal is that the most basic form of self-awareness is my awareness of *who I am to-be.* In José Ortega y Gasset's words: "It is too often

36

forgotten that man is impossible without imagination, without the capacity to invent for himself a conception of life, to 'ideate' the character he is going to be."[18] This sense of identity underlies my awareness of my convictions, commitments, thoughts, and responsibilities. *To be* a person is *to project* a person to be, and so our being is *at issue* for us. This is the fourth ontological trait Heidegger identifies in the opening paragraph of §9: (4) Being is at issue for Dasein. Our being is at issue for us, because we care about our being. In I.6 Heidegger will give the name "care" to Dasein's being and in doing so he refers back to this feature of his analysis from I.1. By "care" Heidegger does not want to refer to the particular emotional phenomena of worry and devotion, but rather to a constitutive or *existential* condition of human life, one that characterizes a carefree and/or detached person as much as one committed to service to others. To care about one's being is for it to matter to one, to make a difference to who one is.

Here in I.1 Heidegger puts the point by way of contrasting us with non-human things: "To entities such as these, their being is 'a matter of indifference,' or more precisely, they 'are' such that their being can be neither a matter of indifference to them, nor the opposite" (68/42). In a discussion of artificial intelligence, John Haugeland once wrote: "The problem with artificial intelligence is that computers don't give a damn."[19] This is an insightful comment about the limitations of artificial intelligence, though Heidegger would want to modify it thus: the problem with artificial intelligence is that computers neither do nor don't give a damn. Our lives *matter* to us, they *concern* us, even when they matter *by* being negligible or irrelevant, whereas non-human things have no concern with anything at all. They cannot even experience their existence as irrelevant.

We care about our lives, our being is an issue for us. We constantly confront the question, or issue, Who am I? (To simplify my formulations, I will refer to this question as "the question of identity.") To confront the question of identity is not to brood over one's identity. Brooding self-questioning is one way to live, but by no means common. We confront the question of identity not in reflecting on ourselves, but rather simply in living a human life. To live a life *is* to answer the question of identity.

This is all a way of saying that my sense of self, with which we began our discussion of §9, is neither cognitive nor specially moral, but rather *practical*. A few pages into §9 Heidegger writes:

In determining itself as an entity, Dasein always does so in the light of a possibility which it *is* itself and which, in its very being, it somehow understands. This is the formal meaning of Dasein's existential constitution. (69/43)

In §12 he adds: "Dasein is an entity which, in its very being, comports itself understandingly towards that being. In saying this, we are calling attention to the formal concept of existence" (78/53). Heidegger chooses to call the sense of self we have been discussing "self-understanding." Dasein's existentiality is the "fact" that it always understands itself one way or another. We are always answering the question of identity by being (or living) some possibility of human life. As we already touched upon in section (i), by "understanding" Heidegger means a form of competence or ability, a practical phenomenon, rather than a cognitive one. Our self-understanding is embodied in the way we live, rather than in how we think or talk about our lives. It is for this reason, moreover, that Macquarrie and Robinson have decided to translate "*sich verhalten*" as "to comport itself," rather than as "to relate itself." Heidegger is talking about a form of comportment or behavior.

How does this Heideggerian sense of self differ from the "moral personality" described by Kant? The Heideggerian-existentialist sense of self is broader and more basic than the self-awareness embodied in the feeling of moral accountability. Your life, your being, is *who you are*, and who you are includes and suffuses how you feel, how you act, how you are disposed, how you talk, with whom you congregate. The difference can be drawn out best in an example: George, Paul, and John are hanging out in a mall. John steals a CD from the music store and gets caught. George is not responsible, for he neither encouraged nor ordered John to steal the CD. Still, he feels implicated in or at issue in this affair. That is because *who he is* is more fundamental than *what he is accountable for*.[20]

Dasein's basic self-awareness is not a form of *awareness* at all, at least not in any usual sense of the word. It is not a form of *subjectivity*, if by that word we have its traditional connotations in mind. Heidegger chooses to use the word "disclosedness," rather than "self-consciousness" or "subjectivity," precisely in order to avoid the traditional associations of those terms. I am disclosed to myself most basically in caring about who I am, that is, in so far as it matters to me who I am. This implies, further, that the question of identity is in play, even if we are not aware of it. Hence the third of Heidegger's ontological characterizations of Dasein in the first paragraph of §9: (3) Dasein is delivered over to its being. This is Heidegger's formulation that inspired Sartre's slogan, "We are condemned to be free." We are "condemned" or delivered over to confronting the question of identity. Because our answer to the question of identity is embodied in how we *live*, rather than how we think or talk; moreover, we cannot avoid the question by not thinking or talking about it.

I mentioned above that one's sense of self suffuses with whom one congregates. That is to say, in caring about who *I* am, I care about who *others* are. In I.4 Heidegger names this care for others "solicitude." In confronting the question of *my* identity, I am also confronting the question of the identity of *others*. His point is that I cannot disentangle who I am from who those around me are. The intimacy of my concern with others can certainly vary from disengaged indifference to deep commitment, but still it *matters* to me who others are. Who others are is open, questionable, at issue in how I lead my life, just as my own life is. As I go about being a father, teacher, and neighbor, how those with whom I engage in being all these things understand themselves is not irrelevant to me. That my sons respond to my fathering by being adoring children, that some of my students respond to my teaching by dedicating themselves to their studies, is crucially important to me in so far as I am a father and teacher.

Furthermore, Heidegger observes in I.4 that we mostly do not rigorously distinguish ourselves from our fellow-travelers in our pursuits. "*Proximally*, factical Dasein is in the with-world, which is uncovered in an average way. *Proximally*, it is not 'I,' in the sense of my own self, that 'am,' but rather the others . . ." (167/129). In living for the sake of being a father, I am living also for the sake of my sons' being children. The disclosure in which I am aware of myself as father is entangled with the disclosure of my sons as my children. In sustaining my being a father, I am sustaining their being children, and in realizing a specific way of being a father, I am realizing a specific way of their being children. My self is not independent of the selves of those around me. Let us call this phenomenon *the immersion of the self in the social world.*

The immersion of the self in the social world is not a psychological thesis about causal interdependence, nor is it a metaphysical thesis about the interdependence of substances. Rather, it is a phenomenological thesis about the way in which I am disclosed to myself. Heidegger does not want to deny that I *can* sometimes be disclosed to myself as isolated. He merely wants to claim that such an isolated disclosure is exceptional. Immersion is an aspect of our everyday experience; it belongs to what Heidegger calls our *averageness*. He describes averageness as, ". . . the undifferentiated character which [Dasein] has proximally and for the most part" (69/43). Averageness constitutes a background condition, a condition that is not only typical of human life, but a standard in terms of which exceptional conditions of human life make sense. For example, Heidegger argues that experiencing oneself as isolated from one's fellows, not just alienated, but rather as being who one is independently of others, is highly atypical. It is not an easy form of self-understanding to sustain, and in any case, it is most commonly found as a *rejection* of the ways of life of those around one, that is, not just as isolation, but as isolation*ism*. Isolationism, such as being a recluse, involves care for the being of others, since it is motivated largely by a moral or existential *reaction* against others.

Immersion in the social world also involves a certain abdication of selfhood. Immersed in the social world, I do not *own* myself, but rather am, in Heidegger's language, "dispersed" in the public. Heidegger contrasts such dispersal with self-ownership, ownedness, or as Macquarrie and Robinson translate it, "authenticity" (*Eigentlichkeit*). Simply in virtue of being human, we face a choice of sorts between self-ownership and dispersal:

> And because Dasein is in each case essentially its own possibility, it *can*, in its very being, "choose" itself and win itself; it can also lose itself and never win itself; or only "seem" to do so. But only in so far as it can be *owned* – that is, something of its own – can it have lost itself and not yet won itself. (68/42–43*)

Heidegger does not tell us very much about this contrast here in §9. We will see below in section (xvii) that self-ownership is consummated in a form of "self-constancy," which Heidegger describes as "steadiness and steadfastness" (369/322). This self-constancy is an achievement that must be won with a struggle. If anything in Heidegger approximates the unity and persistence of the self, it is this existential self-constancy that is gained through self-ownership. This self-constancy is not, however, a given; it is not a logical condition of experience, nor is it the inherence of experiences in a self-substance. It is, rather, an intensification of one's fundamental awareness of oneself. Simply in so far as we live in an average, everyday, undifferentiated fashion, however, we do not experience ourselves in this intensified and owned way.

So, in sum, Heidegger's answer to the Kantian tradition's conception of the unity of self-consciousness is this: we are disclosed to ourselves more fundamentally than in cognitive self-awareness or moral accountability. We are disclosed to ourselves in so far as it matters to us who we are. Our being is an issue for us, an issue we are constantly addressing by living forward into a life that matters to us. Even in the exceptional condition of having lost interest in life, of radical alienation from it, of depression – which Heidegger discusses under the rubric of *anxiety* – the question of identity looms as inescapable, which is why alienation is distressing. This disclosure of myself to myself does not reveal me as a distinct and persisting individual, however, but rather as immersed in a social world that engages me as well. That world, its possibilities, its paraphernalia, and the others who live in that world along with me matter to me simply in so far as my own life matters to me. All of this falls under the heading of *existentiality*.

Study Question

Does Heidegger's conception of "existence" imply that you and I are not identical selves enduring through changes in our experience, personality, physique, and character?

IV. BEING-IN-THE-WORLD

Proximally and for the most part we are immersed in the world. The importance of this observation is hidden from the philosophical tradition, because it has been focused on self-consciousness and moral accountability, in which we experience ourselves as distinct from the world and others. Heidegger's phenomenological approach to the self focuses first on a basic form of self-disclosure: I am what matters to me. Seen thus, I cannot disentangle myself from those around me and the world in which I live. In a phrase, we are *being-in-the-world*. Heidegger describes being-in-the-world as our basic state or constitution. The "being-in" or "inhood" that constitutes being-in-the-world is neither consciousness nor moral accountability, but rather *familiarity* (*Vertrautheit*).

> The [German] expression "*bin*" ["am"] is connected with "*bei*" ["at the home of," or "on the person of"], and so "*ich bin*" ["I am"] means in its turn "I reside" or "dwell amidst" the world, as that which is familiar to me in such and such a way. Being, as the infinitive of "*ich bin*" (that is to say, when it is understood as an *existentiale*), signifies "to reside amidst . . ." "to be familiar with. . . ." (80/54)

Heidegger offers some etymology to add weight to his claims, but it is probably best to stay focused on the phenomenology. We do not just exist or live in a world, but rather *reside* or *dwell* there; that is, we are fundamentally *familiar with the world*.

To develop this idea we need to explore several facets of it. First, Heidegger contrasts the way in which we are *in* our world with the way in which a thing can be in something else. That is, as Hubert Dreyfus effectively formulates the point,[21] Heidegger contrasts an *existential* sense of the word "in" with a *physical* sense. Second, Heidegger states that being-in-the-world is our *basic constitution*, which is to say more than just that we live in our world. All of the other ways in which we go about business, all our other activities, are specific ways of being-in-the-world. Third, a particular application of the second claim is the thesis of §13, namely, that *knowledge* or *cognition* is a "founded" or derivative mode of being-in-the-world. Let us tackle these three points in turn.

For the world to be *mine*, for it to *matter* to me, is more than simply for me to be located within a system of objects. Being located in something is *inclusion*. Elements of a set are logically included in the set, and physical objects can be included within both larger objects and within systems of objects. My computer is located in my study, but it does not experience the study as *its* study; the study does not *matter* to the computer. I am also in my study. I am included within the physical object, my study, and I belong to the set of things contained in my study. More important than such inclusion, however, is that I experience this study as *mine*; it *matters* to me. The word "mine" might suggest legal ownership, and we do not want to focus on that. Even when I take my work to the coffee house near my home, I still experience the coffee house as *mine*, though not as *owned by me*. It is mine in so far as I am *familiar* with it. This familiarity is a pervasive background feature of our experience, one that we do not normally notice. Like many of the phenomena Heidegger describes in *Being and Time*, this familiarity is most apparent in its absence. When I am traveling and find my way to a coffee house in another city, I often experience a certain level of discomfort. The chairs are unfamiliar, the music is different, as are the brews of coffee. The familiarity of my normal stomping grounds is salient for me in its absence.

These contrasts highlight the basic familiarity that characterizes our experience. We do not just occupy a location in a system of objects, but rather *live in a world*. To live in a world is to experience the place one lives as familiar, to know one's way around it. In §14 Heidegger contrasts four different senses of the word "world" (93/64–65), the first and third of which are of interest to us here. The world in Heidegger's first sense – which he decides henceforth to designate by writing the word *world* in scare-quotes, so "world" – refers to "the totality of those entities that can be present-at-hand within the world." That is, the "world" is the system or set of things that are. We may call this (following Dreyfus again) *the universe of things*. The world in the third sense, the world without scare-quotes, is "that '*wherein*' a factical Dasein can be said to 'live.' " The world is a concrete experiential context or milieu. The world in this sense has a distinctive structure that Heidegger explores in I.3. He calls that structure "significance," which underscores the connection between the mineness and mattering of I.1 and the way in which we are in-a-world according to I.2.

The second facet of Heidegger's conception of being-in-the-world is that being-in-the-world is our basic constitution. Macquarrie and Robinson use the term "basic state," but this does not quite convey Heidegger's point. Heidegger's German is actually more literally rendered as "basic constitution" (*Grundverfassung*). The difference in tone is important, because Heidegger's point in §§12 and 13 is that all modes of our experience and activities are determinate forms of being-in-the-world. "Dasein's facticity is such that its being-in-the-world has always dispersed itself or even split itself up into definite ways of being-in" (83/56–57). He gives a list of such "definite ways of being-in," including both activities, such as producing something and making use of something, as well as psychological attitudes, such as considering something.

Among those definite ways of being-in are the various ways in which we relate to objects around us. Heidegger designates a special term for our relation to the things in the world around us, in so far as we are in-the-world: *concern* (83–84/57). Like "solicitude" (*Fürsorge*), which we touched on in section (iii) above, "concern" (*Besorgen*) derives from "care" (*Sorge*). We concern ourselves with the objects that surround us and the states of affairs we confront; we do not just stand in indifferent or inert relations to them. They make a difference or matter to us, even if this mattering is privative, as in Heidegger's examples of neglecting something or leaving something undone. Everything we do and are is suffused with this care.

Heidegger develops this thought in application to Dasein itself, when he writes, "Whenever Dasein is, it is as a Fact; and the factuality of such a Fact is what we shall call Dasein's '*facticity*'"(82/56). He draws a distinction between *facts* (*Tatsachen*) and *Facts* (*Fakta*), which Macquarrie and Robinson track with a distinction in capitalization: facts are determinate aspects of the present-at-hand (and ready-to-hand), whereas Facts are determinate aspects of Dasein. Thus, it is a fact that my computer weighs six pounds., but a Fact that I am a father. Both of these are examples of ways in which entities can be determinate and thus different from other entities, but Heidegger wants to emphasize an important ontological distinction between these two types of determinacy: being a father is a way of being-in-the-world, whereas weighing six pounds. is not.

Now, one might object that *we* have such factual determinations as well: I weigh a certain (top secret) amount, for example. To account for this, Heidegger writes:

. . . for even entities which are not worldless – Dasein itself, for example – are present-at-hand "in" the world, or, more exactly, *can* with some right and within certain limits be *taken* as merely present-at-hand. To do this, one must completely disregard or just not see the existential state of being-in. But the fact that "Dasein" can be taken as something which is present-at-hand and just present-at-hand, is not to be confused with a certain way of "presence-at-hand" which is Dasein's *own*. (82/55)

To describe me as weighing a certain amount is (or at least, can be) to "disregard the existential state of being-in." It is to describe me in the way in which one may describe any physical object. I can weigh x pounds. as living Dasein or as a corpse, it makes no difference. So, if we disregard a person's existentiality and treat him or her simply as a physical object, we can describe that person in terms of his or her factual determinations. In doing so, however, we are missing what makes his or her life *the life* it is. People do not just weigh x pounds.; they live such a weight as being overweight or underweight or as being indifferent to their weight. Weight, as a way of being-in-the-world, is not an indifferent physical property, but rather an existentiell condition. We may similarly distinguish between biological sex and gender, between physical height and stature. Dasein's facticity consists of the determinations of its way of being-in-the-world.

Heidegger formulates the ontological situation here thus: there are two ways to *take* or *consider* Dasein; *as* something present-at-hand and *as* Dasein. This formulation aligns Heidegger quite generally with the tradition of transcendental philosophy deriving from Kant. According to some readings of Kant, his distinction between noumena (things in themselves) and phenomena (appearances) is not a metaphysical distinction between two different sets of entities (e.g., natural and supernatural things), but rather between two different ways of considering or reflecting on the one set of entities that are.[22] Kant takes this approach in his discussion of freedom in the Third Antinomy in the *Critique of Pure Reason*, where he argues that when we explain a person's behavior psychologically, we must ignore considerations of freedom and regard behavior deterministically. When we judge a person's behavior morally, however, we cannot ignore his or her freedom and cannot treat him or her as a deterministic mechanism. It is the same person and the same action we are in each case explaining or judging, but our *attitude* towards the person and his or her action differs.

Heidegger's distinction between factuality and facticity may be construed along the same lines. We may adopt one of two different attitudes towards a person: a scientific-descriptive attitude, which focuses on the person's indifferent properties, such as weight and height, and an existential attitude, which focuses on the person's ways of being-in-the-world. Heidegger characterizes the distinction as *ontological*, whereas Kant construes it as *reflective* or *methodological*, but this difference cuts less deeply than it might at first seem. After all, in the context of phenomenology, ontology is a reflective enterprise: we are exploring the *meaning* of our various ways of experiencing the world, rather than developing a traditional inventory of the universe's furniture.[23]

The third facet of Heidegger's analysis of being-in-the-world that I identified above is the topic of §13 of *Being and Time*: the thesis that cognition is a founded mode of being-in. Before developing Heidegger's argument, we must discuss the words "cognition" and "knowing." In Macquarrie and Robinson's translation, the title of §13 is "A Founded Mode in which being-in is Exemplified. Knowing the World" (86/59). The German translated as "knowing the world" is "*Welterkennen.*" "*Erkennen*" and "*Erkenntnis*" are often used in philosophy to mean knowledge, as in *Erkenntnistheorie*, which is theory of knowledge. They can also be used to mean cognition, however, which is the way in which Kant uses them most often. Recent translators of Kant's writings have begun to use "cognition," where the older and more established translations have used "knowledge."[24] Because Heidegger's discussion of *Erkenntnis* in §13 of *Being and Time* does not focus on any of the special epistemological features of knowledge, such as justification or truth, but rather aims squarely at general aspects of intentionality, it is better to render the term as "cognition" here. (Heidegger discusses knowledge more specifically in §43a in any case.)

Heidegger's thesis in §13 is that cognition is founded or grounded in being-in. This is to say both that familiarity is more basic than cognition, and that cognition is not self-sufficient, but rather a derivative mode of familiarity. Put in a punchier form: Dasein in-a-world is not a subject cognizant of an object. Heidegger uses phenomenology to undercut any attempt to impose a subject–object scheme on our description of our everyday experience. We explored Heidegger's critique of the subject–object model of experience above in chapter 2. If we accept that the subject–object model forces us into awkward and distorted descriptions of our everyday experience, the question becomes: which is more basic, the isolation of a subject attempting to transcend to an object (captured by the subject–object model), or the familiarity of a world that is already disclosed (Heidegger's model)? Should we view subjective isolation as an episodic breakdown in familiarity, or the experience of familiarity as a cognitive achievement to which we do not carefully attend? The chapters that follow *are* Heidegger's attempt to convince us that familiarity is more fundamental than cognition. For now it is worth noting three points.

First, Heidegger maintains that this very question has not heretofore been discussed, because the phenomena of the world and our being-in-the-world have been overlooked. Heidegger views himself as raising this issue for the first time. On this score he is probably correct, although it is also true that other twentieth-century philosophers initiated similar discussions. John Dewey argued that experience is not a matter of knowledge, but rather of practical know-how.[25] Dewey launched his critique of epistemology and the subject–object distinction before Heidegger began to study at the university, but Dewey was writing in an idiom, language, and tradition with which Heidegger and his teachers had no familiarity, and for which they would have had little sympathy. The failure of existential phenomenology and American pragmatism to engage each other in a healthy dialog is one of the great missed opportunities of twentieth-century philosophy. Beginning in the 1930s, Ludwig Wittgenstein also argued that subject and object, knower and known, are philosophical constructs that generate more problems than they solve.[26] He does not try to replace traditional philosophical approaches to subjectivity with newer ones, but rather wants to bring philosophy, as traditionally practiced, to an end. So, Heidegger is not alone in rejecting the subject–object model of experience.

Second, as we noted above in section (ii) and will explore in more detail below in section (xii), the conception of inner objects and the derivative notion of cognitive content are hold-overs from the Aristotelian metaphysics of mind and nature. Both their antiquity and the association with a now-defunct vision of the world make them highly suspect. Nevertheless, we can distinguish between general metaphors of interiority and specific philosophical theories that rely on the notions of *content* and *immanence*. Even though the philosophical theories are suspect, this does not *ipso facto* condemn the general metaphorical economy of the subjective and the interior. If we are less drawn to neologism than Heidegger (and who isn't?) we will want to continue using the language of subjectivity and interiority. We must be careful, however, to inspect our baggage before we board the train and make sure that we are not inadvertently smuggling traditional metaphysical assumptions into our account of human life.

Third and finally, I do not believe that Heidegger attempted to offer anything like a constructive argument against the subject–object interpretation of human life. Several recent exegeses of *Being and*

Time have attributed such an argument to Heidegger, most notably Hubert Dreyfus's *Being-in-the-World* and Mark Okrent's *Heidegger's Pragmatism*.[27] These are fascinating and powerful books, worth studying carefully. In so far as they venture constructive arguments against the subject–object model of experience, they go beyond anything that Heidegger tried, or even would have wanted, to achieve in *Being and Time*. Heidegger's arguments are phenomenological. With respect to the subject–object model of human experience, his argument amounts to the charge that this model does not do justice to our experience, that it forces us to describe our experience in awkward ways, and places the emphasis in our philosophical inquiries on abstract concerns and considerations remote from our everyday lives. Heidegger attempts to drive a methodological wedge between the old ways of doing philosophy and the new way he is offering us.

In sum, our most fundamental experience of ourselves is suffused with mineness and mattering: you experience your life as yours, and that means that it matters to you (is an issue for you) who you are. Since you are proximally immersed in the world in which you live, you also experience the world as yours. The world is not just a "universe of objects," but rather a social milieu. Although you are physically located in a system of things, your fundamental experience of yourself discloses to you the locale in which you live. In order to experience a system of objects in which you are included, you must first experience a disengagement from your immersed and absorbed living. What we need now is a positive phenomenological account of engagement with the world. That is what Heidegger offers us I.3.

Study Question

What other sorts of distinctions parallel that between being overweight/underweight/just right and weighing x pounds?

V. THE WORLD

Heidegger's exploration of the world develops in three phases after the introductory §14. Part A of the chapter directly explores the world phenomenologically. It advances from a description of the entities that are "closest to you" in your experience to an analysis of the structure of the world itself, what Heidegger calls the "worldhood of the world." Part B contrasts Heidegger's phenomenological analysis with Descartes's conception of the world as *res extensa*. Finally, Part C explores Dasein's existential spatiality, that is, the way in which Dasein experiences distance, nearness, and spatiality suffused with mattering. Because of the limitations of this Reader's Guide, I will focus on Part A, skip Part B, and relegate Part C to a few comments in section (vii) below.

Dealings and Equipment

Heidegger calls our engaged interaction with the world "dealings." As Macquarrie and Robinson note in their footnote #2 on page 95, the German word that they translate as "dealings" (*Umgang*) is connected with several other technical terms, such as environment (*Umwelt*) and circumspection (*Umsicht*). The environment is not an ecological phenomenon, as in the dominant sense the word carries today, but rather, our "proximate world," the immediate world by which we are surrounded. By "surrounded" here we do not mean spatially surrounded, but existentially surrounded: the immediate world in which we are immersed and absorbed. Our dealings ("goings-around") take place in the environment ("around-world"). These dealings are guided by a special form of "sight," circumspection ("around-sight"). Heidegger uses "sight" and related words throughout *Being and Time* as metaphors for intelligence. Our engaged everyday dealings are intelligent, but the intelligence that guides them is not cognitive, but rather practical.

What are our dealings like? "The kind of dealing which is closest to us is as we have shown, not a bare perceptual cognition, but rather that kind of concern which manipulates things and puts them to use" (95/67). As Heidegger describes it in *Basic Problems*:

> When we enter here through the door, we do not apprehend the seats, and the same holds for the door-knob. Nevertheless, they are there in this peculiar way: we go by them circumspectively, avoid them circumspectively, stumble against them, and the like. Stairs, corridors, windows, chair and bench, blackboard and much more are not given thematically. (*Basic Problems*, 163)

I often walk into the seminar room in the Philosophy Dept. at Georgetown University while discussing an issue with one of my students. I do not look where I am going; I just walk through the door. I only have to look if something has changed, if for example I bump into a chair or a person. The things in my immediate environment are mostly not objects of cognition for me, but rather things of use, things ready to hand to be used, equipment. When I am in an unfamiliar environment, however, I may look carefully at my surroundings, focusing visually and cognitively on the objects around me, in order to be able to make my way about this strange world effectively.

On page 96, after asking what the proximate objects of our experience are, Heidegger answers: they are Things. Of course, this is not Heidegger's view, but rather a traditional answer. This is typical of Heidegger's pedagogical style in *Being and Time*; he first leads the reader down the conventional path with a traditional analysis of his theme, only to expose the errors of the tradition afterwards. The reader must be alert to this strategy in order to avoid confusion. Heidegger devotes this paragraph and the next to explaining why this traditionalist response is wrong and to settling on new vocabulary to address the phenomena. He considers the analysis of the proximate objects of our experience as "Things invested with value." This formulation is a deliberate echo of Husserl's characterization of the "natural attitude" in his *Ideas*, §28: Husserl describes himself as aware in the first instance of a world of objects spread out in space, some of which are "invested with value." That is, I am aware of a world of things around me, and some of them have functional value: this object right before me is a computer, useful for writing and doing email; this object is a light, useful for illuminating my workspace.

Heidegger rejects this characterization, for it suggests that the entities one deals with in immediate encounters with the environment are objects that also have "value," paradigmatically, use-value. This in turn further suggests we can describe those objects shorn of their value. I can describe my stereo speakers as "mere things" and then add onto that "neutral" description a statement of their function, use, or value. This is a natural way to approach describing the speakers, if one has been exposed to the philosophical tradition. After all, surely the speakers really are rectangular prisms made of wood, with wires and so on inside. These rectangular prisms have a role in my life, but if the human race were to die off, the rectangular prisms would persist, although now they would be useless. Therefore, their use is something added to their underlying reality. What could be clearer?

Recall the guiding principle developed in the previous section: our fundamental access to the world is our familiarity with it, not cognition of it. What is the quality of my familiarity with the speakers? I am familiar with them *as speakers*, not as rectangular prisms that also have a use in my life. Indeed, I am often familiar with the entities in my environment without being able to describe them neutrally. What color are the speakers, what shape is the phone on my desk? I have to stop and figure out answers to those questions, because I do not know. I do not know, because my primary access to those pieces of equipment is not through some neutral description of them with value added on, but rather simply through their role in activity. Seeing use-objects as neutral, value-free entities with value added on requires an artificial stance towards them, a "bare perceptual cognition," a "holding back from manipulation," as Heidegger describes it. So, Heidegger appropriates a special word to pick out these proximate entities that show up in our everyday dealings: *equipment*.

He adds that often equipment is not *present* in my experience at all.

> The peculiarity of what is proximally ready-to-hand is that, in its readiness-to-hand, it must, as it were, withdraw in order to be ready-to-hand quite authentically. That with which our everyday dealings proximally dwell is not the tools themselves. On the contrary, that with which we concern ourselves primarily is the work – that which is to be produced at the time . . . . (99/69)

As I turn on the music in my living room, preparing to hang out with a friend and chat, I do not encounter the speakers at all. The speakers withdraw, recede from my experience. What stands out in my experience is the music on which I am focused and the ambience of my living room. After I get the situation right and sit down to chat, the music and ambience may well recede too, as my friend and I focus on what we are talking about. Equipment, when it is functioning properly, is not salient within my experience. A piece of equipment is often not an object at all.

Further, typically equipment populates our world not as individual objects, but as contexts of equipment (97/68). My living room has a matrix of equipment that makes it the room it is: not only speakers, but sofa, chairs, rug, coffee table, and so on. If someone asks me what I have in my living room, I have to stop and think. I do not know offhand, yet I am familiar with my living room, so familiar in fact that I can enter and settle into it at will. My living room is an entire context of equipment, all arranged and arrayed so that it can serve its appointed purpose. Sofas *belong* in living rooms, which is why we do a double-take when we see a sofa sitting idly by the side of a road, for example. A sofa by the side of a road is *out of place*. One can just walk up to such a sofa and sit in it, but normally one's use of a sofa is always in terms of the sofa's belonging to a living room.

In sum, to encounter a piece of equipment is to use it. To use it, moreover, is to use it for some task, and typically in such use we are immersed in what we are doing and paying little or no attention to the equipment itself (except when it is equipment designed to attract attention, or is malfunctioning – more on both of these conditions later). We understand equipment in terms of the role it plays in our dealings: "A totality of equipment is constituted by various ways of the 'in-order-to,' such as serviceability, conduciveness, usability, manipulability" (97/68).

Heidegger coins a new term to capture the being of equipment: *readiness-to-hand*. He contrasts the readiness-to-hand of equipment with the *presence-at-hand* of mere things. Macquarrie and Robinson have chosen to emphasize the root "hand" in Heidegger's German terms, "*zuhanden*" and "*vorhanden*," what is *to* or *at* my hand vs. what is *before* my hand. In explaining what he means by "ready-to-hand," Heidegger writes: "Only because equipment has *this* being-in-itself [viz., readiness-to-hand] and does not merely occur, is it manipulable in the broadest sense and at our disposal" (98/69). He contrasts what "merely occurs" (*vorkommt*) with what is at our disposal. Thus, "*zuhanden*" means available, and "*vorhanden*" means being occurrent or present. Heidegger's thesis is, then, that what it is for a typical entity in our environment *to be* is for it to be available, at our disposal, for use.

A critic might object by insisting that we cannot deny that the hammer could not *be* available, unless it were also occurrent or present-at-hand at the same time. Heidegger addresses this question in §15:

Yet only by reason of something present-at-hand, "is there" anything ready-to-hand. Does it follow, however, granting this thesis for the nonce, that readiness-to-hand is ontologically founded upon presence-at-hand? (101/71)

Heidegger's phraseology in the second sentence, "granting this thesis for the nonce," undercuts the apparent concession in the first sentence. He is saying that *even if it is true* that entities ready-to-hand can only exist "by reason" or "on the basis" of entities present-at-hand, it does not follow that the *being* of the ready-to-hand is defined in terms of present-at-hand features. One could open up a discussion here of categorial reducibility and ontological supervenience,[28] but whatever their intrinsic interest, such discussions do not reflect Heidegger's phenomenological method. Heidegger aims to describe how we experience equipment, and so the relevant question is whether all equipment shows up as a modification of something present-at-hand.

Phenomenologically speaking, not all pieces of equipment show themselves as also present-at-hand. To see this it is best to move beyond the narrow compass of equipment or tools in the conventional sense. Heidegger focuses on equipment in §15, but in the course of his discussion he progressively broadens his scope to a wider range of entities ready-to-hand, including materials (§15), signs (§17), and what we can call paraphernalia in general (§18). This is a good thing, because for many of us tools in any ordinary sense of the term are not a dominant sort of entity in our lives.

Materials. "In the work there is also a reference or assignment to 'materials': the work is dependent on leather, thread, needles, and the like" (100/70). As I build the shelves with my hammer, I use not only the tools in my workshop, but also the boards, nails, and so on. Heidegger further expands this category of materials to include raw materials: "In equipment that is used, 'nature' is uncovered along with it by that use – the 'nature' we find in natural products" (100/70). As I am cooking in the kitchen, I use not only bowls and frying pans and spatulas, but eggs and spinach and the other food stuffs. Eggs are not normally a tool, unless you are egging your neighbor's house; they are (in the kitchen) a raw material used in cooking, just as is the wood I buy for my fireplace. The eggs with which I cook are eggs for cooking, not natural things with biological properties, as a biologist sees them.

Here, however, nature is not to be understood as that which is just present-at-hand, nor as the *power of nature*. The wood is a forest of timber, the mountain a quarry of rock; the river is water-power, the wind is wind "in the sails." As the "environment" is uncovered, the "nature" thus uncovered is encountered too. (100/70)

Signs. Signs are also equipment of a sort, although not a tool in a conventional sense. "But signs, in the first instance, are themselves items of equipment whose specific character as equipment consists in *showing* or *indicating*" (108/77). Heidegger's example of a sign is a turn signal on a car. A turn signal is a piece of equipment, in that it is at our disposal for use in driving, and its specific function is to indicate which way the driver is going to turn. Heidegger treats signs distinctly from language or "discourse" (which he discusses in I.5), because language is not a set of signs. Language does not consist of tools for communicating or describing; it is, rather, an expressive medium in which we share a world with one another. For this reason Heidegger assimilates conventional signs, such as turn signals, with natural signs, such as storm clouds, because both kinds of sign are available as indicators of other phenomena. He does not classify monuments and symbols as signs, however, because they are expressive; they are discourse rather than equipment.

Paraphernalia.[29] Finally, and most interestingly, Heidegger introduces terminology in §18 that allows him to expand the conception of the ready-to-hand far beyond equipment.

> To say that the being of the ready-to-hand has the structure of assignment means that it has in itself the character of *having been assigned*. An entity is uncovered when it has been assigned to something, and assigned as that entity which it is. *With* any such entity there is an involvement which it has *in* something. The character of being which belongs to the ready-to-hand is *involvement*. (115/83–84*)

Heidegger first uses the term "assignment"[30] in §15, when he writes: "In the 'in-order-to' as a structure there lies an *assignment* of something to something" (97/68). A piece of equipment is an entity that serves a function, an entity "in-order-to" something. A hammer is for driving nails, a garlic press is for pressing garlic. Such functionality is a *kind* of assignment. A piece of equipment's belonging to an equipmental context is also a kind of assignment (97/68). What do both of these sorts of assignment have in common? They are both sorts of involvement: a hammer is involved both in hammering and in the workshop. With this concept of involvement in focus, we can see that a great many other things are involved in our activity without exactly being equipment: paintings and other forms of adornment, religious artifacts, copies of novels, and so on. We do not typically *use* these items for a specific purpose, but to say what they are we need to talk about their roles in human life and not just their physical properties. The paraphernalia of human life is ontologically distinguished by *being* what it is *assigned* to be by our practices; its being is involvement.

We may now return to the question whether "only by reason of something present-at-hand, 'is there' anything ready-to-hand" (101/71). If we are focused only on tools, then it may seem as if to be ready-to-hand requires something present-at-hand that under-lies it and is invested with or assigned value by our practices. If we broaden our focus to paraphernalia in general, however, it is far less obvious that this is so. If you and I are both reading *Hamlet*, are we reading the same book or two different books? There are two exemplars of *Hamlet* between us, but only one drama, *Hamlet*. A traditional metaphysician will puzzle over the relations between exemplars and dramas and will try to assimilate it to some relation that metaphysicians feel they understand better, such as species–specimen or universal–particular. This kind of assimilation, how-ever, is likely to miss the specific texture of the relationship between drama and exemplar, which is, after all, not the same relation as that between red things and the universal red. It is more like the relation between a word-type and word-token, but again not exactly. (*Hamlet* can, after all, be edited, abridged, and translated.) The point is this: when it comes to the drama, *Hamlet*, which you and I are both reading, we do not encounter it as something present-at-hand, something located in this place with these physical characteristics.

In sum, the ready-to-hand is a sort of entity, an entity defined by its involvement in our practices. In order to say what a spatula, an egg, a turn signal, a chalice, or a drama is, we must describe these entities in terms of the role they play in our lives. Heidegger does not emphasize the point here in I.3, but the present-at-hand is what it is independently of our lives and the roles that entities play in our lives.

Galaxies, quarks, electrical charge, and lizards are what they are irrespective of our concerns and interests.

Circumspection and Breakdown

In §13 Heidegger argues that our average everyday dealings in the world are not guided by cognition. Rather, they are a matter of engaged familiarity. When we are going about our business in the world, we encounter and use, but do not always observe the entities around us. Does this mean that our dealings are "automatic," "mindless," or a matter of mechanical habit? No.

> But when we deal with [entities ready-to-hand] by using them and manipulating them, this activity is not a blind one; it has its own kind of sight, by which our manipulation is guided and from which it acquires its specific security. Dealings with equipment subordinate themselves to the manifold assignments of the "in-order-to." And the sight with which they thus accommodate themselves is *circumspection*. (98/69*)

What is circumspection?

By "sight" Heidegger does not mean visual perception. He uses sight as a metaphor for intelligence. He argues that we are familiar with our environment and the paraphernalia that we encounter in it primarily through our skills and abilities, our competences, rather than through cognition. These skills, moreover, are intelligent. As I drive a nail with a hammer, the way in which I hold and wield the hammer is calibrated to the situation in which I am hammering, at least if I am skilled at hammering. I do not need to stop and think about the hammer and how to swing it, and in fact, if I do stop and think, I will swing it wrong. I see my way through the situation and to the goal of my activity by staying focused on the goal and letting my skills navigate the details.

> That with which our everyday dealings proximally dwell is not the tools themselves. On the contrary, that with which we concern ourselves primarily is the work – that which is to be produced at the time; and this is accordingly ready-to-hand too. The work bears with it that referential totality within which the equipment is encountered. (99/69)

Because my skills and capacities in the situation are keyed into the situation, I do not need to know explicitly or cognitively reflect on what I am doing. I focus my cognitive attention on the level of my activity at which my skills are challenged. I focus on the goal for which I am struggling, rather than on the aspects of my activity over which I have mastery.

Sometimes, of course, we do focus on the equipment we are working with. Here I must confess my limited mastery of carpentry. When *I* cut a board, I have to focus intently and bear down on moving the circular saw straight along the line. My saw-cuts have a tendency to slip and slide and be jagged, and when I can, I clamp a guide to the board to steady my cut. When I renovated my house, however, and had the pleasure of observing a master carpenter at work, I noticed that he could joke around and offer personal and political wisdom, while all the while making a perfectly straight cut, often not looking the whole time at what he was doing. This is the achievement of a steady hand, strength, and forty years of experience. So, what we bear down on in our activity is a function of the extent and degree of our mastery. Tools that are unfamiliar require focus, whereas familiar tools do not. Our primordial or originary being-in-the-world is a matter of familiarity, and when it comes to making our way about the world, familiarity is a function of competence or mastery.

Nevertheless, sometimes the equipment forces us to focus on it, when it malfunctions or in some other way resists our work with it. Such phenomena of breakdown or "*un*readiness-to-hand" are the theme of §16: conspicuousness, obtrusiveness, and obstinacy. A piece of equipment is conspicuousness, when it malfunctions: "the tool turns out to be damaged, or the material unusable." A piece of equipment is obtrusive, when another piece of equipment on which it relies is missing, when it ". . . not only [is] not 'handy' ['*handlich*'] but [is] not 'to hand' ['*zur Hand*']" (103/73). In this sort of case, both the missing equipment and the equipment that we do have "to hand," but which we cannot use, are unready-to-hand. Finally, a piece of equipment is obstinate, when it is an obstacle, rather than an instrument of our concern. "That to which our concern refuses to turn, that for which it has 'no time,' is something *un*-ready-to-hand in the manner of what does not belong here, of what has not as yet been attended to" (103/73–74). Through all the details of Heidegger's phenomenology of the unready-to-hand, two points are important.

First, in an encounter with equipment that is unready-to-hand, we are forced to focus or bear down on the equipment. It is unready-to-hand, precisely because it frustrates our activity. Of course, the standards of what counts as malfunctioning are relative to the person. A sticky clutch can be a serious challenge to one driver, but not much of a challenge at all to an experienced driver, especially the owner of the car who has learned to cope with this difficulty. The category of the unready-to-hand, then, is a category that makes sense relative to our capacities and skills, that is, relative to our understanding. The unready-to-hand is whatever challenges our abilities and forces us to bear down on it, rather than on the work to be accomplished.

Second, unreadiness-to-hand is a "deficient mode" of readiness-to-hand, not a mode of presence-at-hand. A broken hammer is not a pile of wood and steel, which would be what it is regardless of what we aim to do. It is a broken hammer. A broken hammer is frustrating, in a way that a pile of wood and steel is not. To malfunction is not to be absent; it is to be unusable. The contrast between what is present and what is absent is different from the contrast between what is available and what is not. A broken coffee maker is present, indeed, so aggravatingly present that it becomes the focus of our attention and activity. Something can be unavailable by being absent, as e.g., when it is missing, but *to be* unavailable is not the same thing as *to be* absent.

Nonetheless, we can get a glimpse of the present-at-hand in breakdown situations.

> Pure presence-at-hand announces itself in such [malfunctioning] equipment, but only to withdraw to the readiness-to-hand of something with which one concerns oneself – that is to say, of the sort of thing we find when we put it back into repair. (103/73)

The practically irrelevant physical properties of the hammer are more salient when the hammer is broken than when it is functioning. It takes me a moment of reflection and searching my mind to remember the color of my hammer (it is brown), because my hammer is in working order and I pay no attention to its color. Its color is practically irrelevant. (Of course, if I am dealing with color-coded equipment, such as wire that is coded for its gauge, then its color is practically relevant and its color is a theme of my activity.) When my hammer breaks, however, and I just dumbly stare at it, its color becomes more salient to me. Its practically irrelevant physical characteristics become accessible. If I fix the hammer, however, then its color once again recedes, and the hammer withdraws into its availability. So, in breakdown experiences, the merely present makes an appearance, usually only to withdraw from the scene again, as my activity gets back underway.

Significance and Worldhood

Circumspection is guided by the totality of assignments that contextualize the task on which we are working. Because I am trying to build a shelf, and because I am able to do so, I refer myself from the task to the equipment and materials. My circumspection is guided by the in-order-to relations that define the equipment and material and their relation to the task at hand. Circumspection is guided by the practical structure of the workshop, a practical structure that I typically already understand, as I dive into my work. Circumspection not only guides me in my immediate activity of building the shelf, but more widely as I move through the environment and pass from one activity to the next. Why do I build a shelf? In order to set up my garage to hold more of that ineliminable American junk we acquire. So, the larger project of making over my garage refers me to the more immediate project of building a shelf, which refers me first to the task of cutting this board down to eight feet. In all of this, I am guided by the structure of in-orders-to that bind the workshop and my activity together.

Often I do not move from larger project to sub-project, but horizontally, as it were, from one project to another. So, after preparing lecture notes for tomorrow's class, I turn to grading papers for my other class. There is no vertical in-order-to relation here. So, what guides me in this transition?

But the totality of involvements itself goes back ultimately to a towards-which in which there is *no* further involvement: this towards-which is not an entity with the kind of being that belongs to what is ready-to-hand within a world; it is rather an entity whose being is defined as being-in-the-world, and to whose ontological constitution worldhood itself belongs. This primary towards-which is not just another towards-this as something in which an involvement is possible. The primary "towards-which" is a for-the-sake-of-which. But the "for-the-sake-of" always pertains to the being of *Dasein*, for which, in its being, that very being is essentially an *issue*. (116–117/84)

I take on both of these nominally independent tasks – preparing this lecture as part of teaching this class, and grading those papers as part of teaching that class – for the sake of being a teacher. The structure of in-orders-to that define the equipment and material and tasks found in this workshop or that office are not just an abstract network of functional roles. Rather, they are bound together by their common involvement in a way of being Dasein for the sake of which I do what I do.

It is unfortunate that Heidegger briefly gives the impression that there is one ultimate for-the-sake-of-which, namely survival. Or at least, it is possible to read one of his comments this way: ". . . and this protection 'is' for the sake of providing shelter for Dasein – that is to say, for the sake of a possibility of Dasein's being" (116/84). This is a misimpression, however. I am also a father, a husband, a son, a neighbor, a youth baseball coach, and so on. Are all of these for-the-sakes-of-which projects that themselves refer back to one ultimate for-the-sake-of-which in my life? There is a temptation to think so, especially when we are forced to deliberate about the overall shape of our lives. When service on the board of directors of our youth baseball league begins to crowd out professional research, I am forced to confront this conflict and ask myself which is more important. If I feel the inclination to try to sort all this out rationally, I will look for the deeper and more comprehensive goal to which to subsume these various projects. It is this sort of reasoning that led Thomas Aquinas, e.g., to posit a "last" or ultimate "end" or goal of human life, a final anchor to which the entire business of rational deliberation could be tied, when needed.[31] It is not necessary to decide here whether rational deliberation requires such a final anchor, for Heidegger does not think that deliberation, rational or otherwise, is the mode in which we confront the deepest questions about who we are and for the sake of what we live. Deliberation is a form of experience that arises in response to breakdown (410/359, §69b). I am normally guided in juggling and balancing my competing interests and projects by the various affects or attunements that I experience: I instinctively lay off the board of directors service to put more time into my professional work, because of the differing ways in which these projects matter to me. We will explore this in more detail below in our discussion of disposedness (section viii). For our purposes here we need only note that there is no reason for Heidegger to commit himself to a conception of an ultimate end of human life.

The structure of in-orders-to is bound together and makes reference back to for-the-sakes-of-which, which themselves are not subordinated to any further goals. We have here, then, the structure of the practical contexts in which we operate. Heidegger calls this structure *significance*. At this point we confront a heap of Heidegger-jargon, and it is worth pausing to collect some of it together. Heidegger writes: "The relational character which these relationships of assigning possess, we take as one of *signifying*" (120/87). The German word he uses is *"bedeuten,"* although he hyphenates it in this its inaugural use (so, *"be-deuten"*). In ordinary German *"bedeuten"* means to mean. Macquarrie and Robinson point out (in their footnote #3 on page 120) that by hyphenating the word, Heidegger may mean to emphasize the root *"deuten"* in the term. *"Deuten"* means to interpret and to point. Further, Heidegger uses the word *"Bedeutsamkeit"* to refer to the "totality of this signifying." *"Bedeutsamkeit"* means significance or importance in ordinary German. So, Heidegger wants to draw attention to the way in which equipment, materials, tasks, and so on become significant or important in virtue of their roles in our activity, and how in virtue of those roles, they also point to one another. The hammer points to driving in nails, and driving in nails points to the hammer; driving nails points to fastening objects, which points to building a shelf, which points, in the end, to being a homeowner or carpenter or construction worker, or what have you. All of the relations Heidegger has been analyzing (for-the-sake-of-which, in-order-to, the whereof of material constitution, and so on) make up the structure of the context in which we operate, the structure of the world.

The world is bound together by these pointings. The structure of the world consists of the totality of these pointings or signifyings. "The relational totality of this signifying we call *significance*. This is what makes up the structure of the world – the structure of that wherein Dasein as such already is" (120/87). There are two ways to approach this definition. Heidegger the phenomenological architect wants to point out the structural pattern of the world, to see the worldhood of the world as a relational scaffolding that is filled, in each case, by the stuff of this world, this context. Heidegger the existential phenomenologist wants to emphasize the texture of significance or importance in the contexts in which we operate.

In order to live in a world in a distinctively human fashion, we must always already be keyed into the structure of significance of the world. When we walk into a workshop that serves some purpose we know not what, we are baffled by the equipment. The workshop is unfamiliar to us, because we do not grasp the in-orders-to and for-the-sakes-of-which that structure the context. To be familiar with a context, with a world, is to grasp the significance, the signifyings, of the things that are located in it. Our ability to experience something as equipment in order to . . . or paraphernalia involved in . . . is based in our prior familiarity with the structure of significance, that is, with our understanding of the roles that things play in our world. Whenever we encounter and deal with a particular piece of paraphernalia, we do so *in terms of* the role that it plays in our activities. That is the difference between confronting a hammer and confronting a hunk of wood and metal. So, a familiarity with the interlocking network of roles and tasks and for-the-sakes-of-which is a condition of the possibility of encountering paraphernalia at all, and it is the heart of our being-in a practical context.

The world is not just a context of paraphernalia; it is also a human context. The workshop is not just a relational system of functions, but rather a fabric of roles held together and grounded in the human possibilities that it subserves. This links the paraphernalia of the world to the people who dwell in the world. Hammers, nails, and boards make no sense apart from carpentry and home-ownership and all the other human possibilities or for-the-sakes-of-which in which they are involved. The same holds in reverse: there is no such thing as being a carpenter apart from the tools and tasks of the carpenter. Someone who describes himself as a carpenter, but who does not work with wood and uses no tools is either a poseur or someone who does not know what carpentry is. So, just as paraphernalia is "uplinked" to human possibilities, human possibilities are "downlinked" to paraphernalia. You live in a complex fabric of overlapping human contexts, the world of school, of work, of the family. These worlds make sense to you in terms of the various facets of your life (your being). Moreover, the various facets of your being make sense in terms of these worlds.

The key to the concept of a world in Heidegger's distinctive sense is precisely this interweaving of human possibility and the roles of paraphernalia.

> *That wherein* Dasein understands itself beforehand in the mode of assigning itself is *that in terms of which* it has let entities be encountered beforehand. *The wherein of an act of understanding which assigns itself, is that in terms of which one lets entities be encountered in the kind of being that belongs to involvements; and this wherein is the phenomenon of the world.* (119/86*)

The world is a horizon of understanding, a space of possibilities, on the background of which we understand both paraphernalia and ourselves. The roles in which paraphernalia are constitutively involved cannot be disentangled from the human possibilities in which we invest ourselves and thereby come to understand who we are. The world is a unitary horizon for making sense of both human life and the paraphernalia with which we surround ourselves.

This implies, finally, that we *are* the sorts of entity who we are only in so far as we go about our business in the world in which we live.

> Dasein as such is always something of this sort; along with its being, a context of the ready-to-hand is already essentially un-covered: Dasein, in so far as it *is*, has always submitted itself already to a "world" which it encounters, and this *submission* belongs essentially to its being. (120–121/87)

To understand ourselves is to submit to a world, or better, to accept or acquiesce in a world. Officially, the passage just quoted focuses on Dasein's relation to the "world," i.e., to the system of objects or paraphernalia that populate our world. This submission to a "world" of paraphernalia is a consequence, however, of our being tied to a world, a world that contextualizes and situates both us and the paraphernalia. We see here, then, a significant element of Heidegger's existentialism, his rejection of the abstraction that dominates so much traditional philosophy. Kant writes about our intelligible character, which somehow stands outside the confines of nature and to which, when we adopt the moral point of view, we ascribe responsibility for having chosen these actions we perform. Husserl writes of the thought-experiment of the annihilation of the world, in which the order and organization of object-directed experience breaks down to such a point that all that remains to our experience is the apperceptive awareness of an ego-point from which a world would be experienced. Thomas Nagel, in a well-known contemporary treatment, writes of the "view from nowhere."[32] These philosophical fantasies of disembodiment, of disentanglement from the world (all prefigured in Plato's philosophy, where Socrates speaks of the body as the prison-house of the soul) are just that, fantasies. To be a human being is precisely to be entangled in a world, to be unable to extricate oneself from the world, to understand oneself and the things around one in terms of the same horizon, the world.

Terminology

In chapter 3 we acquire a new set of technical terms:

Assignment (or reference): the dedication of an entity to its role in our activity.

Circumspection: the "sight" or intelligence that guides our practical dealings in the world and with paraphernalia.

Conspicuousness: the mode of unreadiness-to-hand exhibited when a tool malfunctions.

Dealings: going about business in the world.

Environment: the immediate practical context in which we operate.

For-the-sake-of-which: the relation between the larger scale projects in which we are engaged and the self-understandings that motivate them.

In-order-to: the relation between a piece of equipment and the task it subserves, e.g., between the hammer and driving nails.

Involvement: the relation between a piece of paraphernalia and the role it plays in our activity.

Obstinacy: the mode of unreadiness-to-hand exhibited by something that is an obstacle to our on-going activity.

Obtrusiveness: the mode of unreadiness-to-hand exhibited by a tool when an essential piece of its "co-equipment" is missing.

Presence-at-hand, present-at-hand: the kind of being of mere things, things that are not assigned to roles in human activity.

Readiness-to-hand, ready-to-hand: the kind of being of equipment. Phenomenologically, readiness-to-hand is the availability of something for use in human activity. This is not the same as a thing's presence or occurrence.

Significance: the relational whole of all the relations of signifying. That is, it is the relational web that binds the world together into a whole.

Signify: the relational quality of the in-orders-to, for-the-sakes-of-which, involvements, and so on: the relation of one item in the world "pointing to" or "signifying" another and thereby contributing to its import or significance.

Unreadiness-to-hand, unready-to-hand: The unavailability of something for use in human practice. This is not the same as a thing's absence or non-occurrence.

World: the social context or existential milieu in terms of which we understand both ourselves and the paraphernalia around us.

Worldhood: the being of the world. Significance is the being of the world, hence worldhood. *To be* a world is to be a horizon characterized by significance.

"World": the system of things, the aggregate of objects around us.

Study Question

What should we say philosophically about a piece of paraphernalia that has been forever torn from its context, such as a pottery jug in a museum?

VI. THE SELF AND THE ANYONE

Who is Dasein? Dasein is in each case mine, and that means that *I* am Dasein and so are you, are we not? Yes, but this answer obscures as much as it reveals. When we try to *say* who is in-the-world, we are left with little alternative than to say, "I am in-the-world." The "I" is a "non-committal *formal indicator*, indicating something which may perhaps reveal itself as its 'opposite' in some particular phenomenal context of being" (151–152/116). That is, it is grammatically correct to say that it is I who am in-the-world, but this does not tell us who I am. As we have seen, we are immersed in the world of our concern, and our being does not matter to us as the significance of some isolated point of view from nowhere, but rather, as the life we are living in this world surrounded by this paraphernalia. Proximally and for the most part, we do not experience ourselves as distinct from the world. So, how do we experience ourselves?

We do not typically experience ourselves as isolated from others, but rather as immersed in the world *along with them.* "And so in the end an isolated I without others is just as far from being proximally given" (152/116). What are our encounters with others in the course of our daily business like? Just as paraphernalia are not things invested with value, so others are not bodies invested with psychological properties. Typically we understand others straight away and without further ado. As I walk into my department's office, the work-study student at the desk is taking a message. As I walk out into the courtyard, the man on the bench is eating lunch. I do not have to figure these things out. Mostly others are just there, doing what they are doing, as hammers and tables are just there, being what they are. This is what Heidegger means, when he refers to the "inconspicuousness" and "obviousness" that characterize the being of others as much as the being of paraphernalia (158/121). As with paraphernalia, what others do makes sense in terms of the horizon of the world.

Others are not, of course, paraphernalia. They do not show up as available for use. Rather, others are there with me in the world. "[Others] are neither present-at-hand nor ready-to-hand; on the contrary, they are *like* the very Dasein which frees them, in that *they are there too, and there with it*" (154/118). To say that others are "there too" and "there with" Dasein is to say that we experience others in terms of what they are pursuing, in terms of their for-the-sakes-of-which. When I see the work-study student taking a message, I understand what he is doing as for the sake of his self-understanding as a student. He and I share a social horizon that makes what we do mutually intelligible.

> By reason of this *with-like* being-in-the-world, the world is always the one that I share with others. The world of Dasein is a *with-world*. Being-in is *being-with* others. Their being-in-themselves within-the-world is *Dasein-with*. (155/119)

Others and what they do are normally easily intelligible to me, because we share a world. Heidegger calls others "Dasein-with."

We do not just share a horizon on the background of which what we each do is intelligible, however. Rather, our for-the-sakes-of-which are interwoven with one another as well. In writing this book for the sake of being a teacher and scholar, my being is an issue for me. Since being a teacher and scholar is an activity I pursue in the world, by means of paraphernalia involved in it, and engaged with others who pursue correlated activities, such as being a student, the world is an issue for me simply in so far as I am a teacher and scholar. In pursuing my for-the-sakes-of-which I am engaging and sustaining the for-the-sakes-of-which of students and readers. Since the self-understanding of being a teacher is interwoven with the self-understanding of being a student, to act for the sake of being who I am is to act for the sake of others being who they are as well. "Thus as being-with, Dasein 'is' essentially for-the-sake-of others" (160/123). Simply in so far as Dasein is being-in-the-world, it is also being-with, and simply in so far as its own life matters to it, the lives of others matter to it. Recall that Heidegger calls this mattering "care," and others' mattering to me he calls "solicitude" (*Fürsorge*, literally "caring-for"). It is important to bear in mind that just as "care" does not refer to a specific emotional state, such as worry or devotion, neither does "solicitude." "Solicitude" is just a technical term for the way others matter to us simply in so far as we lead our own lives.

One might object that Dasein cannot *essentially* be being-with, for after all, we are sometimes alone. Heidegger responds, "Being-with is an existential characteristic of Dasein even when factically no other is present-at-hand or perceived" (156/120). Even when we are alone, we are still acting for the sake of some self-understanding that is interwoven with the self-understandings of others. To be with others is not to be in their presence, but rather for what they are pursuing and how they lead their lives to make a difference to me. Even, therefore, if one is a hermit or recluse, having retreated to a cabin in the hills of Idaho to get away from everyone, others matter to one, in this case, as being despicable or to be avoided. Being a recluse is an anti-social way of understanding oneself and one's relations to others. Being anti-social is a "privative" way of being social; it is a stance on the significance of what others pursue.

Does this mean that we are communal beings? Not exactly. The view that we are fundamentally communal and that our self-understanding is at bottom a "we-understanding" is called "communitarianism." Over the past thirty years or so a political and ethical version of communitarianism has come to the fore in Anglo-American philosophy. It has been advocated by a wide range of political and ethical philosophers, including Alasdair MacIntyre, Charles Taylor, and Amitai Etzioni.[33] Heidegger's principal concern

in *Being and Time* is neither political nor ethical, but rather ontological, and so the question we must ask is not whether to embrace
political or ethical communitarianism, but rather "ontological communitarianism." Ontological communitarianism is most closely identified with Hegel, but also developed carefully and in proximity to
our concerns here by Charles Taylor.[34]

Ontological communitarianism is the view that to be a human
being is to be a member of a community. A "community" is a social
group constituted by what Taylor calls "common meanings": "By
these I mean notions of what is significant which are not just shared
in the sense that everyone has them, but are also common in the
sense of being in the common reference world." Taylor uses the
example of the U.S. being constituted by, among other things, a
common reference to a conception of freedom. He points out, moreover, that in order to have the common reference, Americans do not
have to enjoy a consensus about what this common reference means.
In 2006 "red-state Republicans" and "blue-state Democrats" have
divergent conceptions of what a free society means. Our divergent
conceptions of freedom are typically embodied for us in the models
we use to talk about freedom. For a "red-stater" the freedom to pray
in school and the freedom to own and use a gun are examples of
freedom that "blue-staters" do not accept. For a "blue-stater" the
freedom not to be pressured to pray in school and the freedom to
seek an abortion are examples of American freedom that red-staters
do not accept. Blue-staters and red-staters are equally committed to
other examples of freedom, such as the freedom from a state church,
indeed, the freedom to found one's own religious sect and open a
church in the local mall, a freedom that would hardly even occur to a
German. There can be a failure of consensus, precisely because these
are divergent conceptions of American freedom, freedom which is a
common reference point for all of us. Americans who disagree with
the conception – say, neo-Nazis – stand apart from the community,
even if legally they remain citizens. So, common commitments constitute a sense of community, a "we." "We Americans" experience
ourselves as bonded with one another and as differentiated from
other communities precisely by this common commitment.

Heidegger's with-world is not necessarily a community in this
sense. For this reason, Heidegger does not use the term "we" to name
the others, and he does not refer to the world as a "we-world," but
rather as a "with-world." Rather than "we," Heidegger coins a new

term to pick out what he means, in German *"das Man,"* which as I explained above in chapter 2 I will translate as "the Anyone."

These others, moreover, are not *definite* others. . . . "The others" whom one thus designates in order to cover up the fact of one's belonging to them essentially oneself, are those who proximally and for the most part *"are there"* in everyday being-with-one-another. The who is not this one, not that one, not oneself, not some people, and not the sum of them all. The "who" is the neuter, *the Anyone.* (164/126)

The others are not a community constituted by common commitments, but rather the Anyone. The shared social horizon, the with-world, is made up not of some definite group, a sum of persons, but rather by a social structure, a web of paraphernalia-roles, tasks, and for-the-sakes-of-which. This web is what Heidegger calls "significance" in I.3, and here he adds, ". . . the Anyone itself Articulates the referential context of significance" (167/129). We are what we pursue, and what we pursue is constituted by what is an issue in what we do. Heidegger's principal concern in I.4 is to establish that what and how things are an issue for us is governed by the social patterns in which we live.

These social patterns are what we today would call patterns of *social normativity.*

We take pleasure and enjoy ourselves as *one* takes pleasure; we read, see, and judge about literature and art as *one* sees and judges; likewise we shrink back from the "great mass" as *one* shrinks back; we find "shocking" what *one* finds shocking. The Anyone, which is nothing definite, and which all are, though not as the sum, prescribes the kind of being of everydayness. (164/126–127*)

There is a way one does things. There are ways to hammer, ways to drive, ways to drink coffee, and ways to be a teacher. Proximally and for the most part, we do things the way one does them. Because that man is drinking a coffee as one drinks coffee, his presence is unobtrusive, obvious. I "know what he is doing," because he is doing it as one does it. If he is drinking coffee abnormally (say he is lying on the floor of the coffee house while he drinks), then he obtrudes, stands out, and requires interpretation. We can think of these social patterns as a set of "expectations," as long as we do not take the word "expectation" too narrowly to refer to psychological states of expecting.

Heidegger does not merely note the existence of social normativity, but explores phenomenologically how it functions. He focuses on the phenomenon of deviance and how we respond to it. Deviance matters to us, and the care we have about deviance he calls "distantiality." Deviance stands out for us, is conspicuous, and we are disturbed by it. Typically we seek to suppress it. We look askance at people who are inappropriately dressed, we correct mispronunciations, we let people know, subtly or not so subtly, when we think they are "out of line," as we say. This suppression of deviance leads to what Heidegger calls "subjection": "But this distantiality which belongs to being-with, is such that Dasein, as everyday being-with-one-another, stands in *subjection* to others" (164/126). We are subject to the attempts to suppress deviance on the part of others, so much so, in fact, that we suppress deviance in ourselves. Walking down the streets of any town in America, people are mostly dressed very much alike: men wear "men's clothes," women "women's clothes," and no one is walking around naked or in astronaut's gear. Even in "deviant communities" people often dress mostly alike, albeit usually so as to try to shock the larger community from which they are deviating. This similarity, this normalness of human life, Heidegger calls "averageness."

With averageness and our suppressive response to deviance, Heidegger introduces a theme that will occupy him more in Division II: *levelling down*.

Thus the Anyone maintains itself factically in the averageness of that which belongs to it, of that which it regards as valid and that which it does not, and of that to which it grants success and that to which it denies it. In this averageness with which it prescribes what can and may be ventured, it keeps watch over everything exceptional that thrusts itself to the fore. (165/127)

The enforcement of averageness through the suppression of deviance minimizes not only bizarre and off-beat behavior, but also tamps down achievement and greatness.

Every kind of greatness gets noiselessly suppressed. Overnight, everything that is primordial gets glossed over as something that has long been well known. Everything gained by a struggle becomes just something to be manipulated. Every secret loses its force. (165/127*)

Dr. J's spectacular style of playing basketball, which made our eyes fall from their sockets in 1970s, can be seen in every middle school gym now. The intimate, personal, agonized blues song of Skip James, Robert Johnson, and others later became an industry standard, and today there are websites that offer to teach you how to play it.

Now, Heidegger clearly overstates the phenomenon of levelling down in §27. Greatness is not tamped down and innovations are not standardized and averaged out "overnight." The suppression of deviance is often not "noiseless," but rather quite noisy, sometimes involving open conflict and violence. Heidegger's exaggeration of levelling down is an indication of his proximity to his existentialist forebears, Nietzsche and Kierkegaard, who indulge the same rhetoric and have the same bleak view of what Heidegger here calls "publicness." We will look into this in more detail when we explore Heidegger's existentialism. For now we need only acknowledge his observation that the same forces that keep human life recognizable to us all around here and allow us to understand one another without further ado generate a form of conformism and social suppression.

So, who is in the world in an everyday way? Who is the average everyday "subject" of Dasein? Heidegger writes, "The 'who' is the neuter, the Anyone" (164/126). He adds three pages later:

> *Proximally*, factical Dasein is in the with-world, which is un-covered in an average way. *Proximally*, it is not "I," in the sense of my own self, that "am," but rather the others, whose way is that of the Anyone. In terms of the Anyone, and as the Anyone, I am "given" proximally to "myself." Proximally Dasein is the Anyone, and for the most part it remains so. (167/129)

Earlier in the same paragraph, however, he offers a slightly different formulation:

> The self of everyday Dasein is the Anyone-self, which we dis-tinguish from the *owned self* – that is, from the self which has

been taken hold of in its own way. As Anyone-self, the particular Dasein has been *dispersed* into the Anyone, and must first find itself. This dispersal characterizes the "subject" of that kind of being which we know as concernful absorption in the world we encounter as closest to us.

Who is the who of everyday Dasein, the Anyone or the Anyone-self? In §9 of *Being and Time* Heidegger declares, recall, that Dasein is in each case mine. The sorts of achievements (if we can call them that) that Heidegger attributes to the Anyone are not the sorts of things that are mine or that I could own. Indeed, Heidegger's insists on this:

> Everyone is the other, and no one is himself. The *Anyone*, which supplies the answer to the question of the *who* of everyday Dasein, is the *nobody* to whom every Dasein has already surrendered itself in being-among-one-another. (165–166/128)

The public normativity that sets the standard against which deviance is measured is not the sort of thing that you or I can own, and we cannot free ourselves from it or swear off of it. So, it is difficult to see how the Anyone could be in-the-world. *You and I* can, however, be in-the-world in such a way that our lives are dominated by the Anyone, in such a way that we have, as Heidegger says, "lost ourselves" in the Anyone. Thus, by "the Anyone-self" Heidegger must mean an individual self that lives its life in thoroughgoing subjection to the Anyone. We will explore the contrast between the Anyone-self and the owned self below beginning in section (xiii). Here we only need the distinction I have just drawn, between social normativity or the Anyone, on the one hand, and an individual thoroughly subject to that normativity, an Anyone-self. Heidegger's thesis should be, then, that the answer to the question of the Who of everyday life is the Anyone-self.

The main burden of Heidegger's analysis here in §27 is twofold: the world is constituted by a public or social normativity that insists upon a certain averageness in human affairs, and proximally we live in this averageness as an Anyone-self, rather than as some kind of autonomous subject. Heidegger's conception of our sociality differs somewhat from his predecessors' in the German tradition. Hegel thought of our sociality as constituted through what he called "objective spirit," that is, communal values or we-intentions embodied in what we do together and in our institutions. Charles Taylor and other communitarians have followed Hegel's lead on this. Heidegger's contribution to this line of thought is to argue that the social dimension of the world is thinner, as it were, than was conceived by Hegel. Probably because Hegel, like Rousseau before him and communitarians today, was seeking to develop a foundation for a political philosophy, a foundation for identifying the unity of a community through its common institutions and legal culture, these we-intentions, this sense of community was central to him. Heidegger was not a political philosopher; he was not (in *Being and Time*) interested in politics or the state. He was trying to understand, rather, how we make sense of ourselves, how we share an intelligibility, a sense for what is at stake in our lives. This does not require, although it does often involve, a sense of community.

As the political and ethical communitarians bemoan the creeping atomism of contemporary life and the breakdown of communal systems of mutual meaning,[35] Heidegger makes his entrance. He wants to understand how we continue to understand our lives, even as our sense of community literally disintegrates. Clearly, that the world is mine does not require that it be ours. It only requires that it be a with-world.

Study Question

Try to imagine a life utterly unrelated to the life lived by anyone else, that is, an ontologically isolated life. What would such a life have to be like, and why do you think Heidegger does not take seriously the suggestion that the possibility of such a life refutes his thesis that Dasein is essentially being-with?

VII. DISCLOSEDNESS AND THE THERE

As we have seen, Dasein is in its world not primarily by being conscious of it or having beliefs about and intentions to act in it. Rather, Dasein is most fundamentally in its world by being familiar with it. In I.3 Heidegger explored the constitution of the world with which we are familiar and the entities in that world. In I.4 he described the social dimension of the world and the way in which we Dasein are in the first instance Anyone-selves, that is, selves who understand ourselves primarily by way of the public articulation of the world. Here in I.5 Heidegger sets out to analyze our familiarity, as such, in more detail. What is it to be *in-a-world*? What is our being-in? Heidegger's answer: to be-in-a-world is for a world to be *disclosed* to one. §28 is a brief introduction to I.5. In it Heidegger introduces two important concepts: disclosedness and the There.

Disclosedness. Think of disclosedness as Heidegger's replacement for the traditional philosophical conception of consciousness or awareness. As we have seen, Heidegger avoids the language of consciousness, experience, awareness, and intentionality, because he feels that this traditional language brings with it unwelcome philosophical baggage. In particular, it implies a subject–object model of being-in-the-world. To be conscious or aware of a world, to experience it, to have intentional representations of it, are all subjective states directed at objects and an objective world. Here in §28 Heidegger argues that a subject–object model of our being-in-the-world "*splits* the phenomenon asunder, and there is no prospect of putting it together again" (170/132). If we begin with the assumption that we have subjective, representational or intentional states directed at a world, then the question naturally arises: How do we "transcend" the "subjective sphere" in order to grab hold of a world and understand it? Heidegger offers the language of disclosedness as a way of trying to avoid this pre-emptive splitting of the phenomenon. Instead of talking about us being conscious of or intentionally directed at the world, Heidegger writes that the world is disclosed to us.

What is it for the world to be disclosed? I.5 is the answer to that question. Heidegger analyzes disclosedness as having three facets, as I will call them: disposedness, understanding, and discourse. Disposedness is very roughly our sensitivity to the imports of things, the way things matter to us. Understanding is our skillful mastery of the world around us. Discourse is roughly our ability to articulate that world in language. This is to say, then, that Heidegger replaces traditional notions of consciousness and intentionality with a triple-faceted analysis of understanding, mood, and language.

The There. The other new concept in §28 is the There. The term "the There" is derived from "Dasein," Da-sein, being-there. What does disassembling the word "Dasein" and emphasizing the There contribute to our understanding of our being? Heidegger explains it this way:

"Here" and "yonder" are possible only in a "There" – that is to say, only if there is an entity which has made a disclosure of spatiality as the being of the "There." This entity carries in its ownmost being the character of not being closed off. In the expression "There" we have in view this essential disclosedness. By reason of this disclosedness, this entity (Dasein), together with the being-there of the world, is "there" for itself. (171/132)

What the "There" adds to disclosedness is a sense of location, place, spatiality. Due to limitations of space, I chose not to explore Heidegger's phenomenology of spatiality in I.3.C. A few words about it, however, are in order here.

The world with which we are familiar is not just a structure of significance, a scaffolding of in-orders-to and for-the-sakes-of-which. Rather, the world is somewhere. My familiarity with my world is a familiarity with places: my home, my neighborhood, my place of work. These places are not objective geometrical phenomena, but rather existential locales. Our familiarity with place includes a sense of nearness and distance. This nearness and distance is not a matter of a surveyor's measurements, but rather suffused with experiential contours. My kitchen is geometrically closer to my office than my living room is, but because of the layout of my house, it is experientially further away. A shop that is near me by the surveyor's estimate may be experientially far away, if the path from my house to the shop goes up a hill, making it hard to walk or bike the distance. Thus, we can distinguish existential from geometrical nearness and distance, existential from geometrical lay-out.

The essential point for us here is that phenomenologically we are not located in space–time; rather, we are always somewhere with which we are more or less familiar. Our familiarity with the world involves a "here" and "yonder" or "over there." In order to have a "here" and "yonder" we must be located, and Heidegger tries to capture that basic sense of location with the terminology of "the There."

Heidegger also uses the language of the "There" to attempt to supplant traditional metaphors of light with metaphors of location. The philosophical tradition has always used metaphors of sight and the light that enables sight to try to capture our openness to or consciousness of the world. Even Heidegger helps himself to the metaphor of sight in order to describe intelligence. Sight and light, however, encourage thinking of ourselves as at a distance from the world, as being on the far side of a gulf that must be transcended, or perhaps as being trapped in a domain of interiority from out of which we must shine our "intentional ray" (Husserl) and shine a light upon objects. Heidegger offers the metaphor of a clearing in the forest to make the point that we experience ourselves as situated *here* along with things around us, *yonder*, situated together, rather than as standing over against objects apart from us to which we must reach out by means of a mysterious capacity of intentional transcendence.

Working with the metaphors will only get us so far, however. We must now turn to the heavy-lifting in I.5: Heidegger's analyses of understanding, disposedness, and discourse.

Study Question

Does it really make any philosophical difference whether we say "The world is disclosed to me" rather than "I am aware of this object?"

VIII. DISPOSEDNESS

Disposedness (*Befindlichkeit* – I'll discuss the translation below) or mood is one of the basic facets of our familiarity with the world. Philosophical common sense regards moods as the very paradigm of the subjective. A mood is something "in me," a feature of my psychology. Heidegger rejects this way of looking at moods on *phenomenological* grounds. "Having a mood is not related to the psychical in the first instance, and is not itself an inner condition which then reaches forth in an enigmatical way and puts its mark on things and persons" (176/137). Now, this is a funny claim, is it not? What could be more psychical than a mood?

We do not experience moods as secluded inner experiences, encapsulated in the cabinet of consciousness. Heidegger writes: "A mood assails us. It comes neither from 'outside' nor from 'inside,' but arises out of being-in-the-world, as a way of such being" (176/136). Unfortunately, in *Being and Time* he does not offer enough ground-level phenomenology to make his point clearly. He does a much better job in his 1929/1930 lecture series, *The Fundamental Concepts of Metaphysics*, §17. After commenting, as he did in *Being and Time*, that a mood is "*not* at all '*inside*' in some interiority, only to appear in the flash of an eye; but for this reason it is *not at all outside either*," he continues on the next page:

> A human being who – as we say – is in good humour brings a lively atmosphere with them [sic]. Do they, in so doing, bring about an emotional experience which is then transmitted to others, in the manner in which infectious germs wander back and forth from one organism to another? We do indeed say that mood is infectious. Or another human being is with us, someone who through their manner of being makes everything depressing and puts a damper on everything: nobody steps out of their shell. What does this tell us? Moods are not side-effects, but are something which in advance determine our being with one another. It seems as though a mood is in each case already there, so to speak, like an atmosphere in which we first immerse ourselves in each case and which then attunes us through and through.[36]

Phenomenologically, moods are atmospheres in which we are steeped, not interior conditions.

Heidegger is thinking of the way in which a person's mood sets the tone for her environment. Every one of us has presumably had (or been?) a neighbor who is always "down in the dumps," feels like things are too hard, complains. Such a person tends to droop his shoulders, not laugh as readily. When you stop to talk to him and ask a question like, "Hey, how's it going?" the answer you are likely to get is something like, "My boss is such a jerk. You know what he did today?" Conversation becomes immobile in the presence of the downer. Why? Has your neighbor's mood infected you? No. A mood is not an internal disposition, but rather an atmosphere.

According to Heidegger's analysis, mood plays a multifaceted role in our experience. We have seen that our being is an issue for us. For our being to be an issue, it must matter to us. The *ways* in which our being matters are disclosed in mood. We, unlike tables, chairs, and rocks, can "feel like a failure" or be "riding high." Our lives can be burdensome or easy, freed up or boxed-in, guilt-ridden or light. None of these "feelings" is an object in our experience, and none is merely our "internal disposition." Rather, to be liberated or boxed in, to feel like a failure or to be riding high, are ways of carrying oneself in life.

As we saw in section (iii), moreover, we are "delivered over" to our being. To be delivered over is passive; it is to be handed over to something, rather than to claim something. This too is an element of the disclosive work of mood:

> An entity of the character of Dasein is its There in such a way that, whether explicitly or not, it is disposed [*sich befindet*] in its thrownness. In disposedness Dasein is always brought before itself, and has always found itself, not in the sense of coming across itself by perceiving itself, but in the sense of finding itself attuned. (174/135*)

We are thrown into life, which does not merely mean that by the time we become self-conscious, we are already leading a human life. This is true, but not Heidegger's point. Rather, by "thrownness" Heidegger means that we are "subject to" life, that it "burdens" us in the sense that we cannot extricate ourselves from caring about it. Indeed, at any moment we are always already attuned to and disposed in the world. Even the "pallid, evenly balanced lack of mood, which is often persistent and which is not to be mistaken for a bad mood" is a mood (173/134). Business-like indifference is a way of caring about life.

Mood not only sets the tone of life, it also tunes us in to the differential imports of the things, persons, and events around us. An *import* is the way in which something matters to us.[37] For example, in §30 Heidegger analyzes fear in terms of three components: that in the face of which we fear, the fearing itself, and that about which we fear. That "in the face of which" we fear is the object of our fear, namely, the fearsome thing. To be the object of fear *is* to be fearsome. Fear reveals objects in terms of their fearsomeness. A fearless person is someone who does not experience the fearsome; objects that most people fear, the fearless person just passes by. Consider a person who easily confronts her superiors and points out to them their unfairness or callousness. She is fearless. Rather than quaking in her boots before a fearsome boss, she sees the boss as an equal to whom she can make a point. Fear reveals the fearsome, and she who is fearless just does not experience the fearsome as readily as others do.

Not all mattering is as immediate and powerful as fear, of course. When I am working in my garage with my tools, I reach easily and naturally for my hammer, when I need it, because it is reliable. To be reliable is to bear an import in this sense.

But to be affected by the unserviceable, resistant, or threatening character of that which is ready-to-hand, becomes ontologically possible only in so far as being-in as such has been determined existentially beforehand in such a manner that what it encounters within-the-world can *matter to* it in this way. (176/137)

Thus, even serviceability or resistance are imports that pieces of equipment can bear. They are ways in which equipment matters to us in conducting our business. They are disclosed in the moods that characterize our everyday circumspection in the world.

Heidegger sums up his analysis by writing, "*Existentially, disposedness implies a disclosive submission to the world, out of which we can encounter something that matters to us*" (177/137–138). We are thrown into existence, subject to the world, delivered over to life. This is to say that we are entities who encounter the world in terms of how it matters to us. We are tuned in to the way things matter, and our tuning or temper is our mood.

Before we proceed, we should discuss the word "disposedness," as which I have chosen to translate Heidegger's German neologism "*Befindlichkeit.*" Macquarrie and Robinson translate "*Befindlichkeit*" as "state-of-mind," which is rather misleading. Heidegger eschews the language of "minds," and the language of "states" suggests substances with properties. Macquarrie and Robinson nonetheless use "state-of-mind," because its colloquial use does capture one sense that Heidegger is after. Suppose a friend has lost a loved one. We might ask, "What's her state of mind right now? Grief? Anger? Despair?" Used thus, the phrase "state of mind" means something very much like "mood," with an emphasis on one's well-being or "how one is faring." This connotation of "state of mind," if we can dissociate it from the philosophical baggage that comes with minds and states, is very close to what Heidegger means by "*Befindlichkeit.*" Heidegger is surely building on associations with the noun, "*Befinden,*" which is itself built on the reflexive verb, "*sich befinden.*" A person's *Befinden* is her condition; for example, a doctor might ask a patient about her *Befinden.* "*Wie befinden Sie sich?*" means, "How are you doing?" This coincides with one sense of the English adjective "disposed."[38] Disposedness is the ontological characteristic of us that we are always in a mood. "What we indicate *ontologically* by the term disposedness is *ontically* the most familiar and everyday sort of thing: our mood, our being-attuned" (172/134).

Heidegger's premier example of a mood in §§29–30 is fear. It sounds odd to classify fear as a mood, however. How to draw the distinction between moods and emotions is itself a controverted issue, but one way in which moods and emotions are sometimes distinguished in contemporary literature is by looking at the range of responses and behavior-modifications that are elicited by affective states. Moods like depression and elation "are capable of influencing a broad array of potential responses, many of which seem quite unrelated to the mood-precipitating event."[39] If one is mistreated and then descends into depression, the subsequent depression will have an impact upon a wide range of activities and behaviors: one may not want to eat, or one may feel no desire to participate in one's usually favorite activities, such as reading a book. These manifestations of the depression are thematically or topically unrelated to the mistreatment that triggers the depression. By contrast, if one, say, despises another person, the effects of that despising are generally restricted to one's interactions with that individual.

This way of distinguishing moods and emotions is clearly rough and ready, rather than precise, and undoubtedly reflects a continuum of phenomena, rather than two clearly disjoint sets. Nevertheless, the emphasis upon the pervasive impact of mood, the way in which mood sets a tone for the entire range of one's activities, is consonant with Heidegger's phenomenology of mood. Furthermore, the same psychologists who focus on the wider range of effects of mood-states also emphasize the way in which moods perform a "self-monitoring" function.[40] This self-monitoring function just is, I suggest, what Heidegger has in mind by "making manifest 'how one is and how one is faring.'" That is, a mood discloses our general condition to us. This is almost certainly part of the reason that Heidegger chose to use the word "*Befindlichkeit*" in this connection.

This characteristic self-monitoring turns up in Heidegger's analysis of the "about-which" of fear. The about-which of a mood is always one oneself; the mood not only discloses an object as bearing an import, but also discloses something about oneself. In the case of fear, Heidegger suggests that the fear discloses us to ourselves as "endangered and abandoned to" ourselves (180/141). A fearsome object endangers me. This is part of what it is to fear. There is a correlation between the import disclosed by fear, namely, being threatening, and what is disclosed by the self-monitoring, namely, being threatened. This feature is much less present in other emotions, such as love or amusement. The love a parent feels for a child discloses the child, to use an old-fashioned word, as dear. I am not, however, disclosed to myself in so far as my sons are disclosed to me as dear. Similarly, when I am amused by the antics of one of my neighbors' toddlers – say, she is dancing around in circles and singing merrily – the toddler is disclosed as delightful. Very little is disclosed to me about "how I am doing and how I am faring" in experiencing the delightful antics of this toddler, however.

Thus, Heidegger does seem to have something very much like what many psychologists today call "moods" in mind in his analysis: moods disclose entire situations and do so pervasively, and they disclose to us how we are doing and faring. From this vantage point, Heidegger's use of fear as an example of a mood looks to be unfortunate. He may have been misled by the special feature of fear that I am disclosed to myself as endangered, when I fear. He may also have had fearfulness in mind, rather than episodic fear, although in that case it would be difficult to understand why he focuses so strongly on the *object* of fear. Fearfulness does not so much reveal a discrete fearsome object, but rather attunes one to the possibilities of fear. Heidegger analyzes what he calls "anxiety" in some depth in §40 of *Being and Time*, and anxiety is a much better example of a mood than is fear. (It is also worth noting that Heidegger will argue later that the conformist public in which we live tries to turn our attention away from our anxiety by substituting fear for it. This makes it sensible to examine fear in detail, even if it is not a good example of a mood.)

Let us step back and survey Heidegger's conception of mood and disposedness. First, moods are *import-disclosive*: they disclose the way things matter, that is, the imports entities bear. Second, moods are *atmospheric*: they function phenomenologically like atmospheres in which we are steeped, rather than interior private states. Third, moods are *self-monitoring*: they reveal to us "how we are doing and how we are faring," as Heidegger puts it (173/134). Fourth, moods are *passive*: we are delivered over to moods. Heidegger also officially analyzes the threefold structure of a mood as having an "in-the-face-of-which," "about-which," and the mood itself. The in-the-face-of-which is best thought of under the heading of the import-disclosive character of moods, and the about-which is best of thought of under the rubric of self-monitoring.

Further, mood does not "color" or "interpret" independently

given objects of cognition. In the context of fear, Heidegger puts his point thus: "We do not first ascertain a future evil (*malum futurum*) and then fear it. But neither does fearing first take note of what is drawing close; it uncovers it beforehand in its fearsomeness" (180/141). Many children's comics exploit just this, when a character will see, say, an approaching train and only just before being run over, scream. What makes this funny is the tension between our immediate experience of the train as fearsome and the character's apparent obliviousness of the danger. Our experience is not normally like that, however. Although Heidegger does not belabor the point, his observation cuts deeper than simply noting that when we encounter something fearsome, we typically do so "from the start." We can insist upon his point as far as arguing that we cannot separate the "affectively neutral cognitive-content" from the "affective modification" in experience.

Think of the last time you were walking down the street and passed a stranger walking a big strong dog that barked viciously at you as you approached. The stranger pulls back on the dog's leash, says, "hush" or "heel" or something. You are gripped by fear; the dog shows up as fearsome. Its large and appropriately named canine teeth stand out, as do the rippling muscles in its shoulders and legs. Probably at least once or twice when this has happened, the stranger has said to you, "Oh, he's not a mean dog at all. Just barks. Here, sit Sweet Pea." You approach and stick out your hand. The dog sniffs your hand, licks it. You pet the dog. As the dog loses his aspect of fearsomeness, you begin to notice other things about him. The cute pattern on his face, how soft his tongue is. You say to yourself, "Well, his teeth aren't *that* big after all." The point is that the would-be affectively neutral cognitive content of the experience, that is, *what you see*, is in part a function of your fear or comfort. The dog *looks different*, now that you no longer fear him. The content of experience is shot through with import "all the way down."

So, moods (1) disclose imports, (2) function as atmospheres, (3) reveal how we are faring, (4) are passive, (5) have objects, and (6) co-constitute the content of experience.

With these features in mind, we can identify phenomena closely related to mood. We have already explored emotion, which shares mood's characteristics, except self-monitoring, and of which being atmospheric is less characteristic. Consider also *sensibility*, such as a snobbish sensibility or a connoisseur's sensibility. A sensibility has all of the features of a mood except self-monitoring, I believe. Think about what it is like to be with an "old money" person, as opposed to someone who is "middle middle class."[41] In the presence of an "old money" person, we middle-classers tend to feel as if we're talking too loudly, as if we are shabbily dressed. Someone with an old money sensibility creates an atmosphere in which things show up as bearing a distinctive set of imports. Behavior is more likely to show up as either vulgar or refined, whereas in the presence of a middle-classer, this distinction is not salient. People of different social classes are tuned into different aspects of the world, see things differently. The contents of their experience, and the contents of the experiences of those who are steeped in their atmospheres, are shot through with content not available outside the atmosphere. Such sensibilities are slowly and passively acquired, typically early in life, rather than deliberately chosen. (Middle-classers who have done well financially and try to "move on up," typically end up steeped in *nouveau riche* values and sensitivities, rather than those of genuine old money.) One's sensibility does not monitor how one is faring, however, and that clearly distinguishes it from a mood.

Virtues also have some of the characteristics of a mood, but their atmospheric quality is diminished, if not absent altogether. As Aristotle argued in his *Nicomachean Ethics*,[42] and as his contemporary followers have insisted, a virtuous person experiences the world differently than one lacking virtue. A kind person is tuned in to those aspects of our social lives that call upon us to act with kindness toward others. A kind person does not just "see" the same neutral world that everyone else sees, but then draw different conclusions or arrive at different judgments. Like moods, emotions, and sensibilities, virtues can be cultivated, but they are not directly chosen, as courses of action are. They are in this way experientially passive. Virtues sometimes tune us in to aspects of how we and others are faring to which we might otherwise be blind. Virtues, moreover, are not usually atmospheric, though they can be. People whom we describe as "stoical" often do set up an atmosphere in which pain, for example, seems trivial, as honest people often set up an atmosphere in which cheating and stealing seem degrading. But virtue can sometimes be "quiet" and more "personal," less like an atmosphere, and sometimes something one only discovers about a person late in the day.

So, not only moods and emotions, but also sensibilities and virtues (as well as vices), share some of the critical characteristics in which Heidegger is interested under the heading disposedness and mood or attunement. The fundamental disclosive function of mood is to set the tone of expeience, to serve as an atmosphere in which the imports of situations and objects are disclosed and through which we are keyed into how we are faring. Heidegger's account of moods is not neat and clean; he does not properly distinguish moods from emotions, and some of his analysis seems artificial (such as the threefold structure of a mood). His basic thrust is clear enough, however: one of the basic facets of the disclosedness of the world in our experience is our attunement to what matters and how we are faring.

Study Question

Do the phenomena of abnormal psychology refute Heidegger's conception of mood? Can we really regard, e.g., generalized anxiety disorder as something that is not inner and not psychical?

IX. UNDERSTANDING AND INTERPRETATION

What is it to understand something? In philosophical English we use the word "understanding" primarily to refer to an intellectual capacity, a capacity to grasp, manipulate, and use cognitive contents. In contemporary Anglophone philosophy those contents are generally thought of as propositions and their components. Since language affords us our primary grasp on propositions, contemporary philosophers have subcontracted out the exploration of the scope and nature of understanding to the philosophy of language. In many contemporary academic philosophy departments, the philosophy of language has become one of the master sub-disciplines, alongside ethics and logic. This reflects what Richard Rorty long ago named the "linguistic turn" in philosophy.[43] This philosophical usage of "understanding" does not conform, however, to colloquial usage.

In everyday English we use the word "understanding" far more broadly, along with related words, such as "see" and "know." To understand bread, for example, is not limited to possessing a body of knowledge or propositional contents; it is to have quite a lot of know-how as well: to know how to choose the right bread for this dinner; to know how to store bread properly; to know one's way around a bakery. A battery of propositional knowledge is helpful, probably also required, but understanding bread goes beyond the propositions. We sometimes use the word "know" in this context, as in one of my favorite advertising lines, "Bo knows baseball." Bo Jackson did not just know the rules of baseball, and he did not just have a certain amount of historical knowledge of baseball. Bo knew how to play baseball and play it well. This is the sort of understanding in which Heidegger is primarily interested.

The Basic Constitution of Understanding

In Heidegger's everyday use of the word, to understand something is to be able to do or manage or master it.

> When we are talking ontically we sometimes use the expression "understanding something" with the signification of "being able to manage something," "being a match for it," "being competent to do something." In understanding, as an *existentiale*, that of which we are capable is not a What, but being as existing. The kind of being which Dasein has, as ability-to-be, lies existentially in understanding. (183/143*)

In this practical everyday sense understanding is not a specifically cognitive phenomenon.

> Furthermore, the character of understanding as projection is such that the understanding does not grasp thematically that upon which it projects – that is to say, possibilities. Grasping it in such a manner would take away from what is projected its very character as possibility, and would reduce it to the given contents which we have in mind. . . . (185/145)

To grasp something cognitively, to try to capture it in a propositional content or system of propositional contents, flattens out what we understand. In what way? Our clue lies in Heidegger's characterization of understanding as being-toward-possibilities (188/148).

Think about the contrast between what you are able to do and what you can describe as possible. When I think about and plan a bicycle ride, I can imagine and describe turning right onto this bridge and left off of it; I can even imagine that I make these turns more or less sharply, depending on whether the bridge is wet or dry. Of course, this is only the palest image of the range of possibilities that are actually open to me in the event as I ride the bike. I calibrate the precise angle of my turn for all sorts of conditions that I cannot even begin to describe in propositional form. Now, one might be willing to grant this argument for obviously "physical" abilities, such as riding a bike, but still hang on to the idea that in the case of distinctively "intelligent" abilities, the power of conception cannot be discounted. So, let us consider another case: cooking. The recipe calls for searing the chicken in the skillet before placing it in a baking dish with its marinade. When is the searing complete? When can I transfer it to the baking dish? The recipe book says, "when it has lost its pink color and is beginning to brown." How unpink is "beginning to brown?" The only answer here is that it takes experience to know.

The same analysis applies even in "headier" enterprises. It is a now notorious feature of legal adjudication that the concepts used in formulating statutes, the common law, principles, and guidelines do not apply themselves, that their application requires "discretion" or "common sense." This is to say that the propositionally articulable features of a legal situation do not control the process of adjudication; the adjudicator must rely on what we normally call "judgment" to settle cases. Finally, Thomas Kuhn made similar arguments for scientific practice: to know how to work with scientific concepts, laws, and definitions, one must be trained into a scientific practice. "Knowing what modern physics says" just is not genuine understanding.[44]

The space of possibilities in which we operate is wider and richer than can be described by our propositional resources. We do, nonetheless, have a grasp of and, to a certain extent, mastery over this space of possibilities. We are capable of much more than we can describe. Understanding, as Heidegger uses the term, is this mastery of more than we can describe. This is why Heidegger identifies understanding as "the being of such ability-to-be . . ." (183/144). (Note that Macquarrie and Robinson's translation of Heidegger's German term, *Seinkönnen*, as "potentiality-for-Being" is highly misleading. Heidegger is talking about what we are *able to be* or *do*, what we are *capable of*, not what we can develop into.)

Heidegger calls the space of possibilities our "leeway" or "room for maneuver" ("*Spielraum*," 185/145). This space of possibilities

consists indissolubly of one's abilities and the possibilities characteristic of the world.

> Not only is the world, *qua* world, disclosed as possible signifi-
> cance, but when that which is within-the-world is itself freed, this
> entity is freed for *its own possibilities*. That which is ready-to-
> hand is uncovered as such in its service*ability*, its us*ability*, and
> its detriment*ality*. (184/144)

The being of a hammer (what a hammer *is*) is constituted by how
one can use it. How one can use a hammer is bound up with that for
the sake of which we act in using it. That is, the characteristic usability of a hammer is interwoven with being a carpenter, being a homeowner, and what have you. The space of possibilities disclosed to us
in understanding is a unitary field of possible uses of paraphernalia
and possible ways to be Dasein.

Heidegger also uses "understanding" to refer to understanding
this item on this occasion. In these contexts he often uses another
term of art: *projection*. To pro-ject is to throw or cast forth. Thinking
metaphorically, when I drink out of this coffee mug, I am throwing it
forth onto or into its possibility of being a coffee mug, its usability in
the business of drinking. In this act of projection we can identify
what is understood, the coffee mug, and that in terms of which it is
understood, the role of being a coffee mug. In §32 Heidegger gives the
name "meaning" to that in terms of which something is understood
(193/151).

Finally, understanding gives us our "sight." As I indicated in
section (v), sight is Heidegger's metaphor for intelligence. In §31 he
writes: "In giving an existential signification to sight, we have merely
drawn upon the peculiar feature of seeing, that it lets entities which
are accessible to it be encountered unconcealedly in themselves" (187/
147). Our intelligence, our capacity to make sense of things, lies in our
understanding. This intelligence, moreover, is fundamentally not a
cognitive matter; it is a practical matter. In the words of John Dewey,

> Intelligence, in its ordinary use, is a practical term: ability to size
> up matters with respect to the needs and possibilities of the vari-
> ous situations in which one is called to do something; capacity to
> envisage things in terms of the adjustments and adaptations they
> make possible or hinder.[45]

Self-Understanding

To be Dasein is for your *being* to be an issue for you. That is, to be Dasein is for who you *are* and what it is *to be* human to be in question, and for these questions to matter to you. "Understanding always has its attunement" (182/143). If your being did not matter to you, then it might be an open question who you are and what it is to be human, but you would not care what the answers to these questions are. We saw above in section (iii) that to take a stand on the answers to these questions is *not* to reflect upon the questions and develop a formulated answer. Who you are is not a matter of who you *say* or *think* you are, but rather of *how you live*. Heidegger's way of putting this point in §31 is to characterize taking a stand on one's being as "pressing forward into possibilities" (184/145). To be who one is is to project oneself into human possibilities.

For example, I am able to be a father, a teacher of philosophy, a baseball coach, a cook, and other things besides. Being a cook is somewhat obviously a matter of what I can do; it consists of a set of skills and capacities that I exercise from time to time. Whether I *am a cook* or rather cook for the sake, say, of being a father depends on how I go about cooking. Do I cook "for the fun of it," "because I enjoy it for its own sake," as we say, or rather merely to get food on the table for my kids? The answer to that question determines whether I am a cook or cook for the sake of being a father. (Most of us who are cooks in this Heideggerian sense, moreover, also sometimes, even frequently, cook for the sake of being a parent.) These questions are bound up with *how* my cooking *matters* to me. In the previous section we saw that attunement discloses to us how we are doing and faring. If my food tastes unobjectionable, but is abundant, have I failed or succeeded? From the answer to this question we can likely read off my *purpose* in cooking, my for-the-sake-of-which.

Such for-the-sakes-of-which or self-understandings are not social positions. Consider the contrast between someone who is legally and socially a father, but for whom being a father does not matter, and someone for whom being a father is part of his identity. The indifferent father does not do any of the things that fathers do, and when he is confronted with the social and personal demands of being a father, he is as indifferent as he would be to someone insisting that he get involved with Civil War re-enactment. He may be subject, in the eyes of the Anyone and/or of the law, to the obligations of being a father, but those obligations, and the prerogatives that come with them, do not engage him. These social demands and entitlements coincide fairly closely with what Anthony Giddens has called a "social position," and I will follow his usage.[46] Because one can occupy the social position of being a father, without being existentially engaged in being one, and reversewise, a for-the-sake-of-which is not the same thing as a social position.

For-the-sakes-of-which make up our "identities," in the sense of those aspects of human life that engage us existentially and make sense of who we are. In order to be existentially engaged by a way of being, we must "press ahead" into it; we must do the things that one does in being that. Some of the most challenging conflicts in our lives arise when who we are existentially engaged in being stands in tension with who we think of ourselves as being. That they can conflict shows that they are not the same thing, and thus, Heidegger writes, "Projecting has nothing to do with comporting oneself towards a plan that has been thought out, and in accordance with which Dasein arranges its being" (185/145).

Further, our possibilities are "thrown possibilities."

> Possibility, as an *existentiale*, does not signify a free-floating ability-to-be in the sense of the "liberty of indifference" (*libertas indifferentiae*). In every case Dasein, as essentially disposed, has already got itself into definite possibilities. . . . But this means that Dasein is being-possible which has been delivered over to itself – *thrown possibility* through and through. (183/144)

Our possibilities are not laid out in front of us as on a smorgasbord table. We do not choose among them indifferently. Rather, as I confront the existential demands of being a father, those demands already have a grip on me. Getting to the school by 3:20 to pick up my son is urgent; attending my other son's soccer game is exciting. These differential ways in which courses of action matter to me reflect my already being disposed, already being attuned to the ways things matter to me as a father. This is to say, simply put, that I *am* a father, and as a father I press forward into the courses of action and projects to which being a father assigns me.

Thus, Heidegger writes:

> The being-possible which Dasein is existentially in every case, is to

be sharply distinguished both from empty logical possibility and from the contingency of something present-at-hand, so far as with the present-at-hand this or that can "come to pass." As a modal category of presence-at-hand, possibility signifies what is *not yet* actual and what is *not at any time* necessary. It characterizes the *merely* possible. (183/143)

To say that an oak tree can grow to 100 feet high is not to say that it has an ability that it might exercise, whereas to say that I am a father is to say that I have a set of skills and capacities that I do exercise. (Heidegger does not consider *animal* capacities in this context, and that is a serious oversight in his treatment. One of his few comments on animals in *Being and Time* is "the ontology of life is accomplished by way of a privative Interpretation" (75/50). He offers a more extensive analysis in *Fundamental Concepts of Metaphysics*, where he characterizes animals as "poor in world." The chief point should be that even though animals have abilities, and not just present-at-hand contingencies, they do not take a stand on who they are by exercising their abilities.)

Now, of course, we can also talk about people in terms of "mere possibility" or alternatively, "potential." I am not currently able to coach a youth soccer team, but I suppose that if I attended a set of training sessions and spent some time actually playing the game, I could come to be able to coach a youth soccer team. We have here a distinction between those capacities that I have and can exercise, and those capacities that it is possible for me to acquire. Our ordinary uses of "ability" and "potential" correspond pretty well with this distinction: I am able to coach a youth baseball team, but merely have the potential to coach a youth soccer team. Different yet again is the set of my "factual" characteristics: my height, weight, spatiotemporal locations, etc. Among factual characteristics we may distinguish what I actually or factually am from what I actually or factually could come to be. I am actually 5'11", though I could shrink an inch. As we saw in section (iv) above, however, I am not existentially speaking this height or that; rather, existentially I am my stature (if it matters to me at all).

Heidegger is asking us to think of ourselves as *being* our abilities-to-be, rather than being our social positions, our physical characteristics, or our potential. "As projecting, understanding is the kind of being of Dasein in which it *is* its possibilities as possibilities"

(185/145). I am what I act for the sake of being; I am a father, a youth baseball coach, a teacher, etc. Those ways of being are my "possibilities" in the sense of my abilities-to-be, my existential capacities. They are who I am, how I understand myself, even if I do not always interpret or think of myself that way. This is why Heidegger writes that Dasein ". . . is constantly 'more' than it factually is . . ." (185/145). I am more than this height or weight; I am what I am able to be, how I am able to lead my life in the world. The passage continues: "Dasein is never more than it factically is, for to its facticity its ability-to-be belongs essentially. Yet as being-possible, moreover, Dasein is never anything less. . . ." Recall that facticity is Dasein's existential determinateness. So, Heidegger is saying here that our abilities-to-be belong to our existential determinateness, which is just to say over again that I am what I am able to be.

Heidegger develops this theme, when he infers that Dasein "*is* existentially that which, in its ability-to-be, it is *not yet*" (185–186/145). To be *able* to be teacher or coach or father is neither a "static" nor an enduring property of me as an identical subject. His language in this section is shot through with metaphors of motion: understanding is projection, throwing forth, and in projection we press ahead. Further, ". . . only because [Dasein] *is* what it becomes (or alternatively, does not become), can it say to itself 'Become what you are,' and say this with understanding" (186/145). Dasein's being is a matter of its motion into the future, its becoming. In II.5 on historicality, he writes:

> The movement of existence is not the motion of something present-at-hand. It is definable in terms of the way Dasein stretches along. The specific movement in which Dasein *is stretched along and stretches itself along*, we call its *happening*. (427/375*)

We are *not yet* what we are able to be, but this *not yet* and the movement it suggests is not the *not yet* of the present-at-hand. The *not yet* of the present-at-hand is what has not yet occurred, but which will occur in the future. The *not yet* of our existential abilities-to-be, however, are not characteristics that we do not yet possess, like an apple does not yet possess the red color of ripeness, but rather purposes into which we press ahead and that constitute us as who we are *now*.

Understanding, Interpretation, and Cognition

In our discussion of §13 of *Being and Time* (section iv, above), we saw that Heidegger wants in general to reject subject–object models of human experience. Proximally and for the most part, I am not in the world as a disengaged subject trying somehow to transcend to the world; rather, I am already engaged in the world, familiar with it, disposed toward it, and acting in it. Apart from a set of general phenomenological descriptions like this, however, we do not yet know in detail how Heidegger conceives cognition and how he takes it to differ from what he calls "understanding." In order to explore this question, we have to move ahead into §32.

There Heidegger introduces his notion of *interpretation*. He uses the word "interpretation" to name a specific mode of understanding, a mode in which the possibilities disclosed in understanding are "worked out." By "working the possibilities out" he means making them explicit.

> That which is disclosed in understanding – that which is understood – is already accessible in such a way that its "as which" can be made to stand out explicitly. The "as" makes up the structure of the explicitness of something that is understood. It constitutes the interpretation. (189/149)

An interpretation is, thus, an act of understanding in which we make what we understand explicit by understanding it *as* something.

The critical exegetical question we must answer is what Heidegger means by "explicit." Drawing the distinction between Heidegger's uses of the words "understanding" and "interpretation" is an exegetical problem, but it is not a nit-picky textual one. After all, recall that in elaborating on the idea that cognition is founded in being-in-the-world in §13, Heidegger identifies cognition as a form of "interpretation in the broadest sense" (89/62). Seeing how interpretation is an "existential derivative" of understanding, as Heidegger characterizes it here, is thus critical to seeing how cognition is founded in being-in-the-world.

Now, we might be tempted to interpret "explicit" to mean conscious, but that would be a mistake. After all, one might think, to make something explicit is to draw our attention to it. However, if "explicit" means conscious, then Heidegger would be committed to the thesis that all cognition is conscious. This thesis is not only flatly implausible, but the chief proponent of this view, Descartes, did not even inspire his closest successors, Spinoza and Leibniz, to adopt it. Furthermore, there is a word in *Being and Time* that often seems to capture the meaning of conscious: "thematic." So, we must find another interpretation of Heidegger's use of the word "explicit."

Sometimes we use the word "explicit" to contrast with "implicit," in the sense of implied. The word "implied" can be used in many senses, but philosophically it is most commonly used to capture the way a statement can entail or presuppose further statements. This contrast between "explicit" and "implicit" piggy-backs on the logical or inferential relations among statements or propositions. Once we put the point this way, we can see that Heidegger does not intend to contrast understanding with interpretation along these lines. Inferential relations are relations among assertions, and as we will see in the next section, assertion is a form of interpretation, and thus relations among assertions, such as implication, are secondary to the distinction between understanding and interpretation. Viewed historically, moreover, the suggestion that the development of understanding takes place along inferential lines is at the heart of Hegel's philosophy, which explains why logic is for Hegel the master sub-discipline within philosophy. This last observation, finally, makes clear why Heidegger regards Hegel as yet another captive of the tradition's misunderstanding of understanding, despite the otherwise notable sympathies between the thought of these two philosophers.[47]

The connections among assertion, interpretation, and understanding, on which we relied just now to see that by "explicit" Heidegger did not have Hegel's conception of explicitness in mind, point us in a new and better direction. In §13, in the midst of developing his thesis that cognition is derivative of being-in-the-world, Heidegger writes:

> [Taking-in] amounts to *interpretation* in the broadest sense; and on the basis of such interpretation, taking-in becomes an act of *making determinate*. What is thus taken in and made determinate can be expressed in propositions, and can be retained and preserved as what has thus been asserted. (89/62*)

Cognition is a form of "making determinate," *because* it is a sort of interpretation. Further, because cognition "makes determinate," its content can be expressed in propositions. Below, in section (x), we will see what Heidegger means by "making determinate." For now we need only observe that because cognition is a form of interpretation, its content can be expressed in propositions. This claim only makes sense, if Heidegger holds that interpretation always has propositional content. This dovetails nicely with a further observation, that Heidegger's German word that is translated as "explicit" is "*ausdrücklich.*" "*Ausdrücklich*" is derived from "*Ausdruck*," expression. It should, thus, be unsurprising that Heidegger means to connect what is explicit with expression and language.

Heidegger's thesis in §32 is, then, this: understanding that has propositional content (i.e., interpretation) is derivative of understanding that does not. Our ability to grasp the world in such a way that we can characterize it descriptively is derivative of our engaged abilities, our skills and capacities. We can formulate this idea more compactly thus: *representation is derivative of our engaged abilities.* Here I am using the word "representation" the way John Searle uses it in his work on linguistic meaning and mental intentionality, to designate speech acts or mental states that have propositional content.[48] This way of looking at Heidegger's thesis in §32 also intersects nicely with the historical tradition in which Heidegger is writing. Searle's use of "representation" is very close to Kant's use of "cognition." According to Kant, a cognition is a representational state that can be true or false, that can succeed or fail at describing or referring to the world. The paradigm of cognition is a judgment, and judgments are conceptual acts, that is, acts in which we predicate a concept of something. Kant argues further that what he calls "intuitions," namely, perceptual acts, such as seeing a cat, have "the same form of unity" as judgments. Put in more contemporary language, this is to say that all seeing is seeing-as, that perception is mediated by concepts, and that the content of any act of perception is, implicitly, a judgment. To see a cat is to see, say, that this is a cat, or that there is a cat on the mat, or what have you.[49]

Hence, we may restate Heidegger's thesis in §32 thus: there is a level of mastery and intelligence in human life that is not conceptually mediated, that cannot be captured in assertions. As one would expect, his approach to motivating this thesis is phenomenological, and we already considered this phenomenology above. In §32 he places that phenomenology into a structure he calls "the fore-structure of interpretation." The fore-structure connects interpretation with understanding and gives us a more detailed look at the distinction between the two phenomena. The fore-structure consists of three elements: the fore-having, fore-sight, and fore-conception. Heidegger spells out the fore-structure with reference to the example of interpreting the ready-to-hand.

Fore-having. Heidegger writes:

> The ready-to-hand is always understood in terms of a totality of involvements. This totality need not be grasped explicitly by a thematic interpretation. Even if it has undergone such an interpretation, it recedes into an understanding which does not stand out from the background. And this is the very mode in which it is the essential foundation for everyday circumspective interpretation. In every case this interpretation is grounded in *something we have in advance* – in a *fore-having*. (191/150)

Fore-having is the understanding of the background *context* in terms of which any concrete interpretation takes place. In the case of the ready-to-hand, this background context is the totality of involvements, that is, that web of interlocking equipmental roles that define the workshop and make a piece of equipment what it is. Our access to this interlocking web of equipmental roles is our ability to use the equipment and navigate the workshop in which it finds its place.

Fore-sight. Heidegger continues:

> When something is understood but is still veiled, it becomes unveiled by an act of appropriation, and this is always done under the guidance of a point of view, which fixes that with regard to which what is understood is to be interpreted. In every case interpretation is grounded in *something we see in advance* – in a *fore-sight*. The fore-sight "takes the first cut" out of what has been taken into our fore-having, and it does so with a view to a definite way in which this can be interpreted. (191/150)

What does Heidegger mean by describing something as being "understood but still veiled?" The language certainly suggests a situation in which an entity presents us with difficulties. The entity would be understood, because it would fall within the scope of those abilities that give us access to the context, yet still veiled in so far as it is, say, malfunctioning. For example, my carpentry skills give me access to the carpentry workshop, allow me to understand hammers, nails, levels, and so on. This hammer falls within the range of my carpentry skills; I understand it. But since it is malfunctioning – suppose it is cracked – it is still veiled. At this point, the hammer will stand out from the background as an object of "thematic interpretation" for me: I will encounter it as a hammer. The fore-sight "fixes that with regard to which what is understood is to be interpreted," that is, it brings the hammer into view *as a hammer*. The fore-sight introduces the *as-which* into the experience of the hammer.

Fore-conception: Heidegger finishes,

> Anything understood which is held in our fore-having and towards which we set our sights "foresightedly," becomes conceptualizable through the interpretation. In such an interpretation, the way in which the entity we are interpreting is to be conceived can be drawn from the entity itself, or the interpretation can force the entity into concepts to which it is opposed in its manner of being. In either case, the interpretation has already decided for a definite way of conceiving it, either with finality or with reservations; it is grounded in *something we grasp in advance* – in a *fore-conception*. (191/150)

The interpretation has decided for a definite way of conceiving its object. To interpret this *as a hammer* is to deploy a concept, presumably, the concept of a hammer. Interpretation is suffused with conceptuality. This confirms the suggestion that by "interpretation" Heidegger means roughly what Kant means by "cognition," what Searle means by "representation." Interpretation can be captured in propositional form, because it is conceptually articulated.

This way of reconstructing Heidegger's remarks on the fore-structure and the distinction between understanding and interpretation suggests the following objection: surely when we understand something pre-reflectively, we understand it *as* something determinate.[50] As I make a turn on my bike, I understand the bike path on which I am riding as calling for this angle of turn. If I did not understand it as something determinate, then my grasp of it would be entirely vague and I could not respond to it in any definite way. My inability to describe the path in a sufficiently precise way does not mean that I do not grasp it as something determinate. This objection suggests that any concrete act of understanding *is* an interpretation, and that the distinction between what I can describe and what I can interpret is the distinction between assertion and interpretation, not interpretation and understanding. In response to this objection, Heidegger should grant everything but the conclusion. Yes, in making the turn on my bike I grasp the path determinately, indeed, so determinately that I cannot put what I grasp into an assertion. One could say that I understand the path *as* . . ., as long as one does not confuse this "as" with the "as" Heidegger attributes to interpretation. The "as" of interpretation can be expressed in propositions, Heidegger says (89/62 again), which means that I am capable of getting it into a description. The line between understanding and interpretation is just this line, between what can and cannot be expressed in assertion. One might worry here that I have collapsed what Heidegger calls the "existential-hermeneutic" and "apophantical" *as*'s (201/158).[51] The apophantical *as* is the *as* of assertion, that is, the grammatically definite as of predication, whereas the hermeneutic *as* is the *as* of interpretation, which is not grammatically definite. To use this cup as a paper weight in response to a breakdown situation (in which the wind is blowing my manuscript around) is not to assert that this cup is possibly, necessarily, or merely actually a paper weight. Assertion defines the logic of understanding further than does interpretation.[52] Heidegger does not have a special name for the *as* of pre-interpretive understanding; he does not in fact seem to have seen clearly that he needs one. It should be there, however.

In sum, the conceptuality that characterizes cognition is funded by, but does not exhaust, the set of skills and capacities in terms of which we encounter the context of the object in the first place. Thus, I can see this object as a bicycle brake and formulate the judgment, "my brake is malfunctioning," only because I have a set of skills for riding a bicycle. This set of skills cannot be exhaustively spelled out by any set of judgments, no matter how large, and cannot be fully described by any set of assertions, no matter how extensive. The engaged sensitivities and responsiveness that guide me as I ride my bicycle are too refined, too submerged in immediate action, and too fluid to be captured in a theory of bike riding. Practice is more basic or "primordial" than cognition.

Study Question

What should Heidegger say about forms of intelligence and understanding that do appear to be overtly cognitive, such as knowledge of mathematics or physics?

X. LANGUAGE

Language or what Heidegger calls "discourse" is also essential to our familiarity with the world. Heidegger is not alone amongst twentieth-century philosophers in regarding language as absolutely central to our being-in-the-world, or as more traditional philosophers might say, to our consciousness, awareness, or intentionality. John Dewey wrote: "It is safe to say that psychic events, such as are anything more than reactions of a creature susceptible to pain and diffuse comfort, have language for one of their conditions."[53] Wittgenstein, Davidson, and Sellars, hold this view as well. Heidegger's student and philosophical descendant Gadamer put it quite forcefully, "Language is not just one of man's possessions in the world; rather, on it depends the fact that man has a *world* at all."[54] These are all statements of what Charles Guignon has called *linguistic constitutivism*, the thesis that "human existence is possible only within language."[55] By ranking discourse as equi-primordial with disposedness and understanding, Heidegger embraces linguistic constitutivism.

Unfortunately, the text of *Being and Time* is not as clear on this issue as it could be. Not only are there passages which cut against linguistic constitutivism, but it is far from obvious that Heidegger is using the term "discourse" to pick out language. To see what Heidegger's linguistic constitutivism amounts to, it is important to understand that he means something rather broader by "discourse" and "language" than the sort of thing that we think of as "a language," such as English or German.

Discourse (§34)

Heidegger introduces discourse in the crucial second paragraph of §34. His formulation here, along with the rest of §34, involves the use of two related verbs and their derivatives, both of which are translatable as "to articulate": *gliedern* and *artikulieren*. In German the verb *gliedern* means articulation in a structural sense.[56] A *Glied* is a limb or member, and so, *gliedern* and its past participle, *gegliedert*, suggest articulation in the sense in which a skeleton or structure is articulated: consisting of members and joints. *Artikulieren*, on the other hand, suggests somewhat more strongly the dominant sense of putting something into words. Macquarrie and Robinson, in their effort to deal with the complexities of translation, render *gliedern* as "articulate" (with a lower-case "a") and *artikulieren* as "Articulate" (with an upper-case "a"). Although Heidegger's uses of the words do not appear to be entirely consistent, I think we can make some headway by thinking of articulation as structural articulation and Articulation as putting into words or expressing. I will, thus, modify Macquarrie and Robinson's translations by inserting "structural" or "expressive" in square brackets before "articulation," and drop the capitalization, which I think is distracting. Let us work through the second paragraph of §34 methodically.

The second sentence, "The intelligibility of something has always been [structurally] articulated, even before there is any appropriative interpretation of it," reminds us of one the crucial results of §§31–32: what the entity in question is, and how it can be interpreted (the conceptualizable aspects under which it can be taken in), are derivative of the holistic situation to which the entity belongs. This holistic situation is disclosed through understanding, the "fore-having," more fundamentally than through the conceptually articulate interpretation of it. Heidegger adds here that pre-conceptual intelligibility is structurally articulated. The field of intelligibility in terms of which we approach the environment in which we are comporting ourselves is not an undifferentiated mass. It has structure. Its structure, however, is pre-conceptual.

In the third sentence Heidegger defines "discourse": "Discourse is the [expressive] articulation of intelligibility." Pre-conceptual intelligibility is expressively articulated in discourse. If I am right that "Articulation" means *expressive articulation*, then Heidegger's point is that we are able to express the pre-conceptual structure of things. Our capacity to do so is discourse. Because intelligibility is pre-conceptual, moreover, discourse is more basic or primordial than interpretation or assertion (of which more later), for both interpretation and its derivative mode, assertion, are conceptually articulate. Thus, in the fourth sentence, Heidegger writes: "Therefore it underlies both interpretation and assertion."

Now, *what* are we expressing, when we expressively articulate intelligibility? Heidegger's answer: *meaning.* The fifth sentence: "That which can be [expressively] articulated in interpretation, and thus even more primordially in discourse, is what we have called meaning." Heidegger introduced the concept of meaning back in §32 (193/151). When we project (understand) an entity, we do so by making sense of its place in the world: we make sense of the ready-to-hand in terms of its involvement or use; we make sense of Dasein in terms of its for-the-sakes-of-which. We saw that in I.3 Heidegger calls the structural whole of involvements and for-the-sakes-of-which "significance," and so he reminds us here: "That which gets [structurally] articulated as such in discursive [expressive] articulation, we call the totality-of-significations."

To this point, it might seem as if Heidegger's view is that in discourse or language we give expression to a prior structural articulation of the world, which resides in our activity quite independently of anything we might say about it. Indeed, Heidegger encourages this line of thought by writing: "The intelligibility of being-in-the-world . . . *expresses itself as discourse.* The totality of significations of intelligibility is *put into words.* To significations, words accrue." This is *not* Heidegger's considered judgment on the matter, however. At the beginning of the fifth paragraph of §34, he writes: "Discoursing is the way in which we [structurally] articulate 'significantly' the intelligibility of being-in-the-world" (204/161*). (By "significantly" Heidegger seems to mean "according to significance," almost certainly in his technical sense of the term.) This sentence suggests, then, that in discourse we structurally articulate the intelligibility of being-in-the-world and thereby bestow significance on entities. This represents an important correction of the ill-considered formulations of the second paragraph: in discourse we do not just put prior intelligibility into words, but rather structurally articulate it as well.

In other words, expressive articulation *is* structural articulation, which is another way of asserting linguistic constitutivism. It is only in virtue of having a language, or more generally an expressive medium, that we can experience a structurally articulated world, a world in which things make sense by being different from one another, yet also interrelated. In order to understand this idea in more detail, we must have a better grasp on Heidegger's conception of language. Does Heidegger want to say that it is only through, for example, the English language that we are able to experience a differentiated world? There are a few sentences in which he seems to endorse that idea: ". . . discourse too must have essentially a kind of being which is specifically *worldly*. . . . The totality of significations of intelligibility is *put into words*" (second paragraph of §34); and "The way in which discourse gets expressed is language. Language is a totality of words – a totality in which discourse has a 'worldly' being of its own" (third paragraph). To begin to see how these statements are misleading, let us continue with the third paragraph of §34. After writing that "language is a totality of words," he continues, ". . . and as an entity within-the-world, this totality thus becomes something which we may come across as ready-to-hand. Language can be broken up into word-Things which are present-at-hand." At this point it should be clear that Heidegger is using his standard technique of leading us down the path of traditional thought. Language consists of words, words are acoustic disturbances or graphic inscriptions that we use in order to express our thoughts.

To begin to overturn this traditional approach to language, Heidegger states, in the fourth paragraph of §34: "*Hearing* and *keeping silent* are possibilities belonging to discursive speech." Hearing and keeping silent are not acoustic disturbances, they are not graphical inscriptions, they are not even words or anything remotely like words. Yet Heidegger writes: "In these phenomena the constitutive function of discourse for the existentiality of existence becomes entirely plain *for the first time*" (my emphasis). Expressive articulation encompasses far more than the use of words in order to say what we mean. Later in §34, he writes: "Being-in and its disposedness are made known in discourse and indicated in language by intonation, modulation, the tempo of talk, 'the way of speaking' " (205/162). Discourse comprises not only words and their grammar, but also the way in which we use a language to communicate. Such communication involves far more than "semantics" in a narrow sense; it involves everything that we convey in using language.

What is more, although Heidegger does not explicitly say so, there is no reason not to expand his use of the term "language" to cover much more than natural languages. Body-language, the "language of art," dance, gardening, and much more are, in one sense of the term, languages. They are modes of communication that require an analysis that goes beyond merely the dynamics of "what we do." Indeed, Heidegger places communication at the center of his analysis of language or discourse. He analyzes discourse as consisting of three moments: what the discourse is about, what is said in the discourse, and communication (204–205/161–162). Let us focus on communication.

Heidegger makes clear that he means to distance himself from traditional models of communication: "Communication is never anything like a conveying of experiences, such as opinions or wishes, from the interior of one subject into the interior of another" (205/162). If one begins with a subject–object model of experience, then one starts one's analysis of communication with two distinct minds. I think the thought, "my cat Lulu is cute," and this thought is confined within my mind. In order to "share" this thought with you, I have to manipulate words in such a way as to cause you to have the same thought. I must "convey" or transport my meaning to your mind by way of linguistic intermediaries.[57] Heidegger does not want to say that nothing like this ever happens, but he does want to insist that such experiences are atypical of human life. Instead, "Dasein-with is already essentially manifest in a co-disposedness and a co-understanding." That is, we already share a world, and for the most part, we already understand one another.

Heidegger spells out his notion of communication in more detail in §33 on assertion, the section that immediately precedes §34 on discourse. There he writes, communication

> . . . is letting someone see with us what we have pointed out by way of giving it a definite character. Letting someone see with us shares with the other that entity which has been pointed out in its definite character. That which is "shared" is our *being towards* what has been pointed out – a being in which we see it in common. (197/155)

If you and I are sitting in my living room, and I say, "my cat Lulu is cute," I am drawing our joint attention to Lulu and narrowing our joint focus down to her feature, cuteness. I am constituting a shared orientation towards the cat. Now, if you are new to my house and have never met the esteemed Lulu, you might well "learn something" from my assertion. Often, however, we say things we know our audience already knows. So, if you come to my house to watch a World Cup soccer game between Italy and the U.S., I might say, "We don't stand a chance in this game." You already know that. What I am doing in saying this is not conveying anything to you; I am not passing information from my mind to yours. Rather, I am setting the tone of our afternoon together; I am preparing us for a long and futile game. Much of what we do when we express ourselves is set a tone. When I bring in the main course of the dinner I have cooked and announce, somewhat self-mockingly, "And now, the *pièce de résistance*," I actually convey very little, but rather orient us towards the main course, which I hope is something special. When I am dressed meticulously in a business suit with tie and shined leather shoes, I am setting one tone for our meeting; when I am dressed in shorts, sandals, and a torn T-shirt, I am setting quite a different tone. In each case a matrix of imports is disclosed, orienting you in your common experience towards the world in differing ways. To focus narrowly on the "symbol systems" or "semantics" of what we say and do is to miss the bulk of what goes on in communication: joint orientation towards the world in terms of its possibilities and its imports.

In other words, Heidegger wants to re-orient us in our approach to language by shifting the paradigm of linguistic activity. In traditional philosophy, the assertion has served as the paradigm of linguistic activity, but according to Heidegger, assertion is a highly derivative form of communication. If we think instead of poetry, banter, chit-chat, and song, we bring into focus much broader and more amorphous forms of communication. When Robert Johnson sings, "hellhound on my trail" or "blues falling down like hail," he is not making an assertion (and no one would think he is). Rather, he is expressing a mood, a mood that we share as we listen to his haunting song. The question becomes, then, which forms of our expressive activity are more pervasive in our familiarity with the world, assertion or the broader forms of language and expression highlighted by Heidegger? This is not to say, however, that assertion is uninteresting or unworthy of analysis. Far from it.

Assertion (§33)

Assertion has been the focus of philosophical attention to language for a good reason: it is the form of linguistic activity in which the structure of propositions is most apparent, and propositional content has been at the center of traditional accounts of intentionality. Intentionality, or cognition, has been taken to be the foundation of our access to the world, and the logical and justificatory structure of cognition, that is, logic and theory of knowledge, have been two of the core disciplines of philosophy. Yet according to Heidegger, assertion is a highly derivative mode of linguistic activity. Let us explore why.

Heidegger analyzes assertion as a linguistic act in which three things are accomplished: *pointing out, predication,* and *communication.* (These are what he obscurely calls the "three significations" of the word "assertion" on 196/154.) Heidegger's model of an assertion is a subject–predicate assertion, such as "the hammer is too heavy" (his example). This assertion points out the hammer; it predicates being too heavy of the hammer; and it communicates this pointing out and predication.

Pointing out. Assertions point out an entity. "In this we adhere to the primordial meaning of λόγος as ἀπόφασις – letting an entity be seen from itself" (196/154). This formulation might suggest that Heidegger thinks of pointing out as making something present to our senses. He refutes that suggestion by writing (in the same paragraph) that an assertion can point an entity out, even though the entity is neither to hand nor visible. So, what does he mean by "points out," then? A second proposal would be that he means "referring" by "pointing out," as he might mean to suggest when he writes: ". . . the pointing-out has in view the entity itself and not, let us say, a mere representation of it" (ibid.). On this proposal, then, Heidegger is saying that all assertions refer to objects. The problem with this view is that it seems fairly clear that not all assertions do refer to objects, as is clearest in the case of examples such as Bertrand Russell's famous, "The present king of France is bald." The second proposal dictates that Russell's assertion points out the present king of France, but there is no such man.

Heidegger does not tell us here in *Being and Time* what we should do with assertions whose subjects do not refer, but fortunately he does take the question up in *Basic Problems.*

> In essence it is an asserting *about* something and thus is intrinsically referred to some *entity or entities.* Even if that about which an assertion is made should turn out not to be, an empty illusion, this in no way gainsays the intentionality of the structure of assertion but only demonstrates it. For when I judge *about* an appearance I am still related to entities. (*Basic Problems,* 207*)

Even when the subject term of a subject–predicate assertion does not refer to anything, still the assertion relates itself to "entities," which must mean something like "entities in general." He refers to this (in translation) two pages later as the "function of display." The German for "display" is "*Aufzeigung*," which Macquarrie and Robinson translate as "pointing out." I note the divergence in the translations, because Hofstadter's *Basic Problems* indicates a way of thinking about "pointing out": not as reference *per se*, but as display. That is, we do not have to think about pointing out as a relation between an assertion (or a part of an assertion) and an entity. Rather, display can be more general, the function of what Heidegger calls letting entities be seen. Indeed, his reference to "λόγος as ἀπόφασις" in §33 of *Being and Time* points in just this direction. An assertion lets things be seen, that is, directs our attention to them, whether they are seen as they are or in disguise.[58] If this way of understanding pointing out is right, then Heidegger is not arguing for the existence of a word–world relation, such as reference. Rather, he is observing phenomenologically that assertions direct attention, focus, or salience.

This reading allows us to cope with a second potential problem with Heidegger's account, as we might be inclined to read it at first. Heidegger consistently uses subject–predicate sentences as examples of assertions, and this can lead to a lot of mischief, if one is not careful. After all, "If the Republicans win the 2008 presidential election, our country is doomed," is a fine assertion, but it is not a subject–predicate assertion. It is a conditional. Conditionals do not have objects to which their subjects refer, and thus, it is difficult to see how conditionals can be thought of as pointing out or referring to anything. Once again, however, if by "pointing out" Heidegger does not mean a word–world relation, but rather a function of display, then there is no problem. The conditional above does indeed focus our attention or make things salient in the world in a definite way.

One might wonder what the point of Heidegger's analysis is, if we deny that "pointing out" names a reference-like word–world relation. What is Heidegger's motivation at this stage in §33? Again, in *Basic Problems* Heidegger is a little more direct than in *Being and Time*. In the paragraph immediately after he analyzes assertions with non-referring subjects, he writes: "In order for something to be a possible about-which for an assertion, it must *already* be somehow given for the assertion *as unveiled* and accessible" (*Basic Problems*, 208). In other words, in order to be in a position to make an assertion about my cat Lulu, or about the present king of France for that matter, the world must already be disclosed to me in such a way that I can focus our attention on Lulu or the king of France. That is, these entities (or the Republican Party and the Republic, as in the example above of a conditional) must be accessible to assertion already. Assertion does not reach out and grab these entities all on its own; assertion is parasitic upon a prior disclosure of the world in which we live, a disclosure that prefigures the saliencies that I effect through making an assertion.

Assertion is not a free-floating kind of behaviour which, in its own right, might be capable of disclosing entities in general in a primary way: on the contrary it always maintains itself on the basis of being-in-the-world. What we have shown earlier in relation to cognition of the world, holds just as well of assertion. Any assertion requires a fore-having of whatever has been disclosed; and this is what it points out by way of giving something a definite character. (199/156–157*)

Indeed, Heidegger develops the argument further by way of his conception of predication.

The second "signification" of "assertion" is *predication*. Heidegger writes: "We 'assert' a 'predicate' of a 'subject', and the 'subject' is *given a definite character* by the 'predicate' " (196/154). Now, Heidegger's copious scare-quoting here is noteworthy. On a traditional analysis of predication, a predicate-term is predicated of a subject-term; alternatively, a predicate-concept is predicated of a subject-concept. Heidegger's analysis goes in a different direction.

... when we give it [what we have pointed out in the assertion] such a character, our seeing gets *restricted* to it in the first instance, so that by this explicit *restriction* of our view, that which is already manifest may be made *explicitly* manifest in its definite character. (197/155)

Assertion does not merely draw our attention to the world, but does so "under a description." That is, assertion makes some aspect of the world manifest to us, makes it salient, but in some definite respect. When I assert, "Lulu is cute," I am not merely drawing attention to Lulu, but to Lulu as cute. Our attention is narrowed down or "restricted" to some definite feature of Lulu.

Heidegger describes asserting as making something explicit. As we saw above, explicitness is the form of interpretation. Thus, assertion is a form of interpretation: a sort of understanding that makes things explicit. In making things explicit, assertion, like all interpretation, relies on a fore-having, fore-sight, and fore-conception. The fore-having is the background practical understanding of the world and this particular environment, in terms of which I am able to deal with the entities uncovered by the assertion. The fore-sight is the predicate, or determinate respect, in terms of which we make the entities uncovered in the assertion salient. "Thus any assertion requires a fore-sight; in this the predicate which we are to assign and make stand out, gets loosened, so to speak, from its unexpressed inclusion in the entity itself" (199/157). Finally, the predicate that restricts our view of the entities uncovered belongs to a conceptuality or conceptual system that inheres in the language. "When an assertion is made, some fore-conception is always implied; but it remains for the most part inconspicuous, because the language already hides in itself a developed way of conceiving" (ibid.). Heidegger's example of such definite conceptuality goes to the ontological structure of entities uncovered and thereby interpreted in the assertion. The language of engineering and science has different ontological implications than the language of everyday equipment-use; "this hammer is too heavy" is embedded in a different way of conceiving and talking about entities than "this hammer weighs 900 grams."

Now, the relation between assertion and interpretation is fairly close. Interpretation is explicit understanding whose content *can be* expressed propositionally, whereas assertion is a form of language whose content *is* expressed propositionally. Recall, as we examined briefly above in section (iv),

> Taking-in is consummated when one *addresses* oneself to something as something and *discusses* it as such. This amounts to *interpretation* in the broadest sense; and on the basis of such interpretation, taking-in becomes an act of *making determinate*. What is thus taken in and made determinate can be expressed in propositions, and can be retained and preserved as what has thus been asserted. (89/62*)

In order words, cognition (or taking-in) is a form of interpretation, because its content is propositional in nature. Because this content is propositional in nature, it can be expressed in an assertion. This is more than to say merely that all cognition is linguistically mediated. After all, as we saw earlier in this chapter, Heidegger believes that all of human life is linguistically mediated, as long as we embrace a sufficiently broad conception of language (so that it includes body-language and all other forms of expressive behavior). Rather, Heidegger's specific view here is that what distinguishes cognition from pre-cognitive forms of comportment is that its content is propositional, that is, assertable.

With discourse Heidegger completes his analysis of the three facets of disclosedness. In Part B of chapter 5 Heidegger turns to leveled off modes of disclosedness. Rather than turn directly to them, however, it is best to skip ahead to Heidegger's discussions of reality and truth and then return later to I.5.B. Falling and the leveled off modes of disclosedness are thematically closer to the discussion of death and resoluteness. So, let us turn now to §43 of *Being and Time*.

Study Question

Heidegger claims that language is "equiprimordial" with understanding and disposedness. Is human life imaginable without language or discourse in Heidegger's sense of the term?

XI. REALISM AND IDEALISM IN *BEING AND TIME*

§43 of *Being and Time* takes up issues that surround traditional problematics of realism and idealism. In §43a Heidegger addresses the "problem of the existence of the external world," which is to say, epistemological skepticism, and in §43c he tackles the ontological problem whether the world depends on our experience of it. (In §43b Heidegger discusses Dilthey's view that reality is resistance to the will. This view was important in 1927, but not today, and so I will skip §43b.) In both cases, Heidegger does not so much *solve* the traditional problem in view, as *dissolve* it. In this respect, Heidegger is keeping company with other twentieth-century philosophers who have attempted the same general sort of response: Carnap, Wittgenstein, Dewey, Davidson. All these twentieth-century philosophers share the intuition that the traditional problems of whether there is a world outside our minds, and if so, whether we can know it, are pseudo-problems. *Our* job here is to explore Heidegger's distinctive approach to dissolving skepticism and the realism–idealism debate.

Epistemological Skepticism (§43a)

Epistemological skepticism is the philosophical view that we are not able to know whether a world exists beyond our experience. Skepticism finds its canonical modern expression in Descartes's *Meditations on First Philosophy*. In his "First Meditation" Descartes offers a series of three escalating arguments for the conclusion that we are not able to know anything about the world beyond our experience. He begins with worries about perceptual illusion (things not appearing as they are, such as straight sticks that look bent in water), advances to worries about dreaming (there are no internal markers to indicate when we are dreaming, so that we cannot know of any experience whether it is a dream or a veridical experience), and concludes with his "Deceiving Demon Argument." The last argument has been the most successful, historically speaking.[59]

The basic idea behind the Deceiving Demon Argument is this: it is possible, is it not, that an all powerful demon could manipulate our experience so that it is experience as of a world that does not really exist? In order to tell reality from illusion, we use all sorts of clues internal to experience, such as the consistency of this experience with other experiences and with our overall theory of how the world works. If the demon can manipulate our experiences, however, then it can create within us a total set of experiences that pass all of our internal tests for truth, but which are, nonetheless, false. There is a modern science-fiction version of the Deceiving Demon Argument, the Brain-in-a-Vat Argument.[60] Instead of imagining an all-powerful deceiving demon, imagine a brain in a vat with electrodes hooked up to its sensory input channels. The neurophysiologist in the laboratory stimulates the sensory channels of the brain in such as a way as to create the experience as of a world that is not there. A brain in such a vat would not be able to know that its experience is illusory, for there would be no internal clues to what is going on.

These epistemological challenges have vexed modern philosophy since the publication of *The Meditations*, and they have elicited a wide range of responses. Descartes himself tried in his Sixth Meditation to refute the skepticism of the First Meditation by arguing that God, who is all powerful and all good, and whose existence Descartes thinks he has already proven, would not permit such a deception to occur, for deception is a vice. Other philosophers in the Early Modern period either acquiesced in skepticism (Hume) or tried to address it by arguing that physical things just are ideas (or constructions from ideas) in our minds, so that there is no problem about how we know them (Berkeley). Surveying the wreckage of Early Modern epistemology, Kant commented:

> . . . it still remains a scandal to philosophy and to human reason in general that the existence of things outside us . . . must be accepted merely on *faith*, and that if anyone thinks good to doubt their existence, we are unable to counter his doubts by any satisfactory proof.[61]

Kant tried to refute skepticism by means of a highly complex "transcendental argument," which has in turn been the target of much criticism and a source of much confusion.

Heidegger formulates his response to this entire discussion as a direct retort to Kant: "The 'scandal of philosophy' is not that this proof has yet to be given, but that *such proofs are expected and attempted again and again*" (249/205). Skepticism is an answer to a question, the question whether we can know that the world beyond our minds exists. This question is itself defective: "The question whether there is a world at all and whether its being can be proved, makes no sense if it is raised by *Dasein* as being-in-the-world; and who else would raise it?" (246–247/202). The question "makes no sense." Why?

There are passages in §43a in which Heidegger gives the impression that he means that the world is not really independent of Dasein, so that we do not need to prove its existence:

> Such expectations, aims, and demands arise from an ontologically inadequate way of starting with *something* of such a character that independently *of it* and "outside" *of it* a "world" is to be proved as present-at-hand. (249/205)

Such a strategy suggests some form of idealism, perhaps on the model of Kant's "Transcendental Idealism." It is most unlikely that Heidegger has something like this in mind, however, and for two reasons. First, although he concedes that idealism is a more insightful philosophical stance than realism, he really rejects both positions, as he makes clear towards the end of §43a (251/207–208). Second, idealism *refutes* the skeptic, whereas Heidegger aims to dissolve skeptical worries. He does not want to prove the skeptic *wrong*, but rather show that the skeptic's entire question is senseless. This is why he writes: "The 'problem of reality' in the sense of the question whether an external world is present-at-hand and whether such a world can be proved, turns out to be an impossible one . . ." (250/206). The problem of reality itself is impossible. Why?

The question itself must be rejected. To reject the question is to argue that both affirmative and negative answers to the question whether we can know the world to exist are false or otherwise misguided. In continuing the passage just quoted from page 250/206, Heidegger writes that the problem is impossible, ". . . not because its consequences lead to inextricable impasses, but because the very entity which serves as its theme, is one which, as it were, repudiates any such formulation of the question." Dasein is not fundamentally a knowing subject, and the world is not an object of knowledge.

> Even if one should invoke the doctrine that the subject must presuppose and indeed always does unconsciously presuppose the presence-at-hand of the "external world," one would still be starting with the construct of an isolated subject. (249/205–206)

Our "access" to the world is constituted by our being-in, our familiarity, disclosedness. Familiarity, as we have seen at great length, is not a cognitive phenomenon. In virtue of our fundamental familiarity with the world, we "know" our way around it. Such "knowing" is not a form of knowing in the sense of a cognitive attitude, in anything like the sense of justified true belief. We are not talking about beliefs here; we are not talking about intentional attitudes. Thus, asking whether we know (cognitively) whether there is a world is something like asking whether we can smell the color red. It is just an ill-formed question.

There is a nice parallel between this argument and one John Dewey offered in 1912, in "Brief Studies in Realism." In the second of the two "Brief Studies," "Epistemological Realism: the Alleged Ubiquity of the Knowledge Relation," Dewey argues that the flawed premise underlying the entire controversy between skepticism and epistemological realism is the assumption that all of our modes of access to the world around us are forms of knowledge. Dewey argues that since this assumption is false, the entire discussion is based on a mistake. We have many different modes of access to the world. Dewey presents a hilarious send-up of the whole question as a debate between "foodists" and "eaterists," assuming eating to be our sole relationship with the world![62] Heidegger's point is that given that Dasein and world are not subject and object, given that our basic relationship with the world is one of disclosure, rather than cognition, the entire discussion of epistemological skepticism is idle. Heidegger does not aim to refute the skeptic, so much as dismiss him as basing his challenge on a set of assumptions about human life that are ontologically mistaken.

Now, one might well worry that Heidegger has performed a sleight of hand. Suppose he is right that our relationship to the world is not one of either knowledge or cognition more generally, so that it makes no sense to challenge our access to the world skeptically. What does this tell us, however, about the "world," about entities within-the-world, objects? Heidegger's first response would no doubt be that just as the disclosedness of the world is not cognitive, so are our basic relations to entities within-the-world. We "know" equipment by using it, other people by engaging with them. Just as understanding, disposedness, and discourse disclose the world more primordially than does cognition, so they also uncover entities more primordially than does cognition. Thus, if Heidegger's dismissal of the skeptical challenge to our ability to know the world is legitimate, the same strategy should work for any skeptical challenge to our ability to know entities within-the-world (i.e., the "world").

The defender of traditional epistemological concerns need not give up at this point, however. Even if Heidegger is right that we have "access" to entities within-the-world more primordially than by way of cognition, it is nonetheless true that we do sometimes cognize those objects, try to know them. When we do try to know them cognitively, we can entertain skeptical worries about that knowledge. Put a little differently, after conceding Heidegger's central thrust, a skeptic can still urge that Heidegger has not so much dismissed the skeptic as changed the subject. The skeptic challenges *knowledge*, and unless Heidegger means to say that there is no such thing as cognition and knowledge, then we can ask him what he has to say about skeptical challenges to *knowledge*, letting *disclosedness* fall where it may.

Heidegger does not explicitly consider this sort of response in

Being and Time, and so we will have to construct one for him. What gives bite to skeptical challenges to our knowledge of the world? Why have philosophers been worried about skepticism for two and a half millennia? Why do so many young students of philosophy become engaged by skepticism, some even obsessed with it? The answer, presumably, is that epistemological skepticism is a challenge to the security of our connection with the world. The underlying worry is that we might be "cut off" from the world, "out of touch" with it. In humble and everyday ways we are all familiar with the experience of being out of touch with some domain of life or some group of people. What if that experience were fully general? This worry can lead to Pyrrhonian and moral skepticism, and not just the narrower epistemological skepticism developed by Descartes and his successors. To these vaguer and more general worries, Heidegger does have something to say: epistemological skepticism is not that interesting. Maybe clever epistemological arguments can get skeptical concerns about knowledge off the ground, but those concerns do not touch our basic modes of access to and familiarity with the world. There really is no threat that we might be cut off from the world. Or at least, to put it more carefully, the ways in which we can be cut off from the world do not require epistemological reflection, but rather existential reflection, as we will see in Heidegger's discussion of anxiety and resoluteness below.

Metaphysical Idealism and Realism (§43c)

Even if we accept Heidegger's anti-epistemological line of argument in §43a, we have not dispensed with the *metaphysical* problem of realism and idealism. Philosophers have traditionally not only asked whether we can know the world, but also whether the world exists independently of our subjective take on or understanding of it. Early modern realists, such as Descartes and Locke, argued that the world exists independently of our experience of it, whereas the idealists, such as Berkeley and Leibniz, argued that the world of natural phenomena of which we are aware in both ordinary experience and natural science is dependent on our experience of it. Kant tried to split the difference between the realists and idealists by maintaining that although the world is independent of an individual's idiosyncratic experience of it, it is not independent of human understanding in general.

As in his response to epistemological skepticism, Heidegger does not take a position within this debate. Rather, he rejects the entire debate. The key passage on realism and idealism is this:

> Of course only as long as Dasein *is* (that is, only as long as an understanding of being is ontically possible), "is there" being. When Dasein does not exist, "independence" "is" not either, nor "is" "in-itself." In such a case this sort of thing can neither be understood nor not understood. In such a case even entities within-the-world can neither be uncovered nor lie hidden. *In such a case* it cannot be said that entities are, nor can it be said that they are not. But *now*, as long as there is an understanding of being and therefore an understanding of presence-at-hand, it can indeed be said that *in this case* entities will still continue to be.
>
> As we have noted, being (not entities) is dependent upon the understanding of being; that is to say, reality (not the real) is dependent upon care. (255/212)

Being, *but not entities*, is dependent upon the understanding of being, that is, upon Dasein.[63] This passage revolves around a distinction between "this case" and "such a case" (or in the German, "then" and "now"). Heidegger distinguishes between what can and cannot be said in these two cases. He distinguishes the two cases by stipulating that in the one case, Dasein is not, whereas in the other case, Dasein is. He says, then, that "when Dasein does not exist":

- Neither "independence" nor "in-itself" "is."[64]
- "This sort of thing" – presumably the proposition that there are independent things – can neither be understood nor not understood.
- Entities within-the-world can neither be uncovered nor lie hidden.
- It cannot be said either that entities are or that they are not.

There are two ways we can read these claims, which I will call "deflationary" and "robust" ways.

It is easiest to understand the distinction between the deflationary and robust readings by focusing first on the last of the bulleted statements above. Why, when Dasein does not exist, can it be said neither that entities are nor that they are not? Perhaps because

Dasein does not exist, and after all, Dasein would have to do the talking. We could extend this logic to the other three statements. The virtue of this way of reading the passage is that Heidegger's claims, so construed, are obviously true. The drawback of reading the passage thus is that they are trivially true. (Of course nothing can be said when there is no one to say it!) The deflationary reading is *too* deflationary; it robs the passage of any possible philosophical import. What else could Heidegger mean, then?

If we focus on the last sentence of the passage (which is from a second paragraph), Heidegger appears to be making a more interesting claim. Because being depends on Dasein, the being of the present-at-hand depends on Dasein as well. When being "is" not, then entities neither are nor are not. That is,

a. *The being of the present-at-hand depends on Dasein.*

is not to say that,

b. *If Dasein did not exist, entities present-at-hand would not be.*

but rather to say that,

c. *Presence-at-hand depends on Dasein.*

Indeed, we can see how (c) undercuts (b). If presence-at-hand (the being of the present-at-hand) depends on Dasein, then that means that presence-at-hand would not "be," if Dasein did not exist. If presence-at-hand "is" not, then entities can neither be nor not be present-at-hand. More generally, if being depends on Dasein, then when Dasein does not exist, entities can neither be nor not be. Thus, when the antecedent of (b) is true, i.e., when Dasein does not exist, the consequent of (b) is neither true nor false, i.e., entities neither do nor do not exist.

Heidegger rejects both realism and idealism. The realist asserts that if we did not exist, entities would nonetheless be. The realist defends the *independence* of entities. The idealist, in contrast, argues that if we did not exist, objects would not exist either, that they *depend* on us. Heidegger's response to both realism and idealism is that the conditional statements in which they are formulated – (b) above and its contradictory – are both false, because if the antecedent of (b) is true, then neither the consequent of (b) nor its negation can be true.

This analysis does not apply, it is important to note, to the ready-to-hand. The ready-to-hand clearly does depend on Dasein. Anything that is what it is in virtue of being involved in our practices cannot be apart from our practices. A hammer cannot be without carpentry, just as a home run cannot be without the game of baseball. In the case of things ready-to-hand that have an underlying present-at-hand reality, that underlying reality can in principle exist without the practices that define that ready-to-hand item for which it is the underlying reality. So, again in the case of a hammer, the metal and wood can in principle exist without our practices of carpentry, even though the hammer itself cannot do so. In the case of paraphernalia that has no obvious underlying substrate, such as the drama *Hamlet*, as we discussed above in section (v), it cannot exist apart from our practices at all.

These considerations about the dependence of the ready-to-hand on our practices do not apply to the present-at-hand, however. In §69b Heidegger analyzes what he calls "the theoretical uncovering of the present-at-hand within-the-world" (408/356). In this section of *Being and Time*, Heidegger advances two theses about natural science. First, he points out that if his analysis in *Being and Time* is generally correct, then the cognitive and theoretical achievements of natural science depend on a set of scientific *practices*, just as all cognition depends on practice. He thus argues that in order to understand natural science clearly, we must develop an "existential conception of science."[65] Second, Heidegger argues that the domain of entities uncovered by natural science is defined precisely by its independence of our practices. He describes this as the result of a "change-over" in our understanding of being, a change-over in which "the entities of the environment are altogether *released from such confinement*" (413/362). In other words, *to be present-at-hand* is *to be independent of human practices*. Heidegger's rejection of both realism and idealism *does* apply to the present-at-hand.

Now, Heidegger's argument for rejecting the realism/idealism debate turns on statement (c) above. What could it mean to say that being "is" not? And why the scare-quotes? Heidegger puts the verb "to be" in scare-quotes in statements like this, because as we saw in section (i) above, being is not an entity. Since being is not an entity, it neither *is* nor *is not*. Rather, being determines entities as entities, as

Heidegger puts it in chapter 1 of the Introduction to *Being and Time* (25–26/6). Being is the set of standards in terms of which entities make sense as entities. Thus, to refer to conditions in which standards do not determine entities, we cannot write "being is not." Yet Heidegger wants some way to talk about conditions in which ontological standards do not determine entities. To do so, he relies on a idiomatic German phrase, "*es gibt*," which translates as "there is," but does not literally use the German verb "*sein*," "to be"; "*es gibt*" transliterates as "it gives." Indeed, "being" is not the only phenomenon on the "far side" of the Ontological Difference, that is, the difference between being and entities. Among the other phenomena that neither are nor are not we may note especially time. Time, or more precisely, temporality, as Heidegger calls it, belongs to the constitution of being and thus is not an entity. For this reason Heidegger writes "time temporalizes itself," rather than "time is."

What does it mean to say that being "is" or "is not," that is, that ontological standards do or do not determine entities? Heidegger does not address this question here in *Being and Time*, and this is one of the most significant omissions in the treatise. To some extent his approach to this question turns on his analysis of temporality later in division II. He argues that "ordinary time" or "clock-time" depends on "primordial temporality," which is the temporal structure of human life. If this is true, then time depends on human being. I have elsewhere called this thesis *temporal idealism*. Further, if time depends on human being, then so does being, for being is a set of temporal structures. I have called this thesis *ontological idealism*. However, given that Heidegger thinks of temporality as an ontological, rather than ontic, phenomenon, in order to understand properly what it means to say that time depends on human being, we would have to understand more generally what it means to say that being depends on human being. Thus, *Being and Time* provides a lot of apparatus to spell out an argument for the conclusion that being depends on human being, but it does not sufficiently articulate the basic thesis.[66]

As Heidegger's thought went into flux after the publication of *Being and Time*, he maintained his commitment to something like ontological idealism and devoted considerable space to ruminations on the subject. Exploring those ruminations would have to be the focus of a separate study. *Being and Time*'s arguments against the entire realism/idealism discussion are tantalizing, yet incomplete.

Study Question

Is it reasonable to be as cavalier about skepticism as Heidegger is? Is not the history of natural science a story of discovering that the world is not very much like we perceive it to be?

XII. TRUTH

We have seen that according to Heidegger our fundamental access to the world is disclosedness, being-in. Cognition, and the related phenomena of assertion, propositions, judgment, and knowledge, are derivative of being-in-the-world. Heidegger infers from this that the truth or falsity of assertions and propositions is also derivative of a more fundamental sort of truth, which he calls "primordial truth." Heidegger does not offer an alternative theory of truth, however, and in fact in §44 he redeems most of our common-sense conception of truth, even if not the philosophical theory built upon it that is generally called the Correspondence Theory of Truth. Heidegger develops his alternative phenomenology of truth in three stages. In §44a he works out the phenomenology on which he relies to reject the Correspondence Theory. In §44b he argues that the truth of assertions depends upon a more fundamental form of truth, the disclosedness of the world that is at work in our pre-cognitive understanding. In §44c he somewhat misleadingly argues that truth is "relative to" Dasein.

The Traditional Consensus and its Breakdown

Philosophers' views about truth are various, but it is nonetheless possible to identify a position that we might call "the traditional consensus" about truth. The traditional consensus endorses a conception of truth that broadly conforms to what is sometimes called the Correspondence Theory of Truth. The Correspondence Theory states that for a statement or belief to be true is for it to correspond with the world (or reality or the facts). The Correspondence Theory attempts to articulate a philosophical account that expresses a basic intuition about truth, articulated by Aristotle thus: "To say of what is that it is not, or of what is not that it is, is false, while to say of what is that it is, and of what is not that it is not, is true."[67] The Correspondence Theory interprets the basic intuition as an intuition about a relation of correspondence between mind and world. This is to say, then, that it imposes a subject–object model on truth.

Aristotle's theory of how the mind thinks an object reflects his general commitment to "hylomorphism." Hylomorphism is the doctrine that a thing's being may be analyzed as a form informing some matter. In the case of simple physical objects, the form is the object's shape, its matter the material of which it is made. As objects become more complicated, so their forms become more complex and sophisticated. The form of a car is not just its shape, which it can share with a wooden model, but also a specification of its functioning. Much change in the natural world is the imposition of form on matter: when the oven heats the apple pie, the oven transfers the form of heat from itself to the pie. Perception is also a natural process, and Aristotle analyzes it with the same set of tools. When you perceive a tree, the tree affects your eyes, causing a change in them, and the changes in your eyes cause your faculty of perception to take on the form of the tree. When matter is informed by the form of a tree, it is a tree. The mind, however, is a special entity that, when it takes on the form of an object, does not become such an object, but rather becomes a representation of the object. In sum, the mind can perceive and think about an object by realizing the object's form in the special material of the mind.[68]

As odd as Aristotle's theory of perception sounds to us two and a half millennia later, it was part of a comprehensive theory of the world. This theory, moreover, was not just a philosophical theory, but the leading *scientific* theory of its age. The basic outlines of Aristotle's theory of matter, form, change, and mind endured for almost two thousand years, until the Scientific Revolution. During the Scientific Revolution the entire scheme of Aristotle's theory was tossed out in favor of a new mechanical model of physics. The *language* of Aristotle's theory of mind persisted, however, even in the writings of the leading exponents of the Scientific Revolution. Descartes wrote that ideas are "images, as it were" and analyzed them in terms of his theory of formal and objective being. The sun and the idea of the sun, he states in a famous passage from one of his replies to his critics, are the same thing, in the one case (the sun) existing formally, in the other case (the idea) existing objectively.[69] This is Aristotle's theory of mind in new clothes, but also shorn of the overall theoretical context that gave it meaning.

Once the theory is drained of meaning, it becomes mere words, and this allowed Bishop Berkeley to attack it ruthlessly, pointing out that "nothing can be like an idea but another idea."[70] Berkeley inferred that since ideas cannot be like anything beyond themselves, they must be about themselves, and he concluded that the objects of our experience are our ideas and not transcendent material things. Despite all the wrangling about the validity of Berkeley's argument, the bottom line is that no one could develop an adequate response to it, because philosophers of the modern era had no scientific theory of mind (and still have none) with which to replace Aristotle's. Instead, philosophers hung on to the language of "contents" and "immanent objects," but in order to avoid Berkeley's criticisms argued that the "contents" or meanings of ideas, in virtue of which ideas are about objects, are non-real items. As we saw above in section (ii), the content of an idea is neither the (real) object of the idea nor the (real) psychological state of thinking, but rather something else. The content is not a real thing; it does not exist anywhere or anywhen, but is rather "ideal."

The ideality of ideational contents gives philosophers a way to talk about truth as correspondence. Within the classical theory of Aristotle, an idea is true if it shares a form with a real object. Ideas are "like" objects in a somewhat literal sense: they are con-formal (sharing a form) or isomorphic (having one form) with their objects. Once the Aristotelian theory of form-sharing has been drained of its content and reduced to mere words, however, all that can be said is that a true idea "corresponds" to, "agrees" with, or is "similar" to its object. The word "corresponds," however, is just a word, a placeholder for a theory not yet on offer.

I have devoted some space to the history of the theory of truth, because Heidegger's criticism in *Being and Time* of the Correspondence Theory is based on this history, a history with which Heidegger was intimately familiar from his intensive study of and lecturing on the history of philosophy. Heidegger's objection to the Correspondence Theory is that the language of ideal contents and real objects, as well as of a relation of correspondence between them, is "ontologically unclarified."

> Is it accidental that no headway has been made with this problem in over two thousand years? Has the question already been perverted in the very way it has been approached – in the ontologically unclarified separation of the real and the ideal? (259/216–217)

By "ontologically unclarified" Heidegger means that there is no theory behind the language that explains what the ideal contents are, what it is to be ideal, and how ideal items can stand in relations with real objects. Essentially, the language is untethered from its original source of meaning in the Aristotelian theory of mind and is now just verbiage. When we are confronted with empty words, what should we do? Heidegger's answer is always, "return to the phenomena." He offers a phenomenology of truth to replace the Correspondence Theory.

Before proceeding it is worth making one observation about the terminology of correspondence in the second half of the twentieth century. The name "Correspondence Theory of Truth" is also used for a pared down account of truth that is "disquotational." In his path-breaking article on truth, Alfred Tarski offered his Convention (T) as part of his "semantic conception of truth:" "S" is true if and only if S; so for example, "snow is white" is true if and only if snow is white.[71] Tarski proposed Convention (T) as a constraint on any theory of truth one might offer, namely, that it must at a minimum satisfy Convention (T). Convention (T) is really just a formulation of the basic intuition, expressed by Aristotle, with which we began this discussion. Nonetheless, it does quite a bit of work within the context of theories of truth in formal languages, which is the purpose for which Tarski designed it. Some philosophers,[72] however, took up Convention (T) as spelling out what truth is, and some have called this pared down conception of truth the Correspondence Theory. Historically this is somewhat misleading, because to subscribe to Convention (T) is not to posit any mind-, thought-, or content-world relation of correspondence, similarity, or agreement. Really, this approach eschews theories of truth altogether and directs us to content ourselves with the basic intuition.

Heidegger's Phenomenon of Truth

Heidegger agrees that we should stick to the basic intuition and flesh it out with some phenomenology. The phenomenology is not intended to build another theory, but more to support us in our effort to stick with the basic intuition and *not* offer a theory of truth. In effect, what some contemporary analytic philosophers want to do with Convention (T) and our talk about true sentences, Heidegger wants to do with his phenomenology of the experience of truth.

Heidegger approaches the phenomenology of truth by way of the experience of confirmation. His use of confirmation in this context has misled some readers into thinking that he is offering a so-called verificationist theory of truth, according to which for an idea or statement to be true is for us to possess evidence that verifies it directly.[73] This is a misreading, however.

Heidegger approaches truth in terms of the experience of confirmation, because in order to bring truth into focus, we must find experiences in which it is salient, and, like other background conditions in *Being and Time*, truth is normally self-effacing, only salient in breakdown situations. Much of what we say to one another on a daily basis (when we are making assertions) is true, and such truth is not an issue for us. We pay no attention to it. Rather, we pay attention to truth, when it is in question. Suppose my son comes into the house from the backyard and tells me, "The bird feeder is empty." According to §33, my son's assertion uncovers or displays the bird feeder as empty. Now, if I am surprised by my son's report (suppose I just filled the feeder two days ago), I go out into the backyard and check. Indeed, the feeder is empty. What do I experience in so far as I realize my son's assertion was true? According to Heidegger, I do not experience a relation of correspondence between his words and the feeder, or between his thoughts and the feeder, or (especially, I would add) between some ideal meaning and the feeder. Rather, I experience the feeder as empty, the feeder just as my son described it.

> The entity itself which one has in mind shows itself *just as* it is in itself; that is to say, it shows that it, in its selfsameness, is just as *it* gets pointed out in the assertion as being – just as *it* gets uncovered as being. Representations do not get compared, either among themselves or in *relation* to the real thing. What is to be demonstrated is not an agreement of knowing with its object, still less of the psychical with the physical; but neither is it an agreement between "contents of consciousness" among themselves. What is to be demonstrated is solely the being-uncovered of the entity itself – *that entity* in the how of its uncoveredness. (261/218)

This passage is somewhat difficult to read, because Heidegger is appropriating Husserl's language for talking about truth. This language of "selfsameness" is really a distraction, however.

Heidegger formulates his phenomenology of truth quite simply thus: "To say that an assertion *is true* signifies that it uncovers the entity as it is in itself. . . . The *being-true* (*truth*) of the assertion must be understood as *being-uncovering*" (ibid.). In effect, Heidegger is arguing for two claims: that our experience of truth is captured well by Aristotle's formulation of the basic intuition, and that our experience of truth not only does not underwrite the classical Correspondence Theory, but undermines it. This aligns Heidegger fairly well with contemporary exponents of "deflationary" accounts of truth, according to which statements like Tarski's Convention (T) are all there is to say about truth. What Heidegger adds to such deflationary accounts is an analysis of the phenomenology of truth to back deflationary approaches up.

Heidegger seems to be saying a lot more in §44, however. Indeed he is, but the more he says is not an elaboration of a theory of truth, but rather placing the truth of assertions into their philosophical context. As we saw above in section (x), assertion is derivative of interpretation, and interpretation of understanding. The function of display or pointing-out exercised by assertion is possible only on the basis of the "fore-having" of understanding, and so assertions can only be true or false in the context of our pre-assertoric, pre-cognitive understanding of the world. From this Heidegger infers that pre-assertoric understanding is true in a "more primordial" sense than assertions are:

> What makes this very uncovering [by true assertions] possible must necessarily be called "true" in a still more primordial sense. *The most primordial phenomenon of truth is first shown by the existential-ontological foundations of uncovering.* (263/220)

We can read this statement two ways.

Heidegger adheres to a general theory of naming phenomena that the condition for the possibility of *x* should be called "primordial *x*." His boldest statement of this may be found in the context of his account of time:

> If, therefore, we demonstrate that the "time" which is accessible to Dasein's common sense is *not* primordial, but arises rather from authentic temporality, then . . . we are justified in designating as *primordial time* the *temporality* which we have now laid bare. (377/329)

Thus, he calls the existential condition for the possibility of the experience of time in the ordinary sense "primordial time," the existential condition for the possibility of ordinary death (which he calls "demise") "death," etc. This is a recurrent and somewhat misleading strategy of Heidegger's.

In the case of truth, however, there is a somewhat tighter connection between assertoric truth and primordial truth, a connection that has been reflected all along in Heidegger's language of uncovering and disclosedness. Recall that Heidegger reserves the word "disclosedness" for special modes of our access to the world. The world in Heidegger's technical sense, we ourselves, and being are all disclosed; entities within-the-world, that is, the ready-to-hand and present-at-hand, are uncovered. He sometimes refers to both phenomena generically as "unveiling," which, he argues, best captures the meaning of the Greek word "ἀλήθεια." As with his etymologies of German words, I do not regard the interpretation of a Greek word as a substitute for what Heidegger does best, phenomenology.

To see the phenomenological content of Heidegger's conception of primordial truth we may begin with a reflection on language. In order to make an assertion one must use a language. Languages are not, however, merely inert building blocks for making assertions. The very vocabulary we use involves an outlook on the world, an outlook that is implicit in our language. To use a well-worn example, the use of the word "witch" in the early modern period involved a way of looking at some groups of women, an entire conceptuality that intersects with accounts of gender, non-conformism, and mental illness. When we say today that there are no such things as witches, we are not just asserting that it is false that there exists a witch today, as a successful witch-hunter from the days of the Massachusetts Bay Colony would hope to be able to declare after a long and arduous struggle. Rather, we are saying that the concept of a witch gets no grip on the world. The conceptuality in which it inheres distorts the world, rather than discloses it. Similarly, when Freud introduced the notion of the subconscious, he was not just adding an item to the inventory of the mind, as a ornithologist might add a newfound species to the list of birds. Rather, he was changing the way we think about the mind top to bottom.[74]

These observations about conceptual change can be extended to Heidegger's notion of language. Recall that for Heidegger language is not just a tool for saying things, but rather a form of communicative and expressive articulation of the world. This expressive articulation of the world allows us to share the world with one another, and what is more, it structurally articulates the world as well. The assertions we make do their work not just as part of a language of assertions, but more deeply as part of our expressive-communicative behavior. Assertions depend on gesture, styles of clothing and song, poetry, and many other forms of communication besides, and not just on a vocabulary and syntax. Assertions cannot be made and cannot be true apart from these broader forms of communication; they are derivative of them. Further, *and this is the central point*, the broader forms of communication disclose the world as well and at a more basic level than do assertions.

Forms of communication can do a better or worse job of disclosing the world, hence can be true or false in a philosophically extended way of using the words. Some commentators on Heidegger's account of truth have argued that primordial truth – the disclosive work of our understanding of and discourse about the world – does not contrast with any primordial falsity, and thus that Heidegger's use of the word "true" in this context is distorted. In effect, they argue that "true" must always contrast with "false," and since it does not in the case of Heidegger's primordial truth, the word "truth" is misplaced here.[75] The last claim is false, however: there is a form of primordial falsehood.

Before exploring Heidegger's conception of primordial falsehood, we should note that Heidegger's use of "truth" in this context captures some everyday ways of using related words, sometimes even "true" itself. When we say that the Puritans, for example, were "wrong" that there are witches, we do not just mean, as we saw above, that the assertion "There were witches in seventeenth century Massachusetts" is false. We mean that the entire way of looking at the matter in which the Puritans indulged was distorted, misguided, false. Understandings, disclosures of the world can be distorted or not, true or false. Philosophers wedded to the idea that only speech acts and mental states with propositional content, such as assertions, can be true or false, have to engage in conceptual gymnastics to explain what we mean when we say things such as that the Puritans "got it wrong," that they misunderstood things. Heidegger's use of the word "true" tracks this everyday sense of the word. This everyday sense of the word "true" contrasts with forms of falsehood as well, but they are forms of falsehood that cannot be captured by talking about the truth or falsity of assertions. (Nor can they be captured by talking about the truth or falsity our "common sense theories of the world," since they are not theories, as we saw above in sections ix and x.)

What makes Heidegger's discussion of primordial truth and falsity more than just an expression of these observations is that he limits the range along which we should evaluate the truth or falsity of these fundamental world-disclosures. In the case of the Puritans we can talk about how oppressive and ungenerous their way of looking at things was; in other cases we can talk about the success or failure of a scientific approach in generating new and fecund research projects and in helping us to control the forces of nature. These very general political, moral, and pragmatic evaluations of world-disclosures are the normal stock in trade of our arguments about the truth or falsity of entire ways of looking at the world or pieces of it. As we have noted before, and we will discuss again below, moral and political philosophy is peculiarly absent from *Being and Time*. What is more, Heidegger's vision of natural science as aiming for a pure discovery of the world around us, rather than as subservient to our technological and pragmatic aims (as both Dewey and the later Heidegger maintain), closes off the pragmatic avenue for evaluating world-disclosures. Heidegger is left merely with an existential evaluation of world-disclosures, and for this reason he writes:

> The most primordial, and indeed the most owned, disclosedness in which Dasein, as ability-to-be, can be, is the *truth of existence*. This becomes existentially and ontologically definite only in connection with the analysis of Dasein's ownedness. (264/221)

World-disclosures are true to the extent to which they are owned, false otherwise. So, let us now turn to Heidegger's conception of self-ownership.

We cannot leave §44 without commenting briefly on Heidegger's statement in §44c that "truth is relative to Dasein's being" (270/227). With this statement Heidegger does not intend to assert a relativist account of truth, as he indicates three sentences later, when he comments that this relativity does not imply any "subjective discretion" concerning truth. Rather, Heidegger's point in §43c is somewhat simply that if truth is an aspect of some of our assertions, and more basically of our fundamental disclosure of the world, then the bearers of truth are aspects of our being and activity. There are no timeless propositions, we have seen, which could carry truth independently of the languages we use and worlds we disclose, and this means there is nothing that could be a timeless or eternal truth. It does not follow from that, however, either that you and I can believe contradictory things, both of which are true, or that we should say that the views in which we have the greatest confidence, such as the laws of logic, are anything but binding on what we say and think.

Study Question

If the truth of an assertion is its "being-uncovering," how do we distinguish false assertions ("The moon is made of green cheese") from assertions that are neither true nor false ("The king of the U.S. is Elvis Presley")? Both of these assertions do not "uncover."

XIII. EVERYDAY, OWNED, AND DISOWNED LIFE

As we turn to falling, anxiety, death, and resoluteness, we begin to focus on the "existentialist" dimension of the project of *Being and Time*. Heidegger intended this dimension to be located in division II, but for reasons we will explore in a moment, he misplaced some of the existentialist material into division I. Division I is meant to be a "preparatory fundamental analysis of Dasein" (the title of division I), which is to say, a phenomenology of human life in general. Division II is supposed to be a re-analysis of the being of Dasein in terms of time. It turns out that once we come to terms with the possibilities of death and anxiety, and the diverse responses to them that are possible, we see that Dasein must have a "deep" temporal structure that we would otherwise not be able to recognize. Heidegger's analysis of time and temporality has been one of the least influential aspects of *Being and Time*, and not without reason. It is obscure, radical, and what is worse, the arguments for it do not work. Thus, it is not uncommon for readers to put *Being and Time* down after §65, when Heidegger introduces temporality. For this very reason, as well as limitations of space, I will likewise not discuss time and temporality, except in passing, here in this Reader's Guide. The parts of division II that precede §65 have had far greater impact.

In the first half of division II Heidegger develops a "factical ideal" of human life – ownedness or authenticity – in which we live in accordance with our underlying ontological structure. Heidegger argues that we mostly "live away" from ourselves by living in a fashion that does not acknowledge the sorts of entity we are. We do not "own" ourselves. As a *rough* first approximation, one may think of Heidegger as arguing that we do not typically acknowledge the full range of our freedom and live almost as if we were animals, rather than Dasein. This way of putting the basic idea allows Heidegger to resonate with more traditional philosophical visions, such as Kant's. In Kant, if we do not allow our sense of respect for the moral law to lead us to apply the Categorical Imperative in our decision-making, then we are acting heteronomously, rather than autonomously. To act heteronomously is not exactly to live like an animal; animals do not, after all, have practical reason. In applying practical reason merely to satisfy our desires rather than the moral law, however, we are living, we could say, as instrumentally rational animals. Our human freedom lies in our capacity to respond to the demands of the moral law and thereby to rise above the level of such a super-animal.

Similarly, in the condition that Heidegger calls "falling," in I.5.B, we live away from ourselves by failing to acknowledge the full range of our existential freedom. We live in a sort of degraded or leveled down condition, one in which we do not really know who we are. Heidegger has a number of different formulas for this degraded condition: falling, disownedness (inauthenticity), irresoluteness, lostness in the Anyone. The common theme in all of these formulas is that we do not embrace the *sort* of entity we are, namely Dasein, and live as if we did not have the possibility to gather ourselves out of our lostness in the Anyone and resolutely choose an owned life. Exploring this dynamic is the point of I.5.B.

What is the contrary of an owned life? There is an ambiguity in *Being and Time* as to whether a life that is not owned is merely unowned or whether it is more egregiously degraded. We see this tension in §27, on the Anyone, where Heidegger both sometimes characterizes the Anyone as an aggressive form of conformism and also says that the Anyone is a positive constituent of our being. We see the tension again I.5.B, where Heidegger waffles on the nature of falling. For example, he begins §35 by assuring us that by "idle talk" he does not have any "disparaging" connotations in mind. As his analysis proceeds, however, he clearly drifts towards a disparaging understanding of idle talk, as when he describes it as tending towards "complete groundlessness" (212/168). The disparaging character of the adjective "falling" grows as the discussion in I.5.B moves through curiosity and ambiguity, culminating in §38 on "Falling and Thrownness." There he once again declares, at the beginning of the second paragraph, that "falling" "does not express any negative evaluation," but then turns right around and describes fallen Dasein as lost in publicness (220/175), which, as we learned in §27, includes leveling down and the suppression of all greatness and originality. The root problem here is that Heidegger does not seem to have made up his mind whether a life that is not owned is actively disowned. Part of the reason why not is surely that Heidegger held a dim view of everyday life in the early twentieth century. Perhaps Heidegger really meant to describe everyday life as egregiously leveled down and disowned, not unlike the way Kierkegaard and Nietzsche often characterize contemporary life. Most people, according to Nietzsche, belong to the "herd," the weak-willed and unimaginative mass of humanity that does as it is told and tries not to rock the boat. The herd has no taste and no ability to tell what is great from what is ordinary. Nietzsche's rhetoric dovetailed with the revulsion of the German "Mandarins" to Weimar culture.[76] Although Heidegger himself was a small-town, lower middle-class boy, and therefore not a member of the German Mandarin class, he seems to have had sympathy for the Mandarin critique of the decadence of modern urban life. Kierkegaard's concern was less with greatness, taste, and decadence, than with one's ability to rise above the ethical and rational demands of common sense and communal life and commit oneself to a singular, life-defining project, as Abraham did. The reason to mention this existentialist reaction to modern life is that in some passages in *Being and Time* Heidegger appears to endorse elements of Nietzsche's, Kierekegaard's, and the Mandarins' rhetoric. In the grip of such rhetoric, Heidegger may have wanted to assimilate average everyday Dasein to something less admirable, something lower. Seeing philosophically that this is implausible, Heidegger always moderates his critiques with assurances that his characterizations are not meant to be disparaging and that he is describing a "positive" existential phenomenon. The assurances ring hollow, however, in proximity to all the rhetoric.

In his sober moments Heidegger offers philosophical resources for a more balanced view of everyday life. Hubert Dreyfus points to underdeveloped phenomenological resources in *Being and Time* for naming everyday life in a less pejorative way:[77]

This undifferentiated character of Dasein's everydayness is *not nothing*, but a positive phenomenal characteristic of this entity. Out of this kind of being – and back into it again – is all existing, such as it is. We call this everyday undifferentiated character of Dasein *averageness*. (69/43)

If Dasein has an "undifferentiated" character that is neither owned nor disowned, that would indicate a third, and more plausible, description of Dasein's average everydayness. Fortunately, the English words "owned" and "disowned" also suggest a nice third option: "unowned." That is, we may characterize Dasein's average everydayness as unowned, and then reserve "owned" and "disowned" for existentiell modifications of average everydayness. The text of *Being and Time* is ambivalent on this issue, and so we are left to adopt as a working hypothesis the suggestion that there are three modes of life. We shall see in what follows whether it is clarifying to do so.

The hypothesis, then, is this: We live to a large extent in a mode that is unowned. For many of us the wrenching existential challenges that Heidegger describes under the headings of "death" and "anxiety" have not arisen. We glide along through life without having to face the question *whether* to own our lives. When the existential challenges of death and anxiety do arise, however, we are confronted with a choice, whether to own or disown our lives. Heidegger's word for the disowning response is usually "flight." Disowned Dasein flees in the face of death and anxiety and tries to return to everyday life. Having been awakened to the existential challenges, however, one cannot return "naïvely" to everyday life. One must, rather, cover up or bury the existential challenges, and that involves disowning the sorts of entity we are.

XIV. FALLING

I.5.A of *Being and Time* explores the phenomenon of disclosedness, that is, the way in which the world is "there" for us. As we have seen, this disclosedness has three facets, namely, understanding, disposedness, and discourse. In I.5.B Heidegger announces that he will explore disclosedness in its average everyday manifestation, which he calls "falling." He analyzes falling as consisting of "idle talk," "curiosity," and "ambiguity." As we saw in the previous section, however, Heidegger's distinction between everydayness and self-ownership is ambiguous, and there are probably three modes of disclosedness in the neighboring bushes: owned, unowned, and disowned. This is not the only difficulty that besets Heidegger's language of "falling," however.

In I.5.B Heidegger uses "falling" to name a specific mode of disclosedness, but in other places in the text he uses "falling" to refer to our relation to entities within-the-world. In §41, Heidegger identifies care (the being of Dasein) as the structural whole of existence, facticity, and falling. "Falling" here refers to our being-amidst entities within-the-world. Being-amidst is a structural element of Dasein's being, not a degraded or even merely average mode of disclosedness. Nevertheless, the dominant use of "falling" and "fallen" in *Being and Time* is to refer to a degraded mode of disclosedness, rather than to being-amidst. I will use the term in this way.

One would think that idle talk, curiosity, and ambiguity would be fallen versions of the three facets of disclosedness, understanding, mood, and discourse. While idle talk (*Gerede*) is clearly a fallen mode of discourse (*Rede*), and curiosity, as a "tendency towards 'seeing' " (214/170), is plausibly a mode of understanding, ambiguity does not neatly align with mood. Heidegger characterizes it as an inability "to decide what is disclosed in a genuine understanding, and what is not" (217/173), which suggests a mode of understanding, rather than mood. Further, in §38 Heidegger characterizes the mood that goes with falling as tranquility. As he develops his account of resoluteness, he sometimes suggests that we seek out conformity in order to tranquilize anxiety. However, tranquility cannot be the whole story of the mood of fallen everydayness, for the discussion of curiosity in §36 suggests a sort of agitation, rather than tranquility. Thus, I.5.B does not appear to develop a systematic account of the fallen modes of each of the three facets of disclosedness. Rather than treat I.5.B as a systematic extension of I.5.A, then, it is better to treat it as a presentation, albeit confused, of the dominant modes of unowned and disowned life.

The function of discourse is expressively to articulate the intelligibility of the world. Our everyday navigation of the world involves an "original" or "primordial" understanding of some of this world and a merely "positive" understanding of most of it. To have an original understanding of a possibility of human life is to be competent at living or conducting oneself that way. I have an original understanding of driving a car, writing a lecture, helping a child with math homework. Much of my world, however, I do not understand in this original way. I understand how to teach philosophy at the college level, but not how to teach reading at the elementary level. I do, nonetheless, have a grasp of the place of such teaching in our lives, and this enables me to recognize and engage appropriately with elementary school teachers. I do not myself, however, engage with that work, and I do not understand it "from the inside."

The same may be said of our *talk*. Recall that communication is the "[expressive] articulation of being with one another understandingly" (197/155). While talking with a fellow bread-baker about the perils of baking bread, I say things like, "I too often let the dough rise too long." Such statements mutually orient us both towards some aspect of the process. My interlocutor understands what I am saying, shares the situation with me, by coming to be oriented towards it as I am. He might be able to offer advice, since the situation we are sharing means something definite to him. If I make the same comment to someone who does not know how to bake bread our joint orientation towards this situation is shallower. She has a merely positive understanding of baking bread, enough to allow her to understand that baking bread is a process with stages that can go wrong. She will not be able to give me pointers. As Heidegger says, albeit with a twinge of disparagement: "Idle talk is the possibility of understanding everything without previously making the thing one's own" (213/169).

We have only a limited range of original understanding; most of our understanding and most of our talk are merely positive. There are genuinely practical limits on what we can understand originally: we do not have the time or energy to throw ourselves constructively into very many enterprises. People who "stretch themselves too thin" come off as shallow or sophomoric. Our merely positive understanding of things is sufficient, however, to navigate most of our world and negotiate the situations that arise in our experience. A positive understanding of some domain of human affairs is *sufficient* for navigating the world, and it is *impossible* to have an original understanding of all of the world. Thus, sufficient understanding and the positive idle talk that expresses it are constitutive of everyday human life.

Idle talk also has an aggravated or egregiously superficial form. Heidegger describes the slide from positive to degraded idle talk thus:

The being-said, the *dictum*, the pronouncement – all these now stand surety for the genuineness of the discourse and of the understanding which belongs to it, and for its appropriateness to the facts. And because this talk has lost its primary relationship-of-being towards the entity talked about, or else has never achieved such a relationship, it does not communicate in such a way as to let this entity be appropriated in an original manner, but communicates rather by the route of *passing the word along* and *repeating*. . . . Idle talk is constituted by just such passing the world along and repeating – a process by which its initial lack of rootedness becomes aggravated to complete rootlessness. (212/168*)

This characterization might suggest an epistemological worry about how our statements about the world become detached from the experiences that justify them. Just such a thing happens in gossip.[78] Your neighbor tells you that he saw the guy in the house next to him walk out into the backyard naked, and before you know it, the folks at the end of the block are talking about the committed nudist two doors from you. In such a case the reports about the alleged nudist have become detached from the original experiences that justify them (or not). This impression of Heidegger's point is reinforced by Macquarrie and Robinson's translation (which I altered above), according to which the talk's "initial lack of grounds to stand on becomes aggravated to complete groundlessness."

It is not likely, however, that epistemology is foremost in Heidegger's mind, and for two reasons. First, among the philosophical recommendations of *Being and Time*, as we saw in section (xi), is that we should abandon epistemology. So, it would be odd to ascribe an epistemological concern to Heidegger here at such a crucial moment. Second, epistemological concerns about grounding and evidence are appropriate mainly to assertions (and complexes of assertions, such as theories). But as we saw earlier (section ix), discourse is not a set of assertions, nor even a grammatical system and vocabulary for constructing assertions. Thus, it would be highly misleading to reconstruct Heidegger's conception of idle talk by reference to epistemological concerns.

Rather, Heidegger must be thinking about how a merely positive and superficial understanding of some domain of human affairs can be degraded into a mis-understanding. To communicate is to share an orientation to some domain of affairs, and when it is merely positive, it allows us to navigate in and around the domain without being able actually to participate in it, as we saw above. When such positive communication is uprooted from its connection to original discourse, discourse obstructs, rather than facilitates, positive understanding. Let me offer an admittedly rather controversial example. The language of "student-athletes" obstructs the inherent tensions in the lives of so-called student-athletes. Contemporary athletics at the high school level or even below makes demands on athletes that are very difficult to reconcile with a genuine commitment to studies and academic excellence. This tension ranges from the outright scandals that take place at some universities to milder tensions, in which athletes are not able to devote themselves to their studies and perform well because committed to so much practice- and travel-time. As America descends deeper and deeper into its obsession with athletic performance, youth sports coaches sometimes defend holding two or three practices a week for ten and eleven year olds on the grounds that the children are going to have to learn, sooner or later, how to be student-athletes, as if there were something coherent to be there![79]

However one might feel about the particular example I have offered, the model of obstructive idle talk should be clear enough. We sometimes develop ways of talking that give the appearance of expressing a genuine understanding of a phenomenon, but really cover up or obscure aspects of it. Despite the defects of such talk, "what is said-in-the-talk as such, spreads in wider circles and takes on an authoritative character" (212/168). If one has no original understanding of the phenomenon oneself, the mere fact that one talks this way has authority. This is what Heidegger calls "ambiguity."

> When, in our everyday being-with-one-another, we encounter the sort of thing which is accessible to everyone, and about which anyone can say anything, it soon becomes impossible to decide what is disclosed in a genuine understanding, and what is not. (217/173)

As another example, consider all the recent talk in the U.S. about "Nascar dads" and "soccer moms." Such concepts carry the semblance of understanding, the semblance of a rootedness in the context that they purport to disclose, but actually cover up as much as they reveal.

Curiosity deepens our immersion in idle talk. Curiosity, rooted in our fascination with the world, emerges in the possibility of "seeing the 'world' merely as it *looks* while one tarries and takes a rest" (216/ 172). When we merely look at a thing and are, perhaps, delighted by it, we experience a disengaged and at best positive experience of it. We do not, in any case, gain original familiarity this way. There is a heightened form of curiosity, however, in which "curiosity has become free" and we look "*just* in order to see," rather than to understand. Such curiosity leads to distraction, and distraction is a positive roadblock to original understanding. Heightened curiosity thereby contributes to the degradation of understanding.

In order for negative idle talk to take center stage in an account of disowned existence, it must be possible for one to live in idle talk, not just indulge it. That is, it is one thing for one to have a compromised understanding of the conduct and commitments of others, or to have a degraded understanding of this practice or that. It is quite another thing for one to have such an understanding of *one's own* conduct and, especially, one's own for-the-sakes-of-which. I.5.B does not clearly discuss the phenomenon, probably because it is torn between the positive and degraded versions of falling. The degradation of one's own for-the-sakes-of-which is thematically central to the distinction between owned and disowned life, but since I.5.B is officially about average everyday disclosedness, Heidegger pulls back from discussing self-degradation. So, let me weave together some scattered passages in *Being and Time* that describe this phenomenon.

Recall the tension in §27 on the Anyone between the Anyone as the background social normativity that is constitutive and enabling of everyday life and a degraded kind of social pressure, one that Heidegger sometimes calls "publicness" and characterizes as "leveling down" human life. In discussing the latter phenomenon, he writes:

> In this averageness with which [the Anyone] prescribes what can and may be ventured, it keeps watch over everything exceptional that thrusts itself to the fore. Every kind of greatness gets noiselessly suppressed. Overnight, everything that is original gets glossed over as something that has long been well known. Everything gained by a struggle becomes just something to be

manipulated. Every secret loses its force. This care of averageness reveals in turn an essential tendency of Dasein which we call the leveling down of all possibilities of being. (165/127*)

Immersion in the Anyone degrades not only one's understanding of others' lives and worlds, but one's understanding of one's own. Further, in a passage from §55 (II.2), Heidegger suggests that idle talk itself plays a critical role in such lostness in the Anyone: "Losing itself in the publicness and idle talk of the Anyone, [Dasein] fails to hear its own self in listening to the Anyone-self" (315/271). One can listen to the Anyone-self, rather than one's own self.

Film-makers and novelists are generally better at painting such pictures than academic philosophers. So, let us turn to an artistic representation of such disengaged and superficial living. The character of Lester Burnham (played by Kevin Spacey) in the film *American Beauty*[80] leads such a life, and his realization of this inspires his great line, "I feel like I've been in a coma for about twenty years. And I'm just now waking up." To be lost in the Anyone is to live according to a public interpretation of human life that is inflexible and unresponsive to the concrete situation in which one lives.

> *For the Anyone, however, the situation is essentially something that has been closed off.* The Anyone knows only the *"general situation,"* loses itself in those *"opportunities"* which are closest to it, and pays Dasein's way by a reckoning up of "accidents" which it fails to recognize, deems its own achievement, and passes off as such. (346–347/300)

The "general situation" is a generalized or vague, rather than concrete, response to the situation in which one lives. So, Lester Burnham has over the past twenty years gone to work and led an unimaginative and stale life. He has been closed off to other possibilities that were available, which he could have seized, if he had not lived in subjection to the dominant interpretation of life on offer by the Anyone.

> Publicness proximally controls every way in which the world and Dasein get interpreted, and it is always right – not because there is some distinctive and primary relationship of being in which it is related to "things," or because it avails itself of some transparency

on the part of Dasein which it has explicitly appropriated, but because it is insensitive to every difference of level and of genuineness and thus never gets to the "heart of the matter." By publicness everything gets obscured, and what has thus been covered up gets passed off as something familiar and accessible to everyone. (165/127)

Resolute Dasein, whom we will examine in section (xvii) below, discloses "the situation," in which one sees "what is factically possible" for the first time (346/299).

This failure of existential imagination is rather like the way in which someone who has a merely positive understanding of some skill or tool or practice will not see what is genuinely possible; only the experienced practitioner can see that. A novice or unimaginative youth sports coach will see a sulking and bored child and will only think to say to him or her, "If you don't want to play, go sit down on the sidelines." An imaginative and experienced coach will more easily find a way to integrate the bored child into the game or practice, find a role for him or her. In their insightful phenomenology of intuitive expertise, Hubert and Stuart Dreyfus emphasize the way in which an experienced and expert practitioner of a skill will just see and respond to situations that baffle or defeat a novice.[81] It is important to see, however, that this kind of intuitive expertise is not just a matter of doing what is "appropriate" or "called for," but rather that it also enables creative and flexible responses to situations. We can, therefore, see why Heidegger would think of idle talk (and the other phenomena of falling) as constitutive of a less than owned life: in order to *own* a life, we must live that life flexibly and imaginatively, rather than rigidly as a novice would.

In order to develop Heidegger's conception of the "counter-possibility" to such degraded living, namely, self-ownership, we must first explore the existential challenges that raise for the first time the question whether to own one's life or disown it. So, let now turn to anxiety and death.

Study Question

In what ways do you think you might yourself be living an unowned life, one in which you do not recognize what is genuinely possible for you?

XV. ANXIETY

Angst, dread, loneliness, anxiety, despair – these are some of the moods on which the existentialists have characteristically focused. Dostoyevsky's "Underground Man" (the antihero of *Notes from Underground*) is intensely lonely and suffers from what he calls "the disease of too great a lucidity." He is able to see through conventional justifications for action:

> Where will I find the primary reason for action, the justification for it? Where am I to look for it? I exercise my power of reasoning, and in my case, every time I think I have found a primary cause I see another cause that seems to be truly primary, and so on and so forth, indefinitely. This is the very essence of consciousness and thought.

Without such justifications for action, he is left with nothing, except perhaps raw emotion. His raw emotions, however, also fail to move him to act:

> Anger, of course, overcomes all hesitations and can thus replace the primary reason precisely because it is no reason at all. But what can I do if I don't even have anger (that's where I started from, remember)? In me, anger disintegrates chemically, like everything else . . . .[82]

Similarly, Ivan Karamazov has "seen through" the customs of the Russian people, but without having anything to replace them.

> "I understand nothing," Ivan went on, as though in a delirium. "I don't want to understand anything now. I want to stick to the fact. I made up my mind long ago not to understand. If I try to understand anything, I shall be false to the fact and I have determined to stick to the fact."[83]

Ivan has decided to "stick to the fact," that is, not to try to understand anything, not to look for meaning in human life. So, Ivan declares, "The world stands on absurdities," and resolves to take his own life at the age of thirty, when he will have "drunk the cup of life empty."

Other pieces of existentialist literature also focus on the same feelings of despair, anxiety, and solitude: Sartre's *The Flies* and *Nausea*, Camus's *The Stranger*, and almost everything written by Kafka. A quick romp around the Web will also expose a vigorous discussion about movies that might well display such psychological phenomena: *American Beauty* (Mendes), *The Eclipse* (Antonioni), and *Hiroshima Mon Amour* (Resnais), to name a few. What is the *philosophical* significance of such literary and cinematic studies? Heidegger was deeply influenced by existentialist literature, but also concerned to avoid blurring the line between "edifying" writing and philosophy, which is to say phenomenological ontology.[84]

In §40 of *Being and Time* Heidegger offers a phenomenology of existential dread, which he calls "anxiety." However, as we have just seen, we must first ask what anxiety has to do with the ontological concerns of *Being and Time*. The answer is twofold. First, we have seen repeatedly that the ontological structure of a phenomenon stands out in better relief in breakdown situations than in normal. We do not typically encounter equipment in terms of its ontologically constitutive elements; its equipmental character stands out in breakdown, when the ease and transparency of normal interaction slips away. Similarly, I normally experience others as friends, strangers, students, and so on, rather than in the light of their subjection to and enhancement of the Anyone. These features of everyday human life stand out more saliently in the form of social breakdown that Heidegger calls "distantiality," when we encounter deviance.

Here in §40 we discover that a similar pattern holds for Dasein's self-understanding. Our being is existence, and to exist is to constitute oneself as who one is by understanding oneself in a determinate way. We do not normally have the experience of constituting ourselves as who we are; rather, we normally just are who we are and experience the imports of objects and the possibilities of the world as what they are. In anxiety the transparency of self-constitution breaks down, and I become aware of myself as a self-constituter. The phenomenology of anxiety, thus, plays an important evidentiary role in *Being and Time*: it confirms Heidegger's ontological account of existence. (This explains why Heidegger places it in I.6, rather than in division II, where it belongs thematically.)

The discussion of anxiety plays a second important role in *Being and Time* as well, although this role does not emerge clearly until division II. Anxiety, as Heidegger describes it, is a complete collapse of the structure of meaning in which one lives. In anxiety one does not constitute oneself, because one cannot. In a sense, one is unable to exist. Heidegger provocatively labels this inability to exist "death." Death turns out to be the same experience as anxiety. I will refer to this experience as "Dasein's extreme condition," a name I base on Heidegger's characterization of death as "uttermost." Death is the self-understanding that belongs to this experience, anxiety is its mood, and conscience its discourse. That Dasein is able to be, even though it cannot constitute itself as anyone, reveals something important about Dasein, something that eludes the official account of Dasein's being in division I.

In anxiety, the world collapses into total insignificance.

> ... the totality of involvements of the ready-to-hand and the present-at-hand uncovered within the world, is, as such, of no consequence; it collapses into itself; the world has the character of completely lacking significance. (231/186)

The world has significance, because it is *both* that in terms of which we understand equipment *and* that wherein we understand ourselves (119/86). In some existentialist portrayals of anxiety the paraphernalia of human life loses its context: this thing before me no longer presents itself as a coffee mug and degenerates to a mere thing, a hunk of greenish stuff.[85] This does not seem to be the sort of anxiety that Heidegger has in mind, however. Rather, Heidegger emphasizes that in anxiety, "... the world in its worldhood is all that still obtrudes itself" (231/187). The world, the meaningful context of paraphernalia, is still palpably present. I still confront a coffee mug; I still understand paraphernalia in terms of their equipmental roles.

What I cannot do in anxiety is understand myself: "Anxiety thus takes away from Dasein the possibility of understanding itself, as it falls, in terms of the 'world' and the way things have been publicly interpreted" (232/187). Because we cannot understand ourselves in anxiety, we cannot feel "at home" in the world. The world is normally our "home," the place where we dwell, because we understand ourselves therein. Thus, Heidegger characterizes the ambience or atmosphere of anxiety as *uncanniness* or the mode of the "*not-at-home*" (233/188–189). We are, thus, alienated from the world, not because we do not know by what we are surrounded, but rather because the world offers us nothing in terms of which to make sense of our own lives. The world is not only that in terms of which we understand equipment and that wherein we dwell, but also that wherein others dwell. Dasein is being-with-one-another, which means that we experience ourselves as living in a world with others who are in most respects like us. They are "Dasein-with," fellow residents of our common with-world. Just as we can continue to understand what a coffee mug is and what one does with a coffee mug, so we continue to understand what a neighbor is and how one relates appropriately to one. In anxiety our friends, family, neighbors, co-workers, etc., remain just that. But just as our inability to understand ourselves in terms of this given worldly structure alienates us from the context of equipment, so it alienates us as well from others, from our families, friends, etc. "The 'world' can offer nothing more, and neither can the Dasein-with of others" (232/187).

What does this alienation mean? Anxiety is a mood, and as a mood it has the disclosive features of mood, including the disclosure of imports. In our average everydayness the various possibilities of living that are on offer in our lives appeal to or repel us in determinate ways. Being a father is fulfilling, a coach exciting, a neighbor relaxing. Anxiety discloses life's possibilities as well, but without the imports that normally move one to action. In anxiety we cannot press forward into possibilities, because we cannot understand ourselves in terms of the world. Anxiety discloses possibilities as irrelevant or insignificant. The world has nothing to offer, not because there is something defective in the world *per se*, but rather because in anxiety everything about the world, including especially the ways we might carry on in life, are insignificant. They are drained of their meaning, irrelevant. In the psychological literature the condition of "anhedonia" is characterized as an inability to take pleasure in life or "an inability to move things forward."[86] The loss of desire and pleasure are symptoms of the flattening out of experience and the withdrawal from the possibilities of life that have heretofore been meaningful. (In one version of the phenomenon the sufferer hides in vigorous pleasure-seeking, such as hypersexuality or violence, both aspects of the "Karamazov baseness" so vividly on display in Dostoyevsky's novel. Lester Burnham, in *American Beauty*, likewise degenerates into sexual distraction as an antidote to his suffering.)

I am suggesting, then, that some of the core phenomena of

what Heidegger calls "anxiety" are characteristic of what we today call *depression*. What sufferers without the language of Heidegger, Dostoyevsky, and Kierkegaard call a "hopelessness," "intense boredom," "living under a dark cloud," and which clinicians call "flat affect" and "anhedonia," are symptoms of a depressive disorder. In such a condition, one withdraws into isolation, loses interest in the world around one, stops taking pleasure in everyday life, loses motivation to carry on. Heidegger's descriptions of what he calls "anxiety" fit this model quite well: the world "has nothing to offer," and neither do others; one cannot understand oneself anymore; one feels uncanny and not-at-home.

Some of Heidegger's language points in the direction of what psychiatrists today call "anxiety." "That in the face of which one has anxiety is characterized by the fact that what threatens is *nowhere*" (231/186). This threat generates a response typical of anxiety: "Therefore that which threatens cannot bring itself close from a definite direction within what is close by; it is already 'there', and yet nowhere; it is so close that it is oppressive and stifles one's breath, and yet it is nowhere" (ibid.). This sounds a lot like the sort of panic attack that anxious people suffer. It may be that Heidegger really has in mind what is sometimes called "agitated depression."[87] In the end, however, the entire range of phenomena in which Heidegger expresses interest here is not relevant to the ontological conclusions he wants to draw.[88]

Anxiety is of ontological interest, because it exposes the sorts of entity we are, people who can come to find the world and its human possibilities irrelevant. Heidegger is *not* claiming that in anxiety we realize the "deep truth" about our lives, that everything is worthless or meaningless. Rather, just as when the coffee cup leaks and we say to ourselves, "Well, it's *supposed* to hold coffee," thereby making its equipmental character salient, so in anxiety our inability to understand ourselves and press forward into possibilities of life makes plain that we are entities who stand always before the question, "Who am I?" As Heidegger puts it: "Therefore, with that which it is anxious about, anxiety discloses Dasein as *being-possible* . . ." (232/187–188). That we are "being-possible" means that we are entities that are always pressing ahead into a future, or at least trying to do so. In anxiety (or depression, really) that future looms for us, makes a claim on us, but one that we cannot requite. Part of what makes depression a form of *suffering* is that in depression one experiences a demand one cannot address; one feels that one is *supposed* to get up and do something, but nothing appeals to one. One is left in the position of the Underground Man, who declares,

> If only my doing nothing were due to laziness! How I'd respect myself then! Yes, respect, because I would know that I could be lazy at least, that I had at least one definite feature in me, something positive, something I could be sure of. To the question "Who is he?" people would answer, "A lazy man." It would be wonderful to hear that. It would imply that I could be clearly characterized, that there was something to be said about me. "A lazy man." Why, it's a calling, a vocation, a career, ladies and gentlemen! Don't laugh, it's the truth.[89]

This is to say, then, that anxiety confirms the analysis of existence from I.1.

Anxiety points us forward in another direction as well. Anxiety, Heidegger says, brings us face-to-face with our "ownmost ability-to-be."

> Anxiety throws Dasein back upon that which it is anxious about – its owned ability-to-be-in-the-world. Anxiety individualizes Dasein for its ownmost being-in-the-world, which as something that understands, projects itself essentially upon possibilities. Therefore, with that which it is anxious about, anxiety discloses Dasein as *being-possible*, and indeed as the only kind of thing which it can be of its own accord as something individualized in individualization. (232/187–188)

If one comes to *Being and Time* with an inclination to look for a romantic version of the concept of authenticity or self-ownership, then one will read the final sentence of the passage quoted above to imply that in anxiety we come face to face with who we are as unique individuals, as who we are in our individualization. Reading the sentence that way, it makes sense that Heidegger introduces the notion of our *ownmost* ability-to-be: in anxiety we disclose "who we really are," what our "lives are really about." This "deep truth" about us reflects what is most our own.

There is another way to read this sentence, however, one that is grammatically more natural. Anxiety discloses the "only kind of thing" we can be "as something individualized in individualization," all right, but what is that "kind of thing" we can be? Heidegger's answer: being-possible. When we are individualized, when we are stripped of our embeddedness in a community and our reliance upon a world that has been publicly interpreted, we are left with the sheer fact of our being-possible. Our being-possible is not, however, a logical fact, of the sort one might formulate in a metaphysics course: "I am indeed possible (because I am actual)." Rather, our being-possible is our existentiality, our being called forth to take a stand on who we are. This being called forth is salient in anxiety, because we cannot respond to it.

One may think about this in terms of "thick" and "thin" senses of existentiality. "Existence" has a more and less robust sense. The "thin" or less robust sense of existence is that we always stand before the question, Who am I? Normally we answer this question by carry-ing on our lives in a determinate way, thereby taking a stand on who we are, *making* or *constituting* ourselves in the process. This is the "thick" or more robust sense of existence. In anxiety, the thick and thin senses of existence come apart: we stand before the question, Who am I? but we cannot answer it. We have thin existence, but not thick. We are thinned out to mere being-possible.

This analysis implies two further consequences. First, anxiety does not disclose "who we really are," because in anxiety we are no one. We are mere being-possible (thin existence), with no determinate life (thick existence). Anxiety is a kind of breakdown experience, breakdown in the living of a human life, rather than a window onto the truth. Second, in order to be anyone determinate, in order to be able to answer the question, Who am I? we must be embedded within a social context, in a world that has been publicly interpreted, and with others who are likewise constituting themselves as who they are by pressing forward into determinate ways of being human. In other words, Dasein cannot be anyone without a social context. This is to acknowledge the argument made by Charles Taylor in *The Ethics of Authenticity*, that authenticity is only possible in what Taylor calls a "dialogical context."[90]

Anxiety does nonetheless have an important connection with freedom and self-ownership.

> Anxiety makes manifest in Dasein its *being towards* its ownmost ability-to-be – that is, its *being-free for* the freedom of choosing

itself and taking hold of itself. Anxiety brings Dasein face to face with its *being-free for* (*propensio in* . . .) the ownedness of its being, and for this ownedness as a possibility which it always is. (232/188)

Anxiety does not strip us down to our inner, authentic core, as for example natural disasters or great personal losses can. It is common to hear survivors of natural disasters, wars, and the deaths of intimates say, "I understand much better now what is important to me. It's not my job or my status in the community; it's my family." This is an important kind of acknowledgement and personal growth, but it is not what Heidegger is talking about. Rather, anxiety brings us face-to-face with our "ownmost ability-to-be," and this encounter frees us up in some way. But how? In order to answer this question, we must examine our "ownmost ability-to-be" in more detail. Our ownmost ability-to-be is death, and so, we must now turn to Heidegger's account of death.

Study Question

If what Heidegger calls "anxiety" really is depression, shouldn't we just treat it with anti-depressant medications, rather than extract alleged philosophical insights from it?

XVI. DEATH, GUILT, AND CONSCIENCE

Death (II.1)

In anxiety our familiarity with the world around us, our being-at-home in the world, breaks down. Anxiety individualizes us and reveals our ontological constitution: that we always confront the question of identity, although sometimes we are not able to answer this question. When we are not able to answer the question of identity, we are no longer able to press forward into a self-understanding, which is how Heidegger uses the verb "to exist." We are existentially dead, or perhaps dead to the world. Death is ". . . the possibility of no-longer-being-able-to-be-there," or a few sentences later, ". . . the possibility of the absolute impossibility of Dasein" (294/250). Anxiety has the special function of disclosing our death to us: *"But the disposedness which can hold open the utter and constant threat to*

itself arising from Dasein's ownmost individualized being, is anxiety"
(310/265–266). By bringing us face-to-face with our existential death,
anxiety opens up the possibility of *"an impassioned* **freedom towards
death** *– a freedom which has been released from the illusions of the
Anyone . . ."* (311/266).

This is beginning to sound rather grim: we discover our freedom
by being cut off from both our relations to others and our self-
understanding, and confronting our lonely death. What is more,
Heidegger describes our owned relationship to death as "anticipation" (in the English translation) or more literally, "running forth
into" (*vorlaufen in*). Is Heidegger participating in the nihilistic valor-
ization of suicide that one finds in Ivan Karamazov, or in the proto-
fascist idealization of death that one finds in the writings of Ernst
Jünger.[91] If this *were* what Heidegger were suggesting, we would
have reason to be disappointed. Fortunately, it is not. In order to see
this, however, we need first to work through Heidegger's linguistic
gymnastics in II.1.

By "death" Heidegger does not refer to the ending of a human life.
Death is, rather, a condition in which Dasein can find itself: "Death
is a way to be, which Dasein takes over as soon as it is" (289/245).
Death is a *way to be*? One would think that death is a way *not* to be!
Death is not an event that lies off in the future: "Dying is not an
event; it is a phenomenon to be understood existentially . . ." (284/
240). "The possibility of no-longer-being-able-to-be-there" and "the
absolute impossibility of Dasein" do not refer, then, to the termination of life. They refer to some condition in which we can live, but in
which we cannot exist, conceived existentially. If existing in the distinctively existential sense is to go forward with life, to answer the
question of identity, then to die existentially is to be unable to answer
this question. In anxiety we are unable to do this, which implies that
death is another facet of the experience Heidegger calls "anxiety."

If "death" refers to this existential condition, then what does
Heidegger call the ending of a human life? The answer: *demise.*

Dasein too "has" its death, of the kind appropriate to anything
that lives; and it has it, not in ontical isolation, but as codetermined by its primordial kind of being. In so far as this is the case,
Dasein too can end without ownedly dying, though on the other
hand, *qua* Dasein, it does not simply perish. We designate this
intermediate phenomenon as its *demise.* (291/247)

Human beings are alive, and thus, their lives can end; in fact, they always do so. That is, humans do "perish": "In our terminology the ending of anything that is alive, is denoted as perishing" (284/ 240–241). Animals perish, as do specimens of the species *homo sapiens*. But Heidegger insists that we do not "simply" perish. The ending of our lives is "codetermined" by our "original kind of being," i.e., by our being Dasein and not merely an animal. When a human life comes to an end, Heidegger speaks of "demising," rather than merely "perishing."

Thus, Heidegger uses the word "death" in an exotic fashion. He is not the first philosopher to do so: Kierkegaard used the word in a similar way.[92] One can motivate a powerful *metaphorical* use of the term "death," comparable to Lester Burnham's use of the term "coma" in *American Beauty*. Heidegger does not want *his* use of the term to be metaphorical in anything like this sense; that runs the risk of degrading his treatise in ontology into something "merely edifying." So, he sets out to defend his use of "death" on ontological grounds. Death, in *his* sense, is the end of Dasein, as demise is the end of a human life. "It thus becomes more urgent to ask *in what sense, if any, death must be conceived as the ending of Dasein*" (289/244).

Dasein does not end in the sense of being finished or complete. In a detailed set of considerations in §48 in II.1, Heidegger considers several modes of ending in the sense of finishing (or completion). Stopping or termination, as of a process, is one sort of end, as is fulfillment, which takes place when some internal goal has been satisfied. Anything that matures or ripens can be fulfilled or not, as can our projects, which have goals that can be achieved or not. In this sense, as Heidegger comments, "Dasein [conceived as a project] may well have passed its ripeness before the end" (288/244). Because Heidegger describes self-understanding as "projection," or as "project" (his German word "*Entwurf*" can be translated either way), it is tempting to read him as saying that Dasein's end is a special kind of fulfillment. This would be a misreading, however.

A project is a set of activities that are organized around some goal that can be achieved. When the project is completed, it is over. Projects come to an end (or else never end and are forever incomplete, like Bruckner's *Ninth Symphony*). As a teacher, I can design and run a course. We can always ask of these projects whether they have been completed. Dasein, however, is not like this:

By none of these modes of ending can death be suitably characterized as the end of Dasein. If dying, as being-at-an-end, were understood in the sense of an ending of the kind we have discussed, then Dasein would thereby be treated as something present-at-hand or ready-to-hand. In death, Dasein has not been fulfilled nor has it simply disappeared; it has not become finished nor is it wholly at one's disposal as something ready-to-hand. (289/245)

Dasein is not a project, or even a set of projects; it is not something that culminates (or fails to do so). Rather, as Heidegger comments in the sentence directly after this last passage, ". . . Dasein *is* already its not-yet, and is its not-yet constantly as long as it is . . . ."

There is always "more" to a self-understanding than to any project. There is a peculiar open-endedness to our self-understandings. Being a father, teacher, coach, or daughter is not something with a defined goal, such that once that goal has been achieved, the self-understanding is fulfilled or complete. Being a teacher is not teaching a course; it is a way of understanding one's being with students that exceeds the bounds of any project. Indeed, it exceeds the bounds of any profession. I was once at a coaching training session in which the presenter began by asking, "How many of you are teachers?" Ten or so of us raised our hands, and the presenter laughed and said, "Gotchya!" Her point? To coach is to teach, at least when it is done well. This allows us to ask of a coach whether he or she is a teacher or is just marking time or occupying a job.

James Carse develops a related distinction between "finite" and "infinite" games.[93] A finite game is a game with a goal that ends the game, hence winners and losers; one plays finite games in order to win them. An infinite game is a game that one plays for the sake of playing. Infinite games may consist of finite games, but the end of any finite game does not define the end of the infinite game. So, we may distinguish playing a baseball game from being a baseball player. Baseball games can be completed or not, but being a baseball player cannnot. Being a baseball player is (or can be) an infinite game. In a similar vein, Heidegger characterizes Dasein as "existing for the sake of itself," which does not mean that Dasein is self-centered, but rather that it lives for the sake of the self-understanding into which it presses ahead. Self-understandings are infinite games.

Self-understandings can die, however. When a self-understanding stops functioning as a guiding principle in one's life, it is dead. Put a little differently, *one* is dead as, say, a student, when being a student no longer matters to one. The meanings that once structured one's life as a student, the possibilities that once beckoned, and the demands one once felt have become inert. When it is not just this self-understanding or that that has died, but all of them, then one has died. Existential death is more like a "limit-situation" than like the stopping of a process.[94] Existential death is a limit-situation of being-possible, of the ability to be, because in such death one cannot exercise the ability. It thus reveals the limits of existence. No self-understanding is immune to being undercut by anxiety; anything we take for granted about ourselves can be dissolved by the corrosive effects of anxiety. Dasein's existential finitude (limitedness) is its constant, because essential, vulnerability to anxiety/death. Thus, the answer to the question in what sense death is the end of Dasein is this: death is the end of Dasein in the sense of the limit-situation in which the finitude of our being as ability-to-be is exposed.

Heidegger adds that death is certain, indefinite, non-relational, not to be outstripped, and ownmost. Let us consider these aspects of death in turn.

Certain. Heidegger contrasts certainty as an attitude towards evidence and certainty as an existential stance. As an epistemic attitude towards evidence, to be certain is to estimate the probability of an event as 100%. We are epistemically certain of our demise. Of course, maybe someday we will find a way to beat demise, and this means that demise is only "empirically" or "relatively" certain. Heidegger concedes this point (how could he not?) and then comments, *"The fact that demise, as an event which occurs, is 'only' empirically certain, is in no way decisive as to the certainty of death"* (301/257). Why? Because by "death" Heidegger does not mean the event of one's demise, and by "being certain" he does not mean an epistemic attitude towards evidence. By "death" he means the condition of existential anxiety (or depression), and of this condition we cannot be epistemically certain. What percentage of people suffer at some point from major depression? Certainly not 100%.[95] Thus, by "certainty" Heidegger must have something else in mind.

Indefinite. Heidegger characterizes certainty as "holding-for-true." When what we hold for true is an event that occurs, then holding-for-true means believing that the event is probable. When what we hold for true is an existential condition, then to be certain means to disclose as possible. (Recall, primordial truth is disclosedness.) To be existentially certain of death is to understand that it is always possible, that it could strike at any moment. Put from another angle, there is nothing about us that shields or protects us from the threat of existential anxiety. This is a consequence of Heidegger's denial of human nature. If humans were "wired up" so as always to care about something definite, then anxiety would not always be possible. If, as in the popular imagination, "parental instinct" (more commonly, "maternal instinct") or the sex-drive were hard-wired into human psychology, then we would not have to fear that parents might become depressed and abandon their children, or that someone might lose interest in sexuality. We do have to worry about these possibilities, however, because in the relevant sense, no such thing is part of human nature. Thus, existential death is certain, not because 100% probable, but rather because always possible. Human life is vulnerable to radical breakdown. This is why Heidegger connects death's certainty with its indefiniteness: to say that death is always possible is to say that its "when" is indefinite.

Not to be outstripped. This vulnerability to radical breakdown reveals how any possibility of human life can be "outstripped" or "overtaken." Heidegger does not say much by way of explaining his language of "being outstripped," but it certainly suggests the sort of thing that happens when life changes so as to render one's self-understanding unintelligible. The self-understanding of being a steel-worker came crashing to an end in the Monongahela River Valley outside Pittsburgh, Penn. during the early 1980s. Someone who had understood himself that way no longer could; the context stripped it of its livability. One's self-understanding can also be overtaken by one's age, or by fantasies of one's past, as it is for Lou Pascal (Burt Lancaster) in *Atlantic City*.[96] Any for-the-sake-of-which in which one is engaged can dissolve, if one finds oneself in depression. There is only one possibility of human life that can never be outstripped, that is always possible, and that is existential death itself.

Non-relational. Existential death is also "non-relational." "When [Dasein] stands before itself in this way, all its relations to any other Dasein have been undone" (294/250). As a characterization of how people confront or imagine demise, this is highly dubious. Many people demise in the arms of loved ones, comforted by a feeling of fulfillment and a life well lived. Since death is not demise, Heidegger does not mean to deny this. Rather, his point is that in the experience of depression, others can be of no help, as we saw in section (xv).

This means in turn that one cannot relate to anyone else in depression, that one is cut off from them and cannot turn to them for help or illumination in working out one's self-understanding. In a similar vein, Heidegger states that we cannot "be represented" in death, that "*No one can take the other's dying away from him*" (284/240). If we understand "death" to mean the ending of a human life (demise), then of course someone can "die in one's place," e.g., sacrifice his or her life for one (as Heidegger notes in the very next sentence). If Heidegger were arguing that no one could demise for one, then his reflections on death would be vulnerable to Delmore Schwartz's quip that "Existentialism means that no one else can take a bath for you."[97] There are lots of things that others cannot do for one, including taking a bath, having a headache, getting stitches, and demising. Heidegger's point is, rather, that no one can take anxiety away from one. This is true in two senses. First, in a major depressive episode, others are of no use to one, because one ceases to care about them. Direct appeals and offers of help from one's intimates have no power.[98] Second, when one is existentially dead, it is *one's own* life that makes no sense, not someone else's.

Ownmost. Adding up the last two paragraphs, Heidegger concludes that in existential death, Dasein is *individualized*.

Death does not just "belong" to one's own Dasein in an undifferentiated way; death *lays claim* to it as an *individual* Dasein. The non-relational character of death, as understood in anticipation, individualizes Dasein down to itself. This individualizing is a way in which the "There" is disclosed for existence. It makes manifest that all being-amidst the things with which we concern ourselves, and all being-with others, will fail us when our ownmost ability-to-be is the issue. (308/263)

In death we are stripped of all our supports and relations and delivered over to raw being-possible. We confront the existential dimension of our lives, that is, the way in which we *exist* rather than are merely present-at-hand: we always stand before the question, Who am I? Our being is always at issue. We stand before the question of identity, but we cannot answer it.

Dasein is essentially "mine": "The being of any such entity is *in each case mine*" (67/41–42). A page later Heidegger connects mineness to the problematic of ownedness:

And because Dasein is in each case essentially its own possibility, it *can*, in its very being, "choose" itself and win itself; it can also lose itself and never win itself; or only "seem" to do so. But only in so far as it can be *owned* – that is, something of its own – can it have lost itself and not yet won itself. (68/42–43)

We are in each case our "own" possibility. Our being is in each case mine, which means that in some sense your being "belongs" to you. Whatever it is for your being to be yours, it must be present in exist-ential death as well as in everyday living. All that is yours in death is the question of identity, not any answer to it. We saw in section (iv) that to be who you are is to reside in the world, to be familiar with it. In death, however, you are not at home, and so nothing with which you are ordinarily familiar is inherently yours. Death is, therefore, ownmost, most your own.

That death is ownmost does *not* mean that all of our further possibilities, such as being a student, a son or daughter, a teammate, are "not really ours," are somehow shams or cover-ups. One way of hearing the language of "authenticity" and "self-ownership" is to associate it with sincerity or being "true to ourselves." Being true to ourselves requires that we first be honest with ourselves about who we are, what our "real" aspirations and feelings are. With this rhetoric in mind, one might conclude that Heidegger is saying that none of the socially constructed identities or for-the-sakes-of-which in terms of which we understand ourselves are authentic. Any way in which we go about leading our lives involves "selling out" to the Anyone and acquiescing in a public persona that falsifies our identities. This reasoning leads to the gloomy conclusion that "really" we are each "nothing and no one," that once individualized down to our particular essences, there is nothing left. Reading Heidegger this way has a certain plausibility to it and connects with some of Heidegger's formulations: e.g., "*Care itself, in its very essence, is permeated with nullity through and through*" (331/285). This seems to be how Sartre read him as well: we are in the end nothingness,[99] a view captured in the very title of Sartre's treatise in existential phenomenology, *Being and Nothingness*. This is not Heidegger's view, however.

Heidegger is making a slightly different point, namely, that our ownmost capacity is simply our being-possible, and that we confront this aspect of our being starkly in anxiety/death. It is true that all the

for-the-sakes-of-which in terms of which each of us understands
him- or herself are socially mediated.

> If Dasein is familiar with itself as the Anyone-self, this means at
> the same time that the Anyone itself prescribes that way of inter-
> preting the world and being-in-the-world which lies closest. . . . In
> terms of the Anyone and as the Anyone I am "given" proximally
> to "myself." (167/129)

All that is peculiarly our own is that being-possible in virtue of which
we press ahead into who we are, press ahead into some set of possibilities on offer in our culture. It does not follow from this, however,
that we are "really" nothing or that who we "truly" are is revealed in
anxiety/death. We are who we find ourselves to be in the course of
our lives. To see this more clearly, let us turn to the themes of guilt
and conscience in II.2.

Existential Guilt: Being-the-Basis (II.2)

As Heidegger does with the concept of death, he spends considerable
time in II.2 distinguishing everyday guilt from an ontological form
of guilt, existential guilt, which shares a formal structure with everyday guilt, but is really something quite different. Just as demise and
death are both the "end of Dasein," but in very different ways, so
everyday and existential guilt are both "being-the-basis of a nullity."
Everyday guilt is a matter of being responsible for some deprivation
in the life of another, or as Heidegger puts it:

> . . . *being-the-basis* for a lack of something in the [existence][100] of
> an other, and in such a manner that this very being-the-basis
> determines itself as "lacking in some way" in terms of that for
> which it is the basis. (328/282*)

To generate the existential version of being-guilty, Heidegger fills out
what it is to "be the basis" of something and in what ways we are the
basis for "nullities."

Being-the-basis in the ordinary sense is being responsible for
something, or as Heidegger puts it: ". . . being the cause or author
of something, even 'being the occasion' for something" (327/282).
Heidegger offers this variety of formulations in order to indicate that

he does not mean to take sides in any standard debates about the nature of agency. However one analyzes ordinary responsibility, being-the-basis existentially is not ordinary responsibility. Rather,

> In being a basis – that is, in existing as thrown – Dasein constantly lags behind its possibilities. It is never existent *before* its basis, but only *from it* and *as this basis*. Thus, being-the-basis means *never* to have power over one's ownmost being from the ground up. . . . [Dasein] has been *released* from its basis, *not through* itself but *to* itself, so as to be *as this basis*. (330/284–285)

Being-the-basis existentially is to *be* someone, rather than to be responsible for an action or effect, to be someone already *as whom* one must live. Heidegger indicates (between the dashes) that he is really restating the concept of thrownness. We saw in I.5, §31, that Dasein's possibility is thrown possibility. That is, as you confront some significant juncture in your life – for example, whether to move to another city – you are differentially disposed to the possibilities you confront. You are attached to your neighborhood, you are at ease in your workplace, yet you may not feel safe where you live. These differential dispositions are the basis on which you project or press ahead into who you are. "Although [Dasein] has *not* laid the basis *itself*, it reposes in the weight of it, which is made manifest to it as a burden by Dasein's mood" (330/284). The word "burden" feels rather gloomy; it is perhaps better to think of drag, in the sense in which engineers talk about thrust and drag. Who you already are places a drag on your forward trajectory; it situates you and keeps you tied to your context.

In II.2 Heidegger distinguishes two different aspects of thrownness, which he calls "nullities" in §58. This is an odd formulation that easily suggests all the wrong things. He does not want to say that we are really no one and nothing and thus delivered over to nothingness. The "nullities" are "nots" or lacks that limit our being. Dasein is being-possible, that is to say, an ability-to-be; a "not," when applied to an ability, is an *inability*. The "nullities" of which Heidegger speaks are, therefore, inabilities or limitations on our ability-to-be. We have already seen that Heidegger wants to emphasize that we "*never* . . . have power over [our] ownmost being from the ground up." We are not able to take complete control over who we are, because for possibilities to be disclosed for us and be relevant to who we understand ourselves to be, they must already matter to us. We cannot "wipe the slate clean" and start over, because if we did wipe the slate clean, nothing would matter. This is what happens in anxiety or depression, and thus anxiety/depression discloses that our basis is null, limited. Furthermore, our projection is null or limited too. We are not able to be everything we might want to be, nor very much all at once.

> But this implies that in being able-to-be [Dasein] always stands in one possibility or another: it constantly is *not* other possibilities, and it has waived these in its existentiell projection. Not only is the projection, as one that has been thrown, determined by the nullity of being-the-basis; as *projection* it is itself essentially *null*. (331/285)

This passage points to two different sorts of limitation in forward projection. First, in a great many cases, possibilities that we have "waived" or foregone are now irretrievable. Loves and career-paths we do not pursue are typically (though not always) forever gone. Second, we can press forward into only some of the possibilities we can pursue, not all or even many of them. Thus, projection is defined by inability as well: the inability to be possibilities that have been waived and the inability to project oneself into all of what is available to one.

Heidegger summarizes this analysis by saying that Dasein is always "the null basis of a nullity," that is, a limited or finite basis of a limited or finite set of possibilities. Our freedom of maneuver (our "leeway") is limited or contextualized. It is limited by who we already are, which means in part what possibilities we have before us. This is what Heidegger means by our "existential guilt." Recurring then to the discussion of death, Heidegger most definitely does not mean to say that "really" we are "nothing" or "no one." No, really we are who we already are. To be Dasein, to be a person, is to find oneself differentially disposed towards the possibilities the world has to offer, differentially disposed by way of confronting those possibilities in terms of how they matter to one.

Conscience

We have seen Heidegger develop the phenomenology of an extreme or "uttermost" condition of human life, anxiety/death, in which one is not able to understand oneself, because the world has collapsed into insignificance. Like all modes of disclosedness, the extreme condition has three facets. Anxiety is its mood; death is its self-understanding. What, then is the discourse that belongs to this extreme condition? Heidegger calls it *conscience*.

What sort of discourse could accompany anxiety/death? Recall that discourse is language, construed broadly: our expressive articulation of the meaning of experience. In the experience of anxiety/death, however, the world collapses into meaninglessness. It would seem, then, that in anxiety/death there would be nothing to express. Hence, it should come as no surprise when Heidegger writes: "*What does the conscience call to him to whom it appeals? Taken strictly, nothing. . . . Conscience discourses solely and constantly in the mode of keeping silent*" (318/273). The reticence or silence of conscience has a communicative impact nonetheless, Heidegger argues. Dasein is ". . . *summoned* to itself – that is, to its ownmost ability-to-be" (ibid.). What does it mean for conscience to be silent, to "have nothing to tell" (ibid.), yet still to summon Dasein forth to something? It seems as if conscience must have no content, yet still communicate something. How could that be?

We may begin with Heidegger's discussion of *who* is summoned by the call of conscience. He writes:

> The self to which the appeal is made remains indefinite and empty in its what. When Dasein interprets itself in terms of that with which it concerns itself, the call passes over *what* Dasein, proximally and for the most part, understands itself *as*. (319/274)

Conscience does not call to you as a son or daughter, student, lover, or any other way in which you might concretely understand yourself, because in the extreme condition of anxiety/death you are alienated from all these self-understandings. This means that if you are addressed in anxiety, you must be addressed *not* as the determinate person you have been, but rather as the indeterminate person who is now unable to be. The discourse of anxiety must address you as no one definite, that is, as one who is unable to be anyone. Still, "the self has been reached, unequivocally and unmistakably." That is, "while the content of the call is seemingly indefinite, the *direction it takes* is a sure one and is not to be overlooked" (318/274). The call is a *summons*; it *calls you forth* to something. But what? In anxiety/

existential death, you have no "forward motion"; you are not pressing forth into any possibilities that could make you who you are. So, it might seem that there is nothing to which to be called forth. Recall, however, that anxiety is distressing because one feels pull, as it were, but cannot respond to it. The existential pull is forward into being someone, leading a life by pressing forth into the world. Hence, in anxiety/existential death we are called forth into the future, but not in such a way that we can respond.

Heidegger's formula that Dasein is in conscience summoned forth to its ownmost ability-to-be does not mean, then, that Dasein is called to be "true to itself," authentic in one sense of that word. Rather, Dasein is, simply put, called to be. Dasein is at bottom being-possible, and in anxiety we experience that being-possible shorn of its normal realization in our lives. Our being-possible is evident in anxiety/existential death, because the normal call and response of daily life – "Who are you?" "I am the father of these boys, the husband of this woman, the teacher of these students, the coach of these players" – is interrupted by the collapse of meaning and significance. Thus, anxiety/existential death leaves us with a call to which we cannot respond.

The call is, moreover, not merely addressed *to* you as no one in particular, but is addressed *by* you as no one in particular.

> Not only is the call meant for him to whom the appeal is made "without regard for persons," but even the caller maintains itself in conspicuous indefiniteness. If the caller is asked about its name, status, origin, or repute, it not only refuses to answer, but does not even leave the slightest possibility of one's making it into something with which one can be familiar when one's understanding of Dasein has a "worldly" orientation. (319/274)

The existential pull is a pull towards being, that is, existing in Heidegger's sense, not towards being a son or daughter or lover. Thus, you call to yourself in conscience, but the you to whom you call is not you as son or daughter or lover, and the you that does the calling is likewise none of these. You, as being-possible, call to yourself, as being-possible.

If I am right about what Heidegger means by "conscience," it is difficult to see what its connection is to conscience in the moral sense, "conscience" as it is normally used. That Heidegger characterizes what he calls "conscience" as a summons that discloses our being-guilty – that says, as it were, "Guilty!" – is not sufficient to justify his appropriation of the words "conscience" and "guilt." It is true that what Heidegger calls "guilt" is the condition of the possibility of being responsible in the ordinary sense, hence of guilt in the ordinary sense too, being responsible for a deprivation in someone's life. Existential guilt is such a condition of possibility, because unless one were the basis or ground for who one presses ahead into being, one would not be a self that could take action and be responsible. The nullity for which one is the basis, however, and the nullity of the basis one is, are not moral failures, indeed, not failures at all, but constitutive limitations on our ability-to-be. To appropriate the word "guilt" to refer to them is just misleading, and therefore so is Heidegger's appropriation of the word "conscience."[101]

Heidegger's insensitivity to how misleading his appropriations of "conscience" and "guilt" are is a symptom of his tin ear for moral philosophy. Moral philosophy is conspicuously absent from *Being and Time*, which is supposed to be a treatment of the existential dimension of human life, that is, the way in which our self-understanding and what matters to us are constitutive of who we are. If anything, one would think that moral philosophy would lie at the *center* of his considerations. Why doesn't it? There seem to be two factors at work.

First, Heidegger thinks of moral philosophy as an account of how we should conduct ourselves in concrete situations. Thus, in considering whether his phenomenology of conscience is too formal, because it does not touch upon the ways in which our moral conscience highlights for us things we have done wrong, he writes: "We miss a 'positive' content in that which is called [in conscience], *because we expect to be told something currently useful about assured possibilities of 'taking action' which are available and calculable*" (340/ 294). That is, the moral conscience and moral philosophy should give us concrete guidance about how to behave, but existential phenomenology cannot do that. Existential phenomenology is concerned only with our being, and to put it rather baldly, the virtuous and vicious, the well-bahaved and thc ill-, arc all Dasein. Moral philosophy cannot touch upon what makes us Dasein, since it discriminates among competing ways of being Dasein and asks whether they conform to some set of ideals we might articulate.

This is not a convincing reason to eschew moral philosophy,

however. Heidegger himself develops a distinction between owned, unowned, and disowned life, and he concedes that his conception of self-ownership is a "factical ideal" (358/310). Much as Nietzsche's critique of morality often reads more like an attempt to substitute a new vision of morality for an old, so Heidegger's conception of self-ownership often reads like a supplement to or replacement for moral philosophy.

Heidegger probably also felt, as did Nietzsche before him, that moral thought was typically an expression of the Anyone's subjection, leveling down, and domination of human life.[102] There is something to be said for the notion that some aspects of traditional morality, at least, are largely attempts to control forms of deviance that make many of us uncomfortable, such as homosexuality. To tell when moral reactions play this merely conformist role and when they cut deeper requires, of course, that one *do* moral philosophy. (The Roman Catholic Church insists that homosexuality is wrong, not just uncomfortable to the mass of people, and so in order to dispute this, one must argue about the issue morally.) Sometimes Heidegger seems to go further and associate morality *tout court* with the Anyone, conformism, and leveling down, as did Nietzsche. One of the most troubling expressions of this view in *Being and Time*, one that links Heidegger's reflections thematically to Nietzsche's and also to elements of anti-Semitism, is found in the discussion of conscience: "It is easy to see that the conscience which used to be an 'effluence of the divine power' now becomes a slave of Pharisaism" (337/291). Conscience, according to this analysis, is the slave of the democratic impulse, an impulse once controlled by the priests, who spearhead the leveling down of human life through crushing the aristocratic instinct. Once again, to assess this sort of critique, one would have to engage in moral reflection, and this Heidegger does not bother to do.

With these caveats in mind, we can now turn to Heidegger's positive, factical ideal of human life, self-ownership, and resoluteness.

Study Questions

Does Heidegger's conception of death imply that it must always be an illusion to feel, towards the end of one's life, that one has achieved fulfillment and has nothing left to accomplish or be?

Does Heidegger's conception of guilt and the nullity of being-the-basis imply that one can never experience a total self-transformation, as in, perhaps, a religious conversion or rebirth?

XVII. RESOLUTENESS AND SELF-OWNERSHIP

Heidegger's rhetoric of the ownmost ability-to-be, of "authenticity," and of resoluteness certainly might suggest an ideal of "being true to yourself." Consider the following spin on Heidegger's language: in confronting the impending possibility of your own death, you realize what is important to you. Getting clear about what is important to you inspires you to drive out of your life the distractions and accidental preoccupations that build a wall between you and what really matters to you. In doing all this you "choose yourself," are "true to yourself," that is, authentic. Your life achieves a sort of "steadfastness" and self-sufficiency that empowers you to be who you "truly" are. There is certainly something to be said for this vision of authenticity, and many of us have had experiences (not necessarily triggered by an encounter with demise) in which we resolve to put distractions to the side and focus on "what really matters to us." This sort of "self-discovery" – the sort that Charles Taylor explores sympathetically, yet critically, in *The Ethics of Authenticity* – is not, however, what Heidegger has in mind by self-ownership.

Anxiety/death does not by strip away false identities and get us in touch with who we really are, but rather it *strips away ontological distortions* and gets us in touch with *how* we are. "Anticipation [the owned disclosure of death] discloses to existence that its uttermost possibility lies in giving itself up, and thus it shatters all one's tenaciousness to whatever existence one has reached" (308/264). The uttermost or most extreme possibility is death. In death you "give yourself up" not in the sense of surrendering or resigning yourself, but rather in the sense of *giving up on* yourself. When dragged into the alienation and ennui of depression, you give up on being who you are, because who you are no longer matters to you. *Ontologically* your being-a-student is not constitutive of some essence that governs who you are. Normally you do go forward in life as the person you have been, as son or daughter, student, lover, friend, but you cannot count on these dispositions and "the existence you have reached" to remain in place. They are not just *contingent*, as Richard Rorty emphasizes,[103] but also *vulnerable*.

The contingency of the self is an aspect of thrownness. You can only be who you factically are in the cultural, social, historical, and linguistic context in which you live. As Heidegger puts it in II.2, the basis of one's ability-to-be is null. Some commentators, for example, Hubert Dreyfus and Jane Rubin, have interpreted Heideggerian anxiety as the disclosure of this contingency. Anxiety is, they say, the realization that your life has no "ultimate" meaning.[104] It is hard to see, however, why such a realization would produce anxiety, why it would take courage to face up to this discovery, and how Heidegger could interpret much of everyday life as a flight from and cover-up of the inescapability of contingency. Unless, of course, Heidegger were in the grip of a religious vision of human life according to which to have any meaning in life at all is to have meaning that is not contingent. Thus, it makes sense that Dreyfus and Rubin interpret Heidegger as unsuccessfully "secularizing" Kierkegaard's existentialism and as being unable to explain why anxiety is distressing. Contingency is not worrisome, but vulnerability is.

Your self-understanding is vulnerable in two ways. Who you are can be "outstripped" or overtaken by the world, and you can "die to" who you have been. As we saw in section (xvi), when a way of understanding yourself, a for-the-sake-of-which, is overtaken by the world, you can no longer understand yourself in that way. You can also die to who you are by no longer being disposed forward into it. You can die to this aspect of your self-understanding or that (e.g., falling out of love), or more dramatically, you can die to the whole of who you are in existential death or depression. We can characterize both of these sorts of experiences as modes of "becoming impossible," of being unable to go forward as who you have been. It is crucial to the notion of impossibility that you are not merely *disinclined* to go forward, but rather *cannot* go forward. Such experiences are the possibility of the impossibility of any longer being able to be-there as who you have been. Such experiences display your existential vulnerability. Far from calling upon you to be true to yourself, in these sorts of conditions who you have been no longer makes sense and is now impossible.

Facing up to vulnerability requires courage. If you can no longer live as a steel-worker, because that way of life has been outstripped or overtaken by social and economic change, you must be able to give it up and move on. If you don't, you have become "too old for your victories" or are living an illusion. If you fall out of love, you must give up your self-understanding as a lover and move on, and if you fall out of love not with a person, but with some aspect of your self-understanding, you must likewise give it up and move on. To be able to move on and give it up requires existential courage, as anyone whose knees have buckled in such a situation knows. There are many forces that tie us down to who we have been or how we have lived: emotions that entangle us ("This hurts"), financial and legal commitments that shackle us ("I have a mortgage!"), social pressure ("How can you leave him like that?"), and internalized social pressure, guilt ("How can *I* leave him like that?"). What is more, one's harshest critic is often oneself. Recall, "One belongs to the others oneself and enhances their power" (164/126). We can, indeed, leave a failed relationship or a collapsed life behind, but it hurts to do so and it can be socially costly.

I have just been emphasizing the existential flexibility that is required to cope constructively with the several sorts of existential impossibility that threaten us. This emphasis might well seem misplaced, however, as a reading of *Being and Time*. Does Heidegger not deploy a rhetoric of self-constancy and steadfastness, and does this rhetoric not contradict the emphasis I have placed on flexibility and being prepared to give up who one has been?

Heidegger does indeed describe the owned self as self-constant, which he cashes out as steady and steadfast: "*The constancy of the self*, in the double sense of steadiness and steadfastness, is the *owned* counter-possibility to the non-self-constancy which is characteristic of irresolute falling" (369/322). Steadfastness can be both *existentiell* and *existential*. At an existentiell level, you can "win" or "lose" yourself by having, or failing to have, the "nerve" to stick with who you are in the face of social pressure. Heidegger describes this lack of nerve (in §27), when he writes: ". . . by thus disburdening it of its being, the Anyone accommodates Dasein if Dasein has any tendency to take things easily and make them easy" (165/127–128). Standing by who you are, when who you are diverges from the reigning social expectations, is deviance, and the Anyone will try to suppress your deviance, to rein you in.

In discussing the suppression of deviance, or "subjection," as he calls it, Heidegger indulges a sort of rhetoric that one finds in other existentialist writers, especially Nietzsche and Kierkegaard. The "herd," the "social straightjacket," the "universal," pressures us into living pretty much like everyone else does. To resist this pressure takes courage. Nietzsche tended to focus on the more brutal and gruesome means of reining deviance in (punishment, even torture),[105] whereas Kierkegaard and Heidegger focus on the more insidious forms of social control. Think of "experiments in living"[106] such as interracial marriages or lesbian couples who have children in the suburbs. In my suburban neighborhood there are a number of lesbian couples who have children. To make these new arrangements more intelligible to myself, I assimilated them at first to more traditional family patterns: the one parent who holds a full-time job and "brings home the bacon," the other who works not at all or part-time and is the primary "caregiver" at home. One day, however, I was talking to one of my neighbors about a self-help program she had been involved in, and she said to me, "This is what gave us the courage to have our son." It struck me at that moment how much courage was actually involved: explaining to all the school principals and health techs, to the police (when necessary), to the pediatrician, and everyone else, how they live. Doing it over and over. It is the existentiell courage to stand by who one is in the face of the public's distantiality and abuse. I had leveled this courage down in my assimilation of these lesbian families to conventional models; I had fallen prey to the dynamic whereby "overnight, everything that is original gets glossed over as something that has long been well known" (165/127).

So, one contrast we can draw is that between an existentiell life that we *own* in the sense of "stand up for" and one that we *disown*. When we abandon who we are under social pressure, when we falter in the face of criticism of our decisions, we *disown* who we are. With these examples of standing up for who one is, we may seem to have come back to a model of "being true to oneself." Does the lesbian mother not stay true to herself? The answer here depends on how one is thinking of "being true to oneself." In a slogan: the self to which the lesbian mother is true is not her true self. She is owning who she is, but who she is is nothing more than who she finds herself to be. This might seem like a distinction without a difference, until we look at it from another angle.

How would our model existentialist respond, if she were called upon to *abandon* the person she has been? To answer this, we must know who or what might call upon her to do this. The public might do so by regarding her as deviant, unwholesome, or intolerable. If it is a question of public pressure, then she will face this pressure down.

Morality might also call upon her to abandon who she has been. She might become convinced that who she is and how she lives are immoral. (I am not saying that morality does demand this, but merely that she might become convinced that it does, like Julian Lowe in *The Shield*.) In section (xvi) we saw that Heidegger regards the voice of moral conscience to be secondary to the voice of existential conscience, "the call of care." Thus, it is highly unlikely that Heideggerian resoluteness involves conforming to the demands of morality to alter who she has been. The only phenomenon that Heidegger acknowledges as having the standing legitimately to call upon her to change herself is the situation itself.

What could it be for *the situation itself* to call upon her to abandon who she is? If the situation is the space of factical possibilities – what she can do and who she can be here and now – then this situation can only call upon her to abandon who she is, if who she is is not possible in this situation. That is, for the situation to call upon her to abandon who she has been is either for who she has been to have been outstripped by change or for her to have died to who she has been. In such cases, the situation itself demands that she face up to her finitude and give up on who she has been, that she "take it back," as Heidegger says in one passage: "the certainty of the resolution signifies that *one holds oneself free for* the possibility of *taking it back* – a possibility which is factically necessary" (355/307–308).

So, Heidegger valorizes *both* standing by who one is *and* abandoning who one is. Are these not contraries, however? Self-abandonment and standing by oneself appear to be contrary when we formulate the question at issue thus: Does resoluteness require that one stand by or abandon who one has been? Does resoluteness require, in traditional language, persistence or change, being or becoming? The choice between self-ownership and disowning oneself is a choice between persistence and change, only if the self is the sort of entity that can persist or change. The upshot of Heidegger's analysis of the being of the self in *Being and Time*, however, is that the self is not present-at-hand, neither persistent nor changing. The self is not a substance, substance-analog, or candidate substance.

Heidegger makes this point in §65 on temporality, and although we neither want nor need to explore his theory of temporality in detail, this much is useful. The future into which the resolute self presses forward is not tomorrow, and the past from out of which it emerges is not yesterday. As Heidegger formulates the point, the future is not yet-to-come, the past is not gone by. Rather, the primordial past whose analysis Heidegger opens up in §65 (and develops in II.5) is the past of "I am as having been." His choice of terminology here is clever. In German, the perfect tense of the verb "to be" is formulated with a helping verb, as it is in English. In English one writes, "I have been," in German, "*ich bin gewesen.*" The difference between English and German is that whereas English uses "have" as the helping verb, German uses "be." If we were to transliterate "*ich bin gewesen*" into English, it would be, "I am been." Now, this linguistic detail is in and of itself irrelevant, except that it gives Heidegger a means of exploiting the German language to indicate his point. He hyphenates the helping and main verb, so, "*ich bin-gewesen,*" "I have-been." His point is that who I already am, in Heidegger's preferred sense, is not the phases of my life that have gone by. Rather, who I have-been is disclosed by my disposedness, my mood. Who I have-been is who I find myself to be in so far as I press forward into my life.

If we return to the example of the lesbian mother who "stays true" to who she is, resists the social pressure to back down, and remains steadfast, we can see that she is self-constant in two senses. She is stubborn in staying the course with who she has been up to this point, and she is resolute in projecting forth on the basis of who she finds herself to be. We can describe these two patterns as "standing by who one has been" and "standing by who one has-been." In the case of the lesbian mother, the two patterns coincide. Ontologically speaking, however, they are not the same, precisely because to be a self is not to be present-at-hand. This is clear in the other cases we examined briefly. Just as the lesbian mother finds herself disposed to go forward with this socially non-conformist partnership and non-conformist form of motherhood, the resolute lost-lover finds himself disposed to go forward by giving up on the romance in which he has been involved. In both cases, one is called upon by the situation to go forward with the person one finds oneself to be, though not necessarily with the person one has been heretofore. To be Dasein is to be a finite, contingent, and vulnerable basis for pressing ahead into who one is to-be. This basis for pressing ahead is who one has-been. Who one has-been comprises both the world into which one is thrown and the mood or disposition in which one finds oneself.

The contrary of being steady and steadfast is to be lost in the Anyone. In section (xiii) I interpreted being lost in the Anyone as living a superficial and limited life, a life of little imagination, a life lived as one is supposed to live it, that is, according to the general prescriptions of the Anyone. Recall,

> Proximally and for the most part the self is lost in the Anyone. It understands itself in terms of those possibilities of existence which "circulate" in the "average" public way of interpreting Dasein today. These possibilities have mostly been made unrecognizable by ambiguity; yet they are well known to us. (435/383)

Thus, to be lost in the Anyone is to live a life leveled down by idle talk, ambiguity, and curiosity. Being lost in the Anyone is not simply a matter of leading a "normal" life. Rather, the question is whether one leads a "normal" life despite the demands of one's situation and one's disposition. If in leading a normal life one stands by who one has-been, rather than abandoning who one has-been in the face of social pressure or a myopic refusal to acknowledge that one's life has been outstripped or overtaken, then one's normal life can well be resolute. This is why in the passage just quoted Heidegger does not say that to be lost in the Anyone is simply to understand oneself in terms of possibilities that circulate in the culture. Rather, he insists that to be lost, those possibilities must "be made unrecognizable by ambiguity," that is, that one must be closed off to the demands of the situation and of one's disposition.

Thus, to be resolute, to own one's self, is *not* a matter of finding one's true self and insisting upon it, at least not in any conventional sense of those terms. After all, whoever one might take one's "true self" to be can be overtaken by the world. What is more, and perhaps worse, one can die to that self by slipping into a depression that wrenches it away from one. To have found oneself and won oneself is in some cases to stick with who one has been heretofore and do so in the face of daunting social pressure, while in some cases it is to adapt flexibly to a new world or new dispositions. To win oneself is, in and of itself, neither to stick with who one has been nor to "wear the world's clothes lightly." Rather, to find oneself and win oneself is to see what is factically possible and important and to carry through with it, whatever its relation to who one has been heretofore might be. We can put this point by saying that the self one must find and win is who one is *at this moment*, but we cannot let the language of "moments" (*Augenblicke*) mislead us. Just as who I have-been is not who I have been, in the sense of the phases of my life that have gone by, so the moment of vision of which Heidegger writes in §65 is not the now of clock-time, a tipping point between what has gone by and what is to come. This moment of vision, which might better be called a "moment of resolution,"[107] encompasses who I find myself to be and am able to go forward as.

With the phenomena of resoluteness and self-ownership we come full circle to where we began division I: the being of the self. We have learned in division II that the casual, everyday claim that it is "I" who am in the world, although not false, is shallow. Yes, proximally, it is you and I who are in the world, but you and I are mostly Anyone-selves, selves whose self-understanding is shallow and closed off from the genuine range of freedom available in the factical situation in which we live. To see this range of freedom is to see what opportunities the leveled-down public understanding of our lives hides from us, both opportunities to stand by who we have been and opportunities to depart in a new direction. It takes courage to face these opportunities, because doing so activates the repressive forces of distantiality and subjection, the forces that keep us all mostly living like one another, taking few risks, trying few "experiments in living." When we confront our extreme condition of anxiety(depression)/death/conscience, however, we are jolted out of this complacency and forced to face the full range of our freedom. We can hide from these opportunities, once disclosed, disown ourselves, and fall back into a lostness in the Anyone, or we can seize upon our freedom, see for the first time that we are called upon to answer to the situation, and not just the Anyone. Such a steady and steadfast self, true not to who we "really" are, but to *how* we are, is a self we construct through resolutely facing the challenges to our leveled-off complacency.

Study Questions

Why is it necessarily irresolute, an act of self-disowning, to throw oneself into the conformist comforts of one's group or clique? What's wrong with being a "happy conformist?"

Does Heidegger's conception of self-ownership imply that resolute Dasein will always be unique, different, one of a kind? Or might the unobtrusive person next to you on the bus be resolute?

CHAPTER 4

RECEPTION AND INFLUENCE

Being and Time has proven over the almost eighty years since its publication to be an immensely influential text. Jean-Paul Sartre (1905–1980), Maurice Merleau-Ponty (1908–1961), and Hans-Georg Gadamer (1900–2002), three of the leading philosophers of the twentieth century, develop themes central to *Being and Time*. Heidegger's influence extends much further, when we take into consideration his later thought, in light of which we would also have to list Jacques Derrida (1930–2004) and Michel Foucault (1926–1984). I will focus here, however, on the influence of *Being and Time* and Heidegger's other writings from his early period, including *Kant and the Problem of Metaphysics* and "What is Metaphysics?" These early works also elicited a strongly negative reaction, which we will explore, from the empiricist tradition that has found its principal home in so-called analytic philosophy.

As we saw above in chapter 3, Heidegger proposed to use phenomenology in order to carry out his ontological investigations. He hoped to develop a "general ontology," that is, a thorough account of being and its several modes. He undertook to examine human being first, both because he argued that it is essential to have a clear understanding of our "point of access" to being, before investigating being directly, and because he embraced ontological idealism, according to which being depends on the understanding of being, that is, upon human being. Because he never completed *Being and Time* his general ontological aspirations were far less influential than his concrete phenomenology of human life. Sartre and Merleau-Ponty responded to the latter and not to Heidegger's more traditional ontological vision. They responded, however, in very different ways.

In his early treatise *Being and Nothingness* Sartre carried out a form of existential phenomenology. His method is far closer to Husserl than to Heidegger, even though some of his topical themes show the strong influence of *Being and Time*. Sartre focuses his phenomenological inquires on an examination of the "*ego cogito*," the "I think." He regards human being as a "for-itself," that is, a form of self-consciousness. In this regard Sartre's philosophy is very traditional, another example of the subjectivist approach to human life that began with Descartes, passed through Kant, and culminated in Husserl. Sartre insists that he is faithful to *Being and Time* in this orientation, but either he did not understand *Being and Time* or deliberately distorted it. If there is one consistent message throughout *Being and Time*, it is that the subject–object model of human experience, along with its attendant notions of inwardness and self-consciousness, must be discarded in favor of a model of human openness to a world that is always already there. Sartre does show Heidegger's influence in his strategy of trying to capture human experience in its daily reality, rather than in its logical structure (as is much more the focus of Husserl), but he tends to interpret that daily reality as the experience of an I, rather than as being-in-the-world.

Sartre embraces the central thesis of philosophical existentialism, that our essence is to-be, as well as some of existentialism's topical themes, and here he does carry forward the influence of *Being and Time*. Sartre offered perhaps the best known version of the central existentialist thesis in his formula, "existence precedes essence."[1] This formulation is a direct echo of Heidegger's statement from §9 of *Being and Time*, that "*the 'essence' of Dasein lies in its existence*" (67/42). Sartre clarified this Heideggerian idea by explaining it as a denial that we are "hard wired," as are animals, with instincts and passions that determine what we make of ourselves. All of our psychological and physical traits – our factual determinations, as Heidegger calls them – are subject to interpretation. (Recall the distinction between height and stature from section iv of chapter 3 above.) We are free to re-evaluate the significance of these factual determinations. This freedom is the distinctively human freedom of an entity that lives in a world of significance and not just in a world of "in-themselves" or inert objects.

Like Heidegger and the other existentialists, Sartre believes that in the extreme experiences of dread and alienation we gain insight into the nature and scope of our freedom and responsibility. In particular, in dread, in which our self-interpretation peels away and the world confronts us in its meaninglessness, we see that we are radically free and responsible for our entire world through our power to interpret it. Radical freedom does not mean, as it might be interpreted in a more conventional context, that we are able *to do* whatever we like, but rather that nothing we do, think, feel, or are is beyond the scope of possible re-interpretation. In "Existentialism is a Humanism" Sartre argues that we cannot be guided in our decision-making by who we have been or how we feel, because it is always up to us to assign value to these factors.

After the Second World War, Sartre moved away from his early investment in existentialism, but the influence of *Being and Nothingness* remained strong. The English-speaking world's first introduction to *Being and Time* was through its influence upon Sartre, and many of the early readers in the U.S. and U.K. of Heidegger's philosophy were steeped in Sartre and read Heidegger through Sartre's eyes. It was not until later that Anglophone philosophers took a new look at *Being and Time* and saw something very different than Sartre did. (We shall return below to the state of contemporary Heidegger scholarship.)

In France Sartre found a worthy rival in Merleau-Ponty. Merleau-Ponty devotes considerable attention in his early masterpiece, *The Phenomenology of Perception*, to rebutting Sartre. He argues that Sartre's conception of freedom makes no sense, because it would imply that right after making a decision, the fact that I have just made a decision carries no weight and must be re-evaluated all over again. Looking back to *Being and Time*, Merleau-Ponty's point is that Sartre does not distinguish between who I have been and who I have-been (above, chapter 3, section xvii). The only way to go forward in life is as the person I find myself already to be. We cannot take control of our being from the ground up, as Heidegger says. Sartre misses this absolutely critical insight, and Merleau-Ponty uses this oversight to sink Sartre's account of freedom.

Merleau-Ponty was a more careful reader of Heidegger than was Sartre, or perhaps he just agreed with Heidegger more. He pays homage to Heidegger less than does Sartre, and that may be because he identified a serious lacuna in Heidegger's phenomenology of engaged living. Many of the examples I offered above of engaged dealings in the world were examples in which bodily abilities play a central role. Indeed, Heidegger's position, as I have explained it, implies that cognitive capacities cannot be disentangled from bodily ones in our everyday engaged activity. Merleau-Ponty saw this and understood that it requires us to develop a phenomenology of the body and the way in which the body plays a central role in disclosing the world to us. In *The Phenomenology of Perception* he develops the concept of "motor intentionality," which is the way in which our motor skills understand the world around us. In effect, Merleau-Ponty pursued the general project of division I of *Being and Time* in an essential direction neglected by Heidegger, but without which Heidegger's phenomenology is seriously compromised.

Another author who developed some of the themes of *Being and Time* further than did Heidegger was Heidegger's own student, Gadamer. Gadamer first met Heidegger while the latter was still Husserl's assistant at Freiburg, and he followed Heidegger to Marburg, when Heidegger took up his first professorship there. Gadamer wrote his *Habilitation* at Marburg during this period, which was the apogee of Heidegger's interest in hermeneutics. Hermeneutics became the focus of Gadamer's intellectual energy. Indeed, it is due to Gadamer's subsequent influence that *Being and Time* is regarded as an important step in the development of hermeneutics, for there is, one must admit, precious little in *Being and Time* to warrant this accolade. Heidegger's few scattered comments on hermeneutics in *Being and Time* hardly add up to a theory of interpretation. He does insist that the articulation of the meaning of human activity must be interpretive, as well as that phenomenology is necessarily hermeneutic. He does not develop these lines of thought very well, however, and he adds very little to our understanding of (what he calls) Interpretation (with a capital "I" in translation), which is the understanding of linguistic and cultural products.

Gadamer's *Truth and Method* is a treatise exploring the history of hermeneutics and the nature of interpretation. It has been one of the most influential books of the post-War period and has given rise to the use of the term "hermeneutics" to designate a philosophical movement, rather than a technique or discipline. Gadamer seized upon Heidegger's claim that all interpretation, whether it be interpretation or Interpretation, relies upon a taken-for-granted context and a set of "assumptions" held about the object of interpretation by the interpreter. Gadamer calls these assumptions "prejudices," and he argues that they enable Interpretation, rather than distort it. Just as all overt Interpretation relies on such assumptions, so interpersonal and cultural understanding relies upon a cultural context, a tradition in which we live. Gadamer thus develops a traditionalist view in *Truth and Method*. We must always find our orientation within the linguistic and cultural tradition to which we belong, rather than attempting to start afresh or align our culture with ideals that are crafted from the outside. (This pitted Gadamer over against the Frankfurt school of neo-Marxist critical theory, represented most prominently over the past quarter century by Jürgen Habermas (1929–). The debate between Gadamer and Habermas, as well as their followers, has been one of the more interesting and lively debates of the past half century.) It is not clear that *Being and Time* implies this sort of traditionalism; the general impression that it does is due to Gadamer's influence as a conduit of Heidegger's thought.

In Sartre, Merleau-Ponty, and Gadamer we have been looking at three philosophers who were constructively influenced by Heidegger to develop further the existentialism, phenomenology, and hermeneutics first broached in *Being and Time*. Heidegger has also inspired an equally negative reaction amongst generally empiricist philosophers, and this negative reputation has carried over to some of the prejudice against *Being and Time* that students are likely to encounter in many English-speaking academic philosophy departments today.

One of Heidegger's central interests during the 1920s was his phenomenological appropriation of Kant's philosophy. Heidegger addresses Kant's philosophy in detail in several of his early lecture series (*Logic, Basic Problems,* and *Phenomenological Interpretation of Kant's "Critique of Pure Reason"*). His reflections on Kant culminated in his 1929 *Kant and the Problem of Metaphysics*. In all of these treatments, but most aggressively in the 1929 book, Heidegger works up an interpretation of Kant's *Critique of Pure Reason* as a treatise in ontology. The dominant reading of Kant in Germany at the time was the "neo-Kantian" approach, pioneered in the late nineteenth century, but represented in the twenties by Ernst Cassirer. The neo-Kantians read Kant, as do most scholars of Kant today in the U.S. and U.K., as chiefly a theorist of knowledge, morality, and aesthetics, not as a contributor to metaphysics. Indeed, Kant is usually read as having rejected metaphysics by arguing that we are unable to know anything about "things in themselves" and must limit ourselves to knowledge of things as they appear. As we noted earlier, Kant declared that "The proud name of ontology must give way to the modest one of a mere analytic of pure understanding."[2] Heidegger's assault on neo-Kantian orthodoxy was sensational enough that a debate was arranged between Heidegger and Cassirer in Davos, Switzerland, in 1929.[3] Why would a dispute about the proper way to read Kant be seen as so important?

Heidegger's claim on Kant was really a stalking horse for a much larger debate, one that lies at the center of the contemporary division in philosophy between so-called Continental and self-styled analytic philosophy. The reason Heidegger did not accept at face-value Kant's rejection of what he called "ontology" in favor of what he called "a mere analytic of the pure understanding" was that Heidegger regarded the understanding as Kant examined it to be a derivative human capacity. The ability to form and manipulate concepts, to arrange and evaluate propositions logically, to make claims to knowledge and to assess the evidence possessed for those claims, these are all achievements of the "faculty of concepts," as Kant called it. They are important achievements, certainly, but they all rest on a more basic familiarity with the world, as we have seen Heidegger argue. The crux of Heidegger's dispute with Cassirer and the neo-Kantians over Kant-interpretation was Heidegger's claim that Kant accepted that conceptual understanding is founded in something more fundamental, and even gave it a name ("the imagination"), but balked at revising his anti-ontological assertions in light of this insight. However one comes out on issues of Kant-exegesis, and not many have agreed with Heidegger, it is the implications of the view Heidegger *attributes* to Kant and develops elsewhere that had a significant impact on the philosophical scene.

Heidegger argues that there is a form of understanding more basic or "primordial" than Kantian understanding (see section ix of chapter 3 above). Although he does not place his critique of philosophical logic front and center in *Being and Time*, it is prominent in other texts from Heidegger's early period, especially "What is Metaphysics?" A mastery of the basic elements of formal logic is a standard prerequisite for the philosophy major at Anglo-American universities, and the ability to formulate one's inferences in formal-logical terms is often considered evidence of an argument's seriousness. Thus, when Heidegger writes:

> If the power of the intellect in the field of inquiry into the nothing and into being is thus shattered, then the destiny of the reign of "logic" in philosophy is thereby decided. The idea of "logic" itself disintegrates in the turbulence of a more originary questioning.[4]

This is often taken as evidence that he is not really doing philosophy, that he is engaged in some sort of crypto-religious, mystical, or simply confused project.

In order to evaluate this reaction, we must put Heidegger's views into perspective. The issue here is not really one about the formal predicate calculus that is standard fare in contemporary introductory logic courses. Rather, the issue is a core commitment of traditional logic, one shared by mathematical logic, or at least its philosophical reception. According to traditional logic, the fundamental unit of analysis is the judgment (or statement, sentence, assertion, proposition); in the formal predicate calculus this means "well-formed formulae." Thus, concepts, or as Kant identified them, "predicates of possible judgments," are essential to the formation of thoughts or sentences that can be true or false, that is, that can succeed at or fail in describing the world. Intentionality is ineliminably conceptual. This is the core commitment of the philosophical tradition that Heidegger rejects.

Heidegger argues that the most fundamental aspects of our experience and the originary locus of truth are pre-logical. Logic, whether it be Aristotelian logic or the predicate calculus, cannot get a grip on primary understanding, because primary understanding is pre-conceptual. This is a large component of Heidegger's critique of the neo-Kantian interpretation of Kant, and we now know that Rudolf Carnap's early exposure to the Heidegger–Cassirer debate in Davos, Switzerland, in 1929 played a formative role in his development and pushed him towards his strongly-worded rejection of Heidegger's philosophy in 1931.[5] Carnap's denunciations of Heidegger are not a small-minded failure to understand Heidegger's ideas, even if Carnap does sometimes miss Heidegger's moves. Rather, Carnap's reaction indicates a genuine sensitivity to the revolutionary character of Heidegger's thought. When revolutionaries challenge the very foundation of one's commitments, reactions tend to extremes, as they do here. There is much that analytic philosophers can learn from Heidegger, but it is no use denying that if Heidegger is right, then much of traditional philosophy suddenly seems superficial, and the core commitments of the logical tradition crumble.

The fundamental disclosure of the world and what is important in human life does not take place in theories or judgments; it cannot be captured in assertions, Heidegger insists. Thus, it is not subject to regulation by logic. This is not a license to flout logic and to assert contradictions. Contradictions are defective assertions. Heidegger aims for something more basic than assertions or what can be captured in them. He is trying to talk about something a-logical, because pre-logical. Our most fundamental forms of "sight," or intelligence, reside at the practical, engaged, pre-conceptual, and hence pre-logical level of experience. It is for this reason that after about 1930, Heidegger turns from traditional philosophy to poetry, cultural criticism, mysticism, and philosophers like Nietzsche, who are engaged in a rather different enterprise than were Aristotle, Kant, and Husserl.

This turn (Heidegger's "turn") away from traditional philosophy and its logical methods makes Heidegger almost unintelligible to mainstream academic philosophers trained in traditional philosophy, especially those reared on formal logic and the generally empiricist epistemology that is standard fare in the world of English-speaking philosophy. It is, thus, unsurprising that these philosophers have found Heidegger hard to understand, even though the shallowness of some of their critiques at times borders on being puerile.[6]

This explains why Heidegger's first arrival in the world of Anglophone philosophy came from sources outside the empiricist tradition. Among the earliest conduits of Heidegger's thought into the English language was William Richardson's 1963 *Heidegger: Through Phenomenology to Thought*. Heidegger himself wrote a letter which served as a preface to Richardson's book, a letter which cast considerable light on Heidegger's development as a thinker. Richardson's work was followed closely by other commentators, such as Joseph Kockelmans, who published his *Martin Heidegger* in 1965.[7] Richardson, Kockelmans, and others were not operating from within the empiricist tradition of Anglo-American philosophy, and their style strikes many trained in that tradition as somewhat old-fashioned. In particular, Richardson and Kockelmans offer an older style of commentary, what is sometimes called a "summary."[8] Whereas mainstream Anglo-American philosophers will happily diverge from an historical text and import concepts and ideas from contemporary philosophy in order to reconstruct and amend, where necessary, the author's own words, Richardson and Kockelmans stay closer to the text, as is also the norm in Germany to this day.[9]

The reception of Heidegger's thought into the largely empiricist world of Anglo-American philosophy was stymied by the strongly anti-logicist direction it took after *Being and Time*. In *Being and*

Time Heidegger still aspired to what he was pleased to call a "science of ontology." The German word for science (*Wissenschaft*) does not refer exclusively to the natural sciences, as the word "science" sometimes does in English. Rather, it refers to any disciplined inquiry. (In German, theology and literary studies are *Wissenschaften*.) In the period of *Being and Time* Heidegger affirms that a science is a conceptually articulate account of a domain of inquiry. Further, "philosophy is the theoretical conceptual interpretation of being . . ."; thus, "that philosophy is scientific is implied in its very concept" (*Basic Problems*, 11–12). *Being and Time* has not yet made the full move to the anti-logicist position, and the question remains whether it must make that move. I have elsewhere argued that if Heidegger holds on to the priority of practice over cognition, then he must either abandon the idea that philosophy is scientific (in his sense) or the thesis that the understanding of being is *a priori*.[10] The later Heidegger gave up on the former notion, but most academic philosophers in the English-speaking world would much prefer to forsake the latter thesis, and this makes it possible for them to read and learn from *Being and Time* without having to accept the anti-logicist conclusions at which Heidegger himself arrived.

This explains how *Being and Time* can have achieved a belated reception in the world of analytic philosophy. Beginning in the 1960s philosophers who had been trained in the generally empiricist and logicist ways of Anglophone philosophy discovered Heidegger and began to write about him. Hubert Dreyfus made significant use of Heidegger's phenomenology of engaged activity in his critique of the program of artificial intelligence in *What Computers Can't Do*, first published in 1972.[11] Dreyfus saw the extensive and diverse connections between Heidegger's critique of the subject–object model of experience and related analyses that had emerged in the empiricist tradition, for example, in differing ways in Wittgenstein, Quine, and Kuhn. As the empiricist tradition played itself out and generated internal criticisms, some philosophers trained in that tradition began to look for new sources of insight. Most prominent among these philosophers is no doubt Richard Rorty. Rorty's *Philosophy and the Mirror of Nature* (1979), which has tellingly generated reactions as strongly negative as Heidegger's writings from the late 1920s, argued that traditional philosophy, with its commitment to the Correspondence Theory of Truth, has hit a dead end and that we must turn to "edifying" discourse, such as hermeneutics, in order to address many of the humanistic questions of our intellectual tradition more broadly, a tradition from which mainstream, empiricist, logicist philosophy has become alienated. Rorty has written extensively on Heidegger, as is evidenced in the title of one of his volumes of collected papers, *Essays on Heidegger and Others*. The combined influence of Dreyfus (whose work on Heidegger is captured late in the day by his 1991 *Being-in-the-World*) and Rorty has led to an explosion of work on Heidegger among those reared in the empiricist tradition. Among the books that should be mentioned in this connection are: Charles Guignon's *Heidegger and the Problem of Knowledge*, Mark Okrent's *Heidegger's Pragmatism*, Taylor Carman's *Heidegger's Analytic*, and Steven Crowell's *Husserl, Heidegger, and the Space of Meaning*. My own approach to *Being and Time* here in this Reader's Guide is a product of the influence of Dreyfus, Rorty, and other like-minded commentators. The shared aspiration of us all is to show how *Being and Time* offers new and insightful positions on philosophical questions of common concern across the spectrum, including the nature of human subjectivity, truth, sociality, and the challenges that confront us in our efforts to live a steadfast life, true to a compelling ideal of freedom.

NOTES

CHAPTER I

1 I will work off of the standard English translation, *Being and Time*, translated by John Macquarrie and Edward Robinson (New York: Harper & Row, 1962). This is a translation of *Sein und Zeit*, originally published in 1927 in the *Yearbook for Philosophy and Phenomenological Research* (vol. 8, 1927). The standard German edition is now published by Max Niemeyer and is in its fifteenth edition. Page references to *Being and Time* throughout the Reader's Guide are given in brackets following each citation: (171/132). The first number refers to the English translation, the second the original German.

2 Michael Friedman, *A Parting of the Ways: Carnap, Cassirer, and Heidegger* (Chicago: Open Court, 2000).

3 One may find a translation of Heidegger's *Habilitation* in *Supplements: From the Earliest Essays to "Being and Time" and Beyond*, ed. John van Buren (Albany: SUNY Press, 2002).

4 Martin Heidegger, "My Way to Phenomenology," in *Time and Being* (New York: Harper & Row, 1972), p. 74. The book of Brentano's whose title is usually rendered *On the Manifold Senses of Being in Aristotle* has been translated into English as Franz Clemens Brentano, *On the Several Senses of Being in Aristotle*, trans. by Rolf George (Berkeley: University of California Press, 1975).

5 Immanuel Kant, *Critique of Pure Reason*, trans. by Norman Kemp Smith (New York: St. Martin's Press, 1929), p. A247/B303.

6 Martin Heidegger, "Letter to Father Engelbert Krebs (1919)," in *Supplements*.

7 See Heidegger's 1921 lecture series *The Phenomenology of Religious Life*, trans. by Matthias Fritsch and Jennifer Anna Gosetti (Bloomington: Indiana University Press, 2004) and his public lecture in 1927, "Phenomenology and Theology," in *Pathmarks*, ed. William McNeill (Cambridge, UK: Cambridge University Press, 1998).

8 *Martin Heidegger, Karl Jaspers: Briefwechsel: 1920–1963* (Frankfurt am Main: Vittorio Klostermann, 1990).

9 Among other things, Hannah Arendt, as well as a number of his most successful students, such as Herbert Marcuse and Karl Löwith, were Jewish.

10 The two best treatments of this topic are Iain Thomson, *Heidegger on Ontotheology: Technology and the Politics of Education* (Cambridge, UK: Cambridge University Press, 2005) and Hans D. Sluga, *Heidegger's Crisis: Philosophy and Politics in Nazi Germany* (Cambridge, MA: Harvard University Press, 1993).

11 "Nur ein Gott Kann uns retten," *Der Spiegel* (1976).

CHAPTER 2

1 In his Replies to the First Objections, in René Descartes, *Meditations on First Philosophy with Selections from the Objections and Replies*, rev. ed., trans. by John Cottingham (Cambridge, UK: Cambridge University Press, 1996).

2 Donald Davidson, *Inquiries into Truth and Interpretation* (Oxford: Oxford University Press (Clarendon Press), 1984).

3 The reader may find a detailed treatment in my *Heidegger's Temporal Idealism* (Cambridge, UK: Cambridge University Press, 1999).

4 Much better, in any case, than *Being and Time: a Translation of "Sein und Zeit,"* trans. by Joan Stambaugh (Albany, NY: SUNY Press, 1996).

5 Following John Haugeland, "Heidegger on Being a Person," *Noûs*, 16 (1982).

6 Following Charles B. Guignon, *Heidegger and the Problem of Knowledge* (Indianapolis: Hackett Publishing Co., 1983).

7 Following Taylor Carman, *Heidegger's Analytic* (Cambridge, UK: Cambridge University Press, 2003).

CHAPTER 3

1 See "Kant's Thesis About Being," in *Pathmarks*. For more on this theme, see Thomson, *Ontotheology*.

2 See Thomas Kuhn, *The Structure of Scientific Revolutions*, 2nd, enlarged ed. (Chicago: University of Chicago Press, 1970).

3 See, for example, John Dewey's account of the history of metaphysics as the codification of the experiences of those who did not have to work with their hands (which is pretty much the antithesis of Heidegger's account in *Basic Problems*): *The Quest for Certainty*, in *Later Works, 1924–1953*, vol. 4 (Carbondale, IL: Southern Illinois University Press, 1988).

4 *Temporalität*, which Macquarrie and Robinson render as "Temporality" with a capital "T," to distinguish it from *Zeitlichkeit*, "temporality" with a lower-case "T"; (t)emporality is the temporal structure of *our* being.

5 Franz Brentano, *Psychology from an Empirical Standpoint*, trans. by D.B. Terrell, Antos C. Rancurello, and Linda L. Mcalister (London: Routledge and Kegan Paul, 1973).

6 Husserl, *Ideas Pertaining to a Pure Phenomenology and to a Phenomeno-logical Philosophy; First Book, General Introduction to a Pure Phenom-enology*, trans. by F. Kersten (The Hague: Martinus Nijhoff, 1982). Note that Heidegger does not accept the phenomenological reduction *per se*, because, he argues, in the case of our own being, we cannot describe what it is to be human without taking a stand on our own existence. See *History of the Concept of Time: Prolegomena*, trans. by Theodore Kisiel (Bloomington: Indiana University Press, 1985).

7 See "My Way to Phenomenology," in *Time and Being*.

8 See "The Ideal of Pure Reason," in *Critique of Pure Reason*.

9 Heidegger offers as an analogy the forms of intuition in Kant, but this analogy presupposes Heidegger's interpretation of the forms of intu-ition, which is not generally accepted. See *Phenomenological Inter-pretation of Kant's "Critique of Pure Reason,"* trans. by Parvis Emad and Kenneth Maly (Bloomington: Indiana University Press, 1997), §§7–9.

10 As an example, see David Lewis, "General Semantics," *Synthese* (1970).

11 Heidegger's doctoral dissertation was a critique of psychologism in a Husserlian mold. "Die Lehre vom Urteil im Psychologismus," in *Frühe Schriften* (Frankfurt am Main: Vittorio Klostermann, 1978).

12 E.g., David Brooks, *On Paradise Drive: How We Live Now (and Always Have) in the Future Tense* (New York: Simon and Schuster, 2004).

13 Peter Humfrey, *Painting in Renaissance Venice* (New Haven: Yale University Press, 1995), p. 226. The painting is on plate 164.

14 Kant, *Critique of Pure Reason*, p. B408. For Hume, see *A Treatise of Human Nature*, 2nd ed. (Oxford: Oxford University Press, 1978), Book I, Part IV, Section VI.

15 Kant, *Critique of Pure Reason*, p. B131.

16 Heidegger attributes the cleanest version of this thesis to Max Scheler, who writes that the person "is rather the *unity* of living-through [ex-periencing] which is immediately experienced in and with our experi-ences – not a thing merely thought of behind and outside what is immediately experienced" (*Formalism in Ethics and Non-formal Ethics of Values: a New Attempt Toward the Foundation of an Ethical Personalism*, 5th rev. ed., trans. by Manfred S. Frings and Roger L. Funk [Evanston: Northwestern University Press, 1973], as quoted by Heidegger in *Being and Time*, 73/47).

17 Søren Kierkegaard, *The Sickness Unto Death*, trans. by Howard V. Hong and Edna H. Hong (Princeton: Princeton University Press, 1980), p. 13.

18 Jose Ortega y Gasset, "History as a System," in *History as a System and Other Essays Toward a Philosophy of History* (New York: W. W. Norton, 1961), p. 203.

19 John Haugeland, "Understanding Natural Language," *Journal of Philosophy*, vol. 76 (1979).

20 Of course, one can reconfigure moral considerations to train on this sense of self. Thus, my claim here is not that Heidegger's reflections on self-identity "transcend" moral philosophy, but merely that they dig deeper than Kant's notion of the moral personality. In fact, some of

the impetus behind the return to virtue theory in contemporary moral philosophy lies in considerations such as these, and there is no principled reason why one could not develop a Heidegger-friendly moral philosophy.

21 Hubert L. Dreyfus, *Being-in-the-World* (Cambridge, MA: Massachusetts Institute of Technology Press, 1991), ch. 3.

22 See Henry E. Allison, *Kant's Transcendental Idealism* (New Haven: Yale University Press, 1983). Heidegger seems to take a similar approach to Kant in *Phenomenological Interpretation of Kant's "Critique of Pure Reason."*

23 Moreover, it follows from Heidegger's interpretation of the transcendental reflective inquiry as ontology that we cannot say that it is the same *entity*, in this case I, who am a father and weigh x pounds. We cannot talk about the numerical identity of two items with different ways of being.

24 For example, *Critique of Pure Reason*, trans. by Paul Guyer and Allen W. Wood (Cambridge, UK: Cambridge University Press, 1998).

25 See Dewey, *The Quest for Certainty* and *Experience and Nature*, in *Later Works: 1924–1953*, vol. 1 (Carbondale and Edwardsville: Southern Illinois University Press, 1981).

26 See Wittgenstein, *Philosophical Investigations*, 2nd ed., trans. by G. E. M. Anscombe (Oxford, UK: Blackwell, 1997) and *Preliminary Studies for the "Philosophical investigations," generally known as the Blue and Brown Books*, 2nd ed. (New York: Barnes & Noble, 1969).

27 Dreyfus, *Being-in-the-World* and Mark Okrent, *Heidegger's Pragmatism* (Ithaca: Cornell University Press, 1988).

28 See John Haugeland, "Ontological Supervenience," *Southern Journal of Philosophy*, vol. 22 (1983 Supplement) and "Weak Supervenience," *American Philosophical Quarterly*, vol. 19 (1982).

29 I borrow this word from Haugeland, "Heidegger on Being a Person."

30 "*Verweisung*," which Macquarrie and Robinson usually render by the phrase "assignment or reference." I will just use "assignment," both because Heidegger's concept is close to the idea of a social convention, and because in English it is easy to confuse "reference" with Frege's term.

31 See Thomas Aquinas, *Treatise on Happiness*, trans. by John A. Oesterle (Notre Dame: University of Notre Dame Press, 1964), p. 9 (Question 1, Art. 4).

32 Thomas Nagel, *The View from Nowhere* (New York: Oxford University Press, 1986).

33 See Alasdair C. Macintyre, *After Virtue: A Study in Moral Theory*, 2nd ed. (Notre Dame, IN: University of Notre Dame Press, 1984), Charles Taylor, *The Ethics of Authenticity* (Cambridge, MA: Harvard University Press, 1992), and Amitai Etzioni, *The Common Good* (Oxford: Blackwell Publishing, 2004).

34 In addition to *The Ethics of Authenticity*, see *Sources of the Self: The Making of the Modern Identity* (Cambridge, MA: Harvard University Press, 1989) and "Interpretation and the Sciences of Man," *Philosophy*

and the Human Sciences: Philosophical Papers, vol. 2 (Cambridge, UK: Cambridge University Press, 1985), from which the quote in the next paragraph is drawn.

35 See Robert N. Bellah, *Habits of the Heart: Individualism and Commitment in American Life*, 1st Calif. pbk., updated edition with a new introduction (Berkeley: University of California Press, 1996).

36 *The Fundamental Concepts of Metaphysics: World, Finitude, Solitude*, trans. by William Mcneill and Nicholas Walker (Bloomington: Indiana University Press, 1995), pp. 66–67.

37 I take the term "import" from Taylor, "Interpretation and Sciences of Man."

38 See "The Oxford English Dictionary," <*http://www.oed.com/*>, under the heading "disposed." My favorite citation of this use, use #2, is from Chaucer: "Thy breeth ful soure stynketh, That sheweth wel thou art nat wel disposed" (c 1400).

39 William N. Morris and Paula P. Schnurr, *Mood: The Frame of Mind* (New York: Springer-Verlag, 1989), p. 3.

40 Moods "inform us about our general state of being" and "are thought to be involved in the instigation of self-regulatory processes" (ibid., pp. 2–3). See the literature cited by Morris.

41 See PBS, "People Like Us," (2001).

42 *The Nicomachean Ethics of Aristotle*, trans. by W. D. Ross (London: Oxford University Press, 1963).

43 See Richard Rorty (ed.), *The Linguistic Turn: Recent Essays in Philosophical Method* (Chicago: University of Chicago Press, 1967)

44 See Kuhn, *Scientific Revolutions*.

45 John Dewey, "Does Reality Possess Practical Character?" in Jo Ann Boydston (ed.), *The Middle Works, 1899–1924*, vol. 4 (Carbondale, IL: Southern Illinois University Press, 1977), p. 130.

46 Anthony Giddens, *The Constitution of Society* (Berkeley: University of California Press, 1984), p. 84.

47 See *Hegel's Science of Logic*, trans. by Arnold V. Miller (Atlantic Highlands, NJ: Humanities Press International, 1989). For Heidegger's critique of Hegel, see *Hegel's Concept of Experience*, 1st ed. (New York: Harper & Row, 1970). For an influential contemporary account of the dynamics of making things explicit in this sense of the term, see Robert Brandom, *Articulating Reasons: An Introduction to Inferentialism* (Cambridge, MA: Harvard University Press, 2000).

48 And what he calls "a direction of fit," but we do not need to focus on that feature. See Searle, *Intentionality* (Cambridge, UK: Cambridge University Press, 1983), pp. 11–12.

49 Kant, *Critique of Pure Reason*, pp. A79/B104–105, B376–377, and §19 of the B-Deduction.

50 I consider these objections in my "Is Heidegger a Representationalist?" *Philosophical Topics*, 27 (1999).

51 The connection with the two different *as*'s was first suggested to me by Cristina Lafont during a discussion at a conference. For a version of the view I am rejecting, see Lafont, *Heidegger, Language,*

and World-Disclosure, trans. by Graham Harman (Cambridge, UK: Cambridge University Press, 2000).

52 This tracks Kant's distinction between the "undetermined object of an empirical intuition" (an appearance) and the determinate object of a judgment. Kant, *Critique of Pure Reason*, pp. A20/B34 and §19 of the B-Deduction.

53 Dewey, *Experience and Nature*, p. 134.

54 Wittgenstein, *Investigations*; Davidson, *Truth and Interpretation*; Wilfrid Sellars, "Empiricism and the Philosophy of Mind," in *Science, Perception and Reality* (Atascadero, CA: Ridgeview, 1991), and Hans-Georg Gadamer, *Truth and Method*, trans. by Garrett Barden and John Cumming (New York: Crossroad Publishing, 1975) (the quote is from p. 443).

55 Guignon, *Heidegger and Knowledge*, p. 125.

56 Thus, Macquarrie and Robinson's distinction between the verbs is too weak. I am grateful to Prof. James Lyon of the Brigham Young German Dept. for confirming this for me through an examination of the historical record.

57 The most influential modern model of communication along these lines is H. P. Grice, *Studies in the Way of Words* (Cambridge, MA: Harvard University Press, 1989).

58 Heidegger's analysis here is similar to Husserl's analysis of the "x" of the noema. See John J. Drummond, *Husserlian Intentionality and Nonfoundational Realism: Noema and Object* (Dordrecht: Kluwer Academic Publishers, 1990).

59 For Descartes, see "First Mediation." For an interesting and sophisticated discussion of skepticism, see Barry Stroud, *The Significance of Philosophical Scepticism* (Oxford: Oxford University Press, Clarendon Press, 1984).

60 Due to Hilary Putnam, I believe: see *Reason, Truth, and History* (Cambridge, UK: Cambridge University Press, 1983), ch. 1.

61 Kant, *Critique of Pure Reason*, p. Bxxxix.

62 See "Brief Studies in Realism," in Jo Ann Boydston (ed.), *The Middle Works, 1899–1924*, vol. 6 (Carbondale and Edwardsville: Southern Illinois University Press, 1978).

63 The analysis that follows is a simplified version of the argument presented in two of my published essays: "Is Heidegger a Kantian Idealist?" *Inquiry*, 37 (1994), and "Heidegger's Kantian Idealism Revisited," *Inquiry*, 47 (2004).

64 Macquarrie and Robinson write, "nor 'is' the 'in-itself.'" Heidegger does not use a definite article before "in-itself," because he is not trying to refer to *the* in-itself, that is, entities that exist in themselves, but rather to the *category* of the in-itself.

65 Which is precisely one way to look at Kuhn's Scientific Revolutions. For more on Heidegger's philosophy of science, see Joseph Rouse, *Knowledge and Power* (Ithaca: Cornell University Press, 1987).

66 I have analyzed this argument in considerable detail in *Heidegger's Temporal Idealism*.

67 *Metaphysics*, Book 4, 1001b25.

68 For a clear summary of Aristotle's psychology, see Christopher Shields, "Aristotle's Psychology," *Stanford Encyclopedia of Philosophy* (Winter 2005), Metaphysics Research Lab, Center for the Study of Language and Information <*http://plato.stanford.edu/entries/aristotle-psychology/*>, accessed Winter 2005.

69 The first quote is from the Third Meditation, the second from the Replies to the First Objections.

70 See *A Treatise Concerning the Principles of Human Knowledge* (Oxford: Oxford University Press, 1998).

71 "The Semantic Conception of Truth," *Philosophy and Phenomenological Research* 4 (1944).

72 E.g., Davidson, *Truth and Interpretation*.

73 See Okrent, *Heidegger's Pragmatism*.

74 For a clear discussion of this point, see Richard Rorty, *Contingency, Irony, and Solidarity* (Cambridge, UK: Cambridge University Press, 1989), ch. 1, "The Contingency of Language."

75 An argument originally advanced by Ernst Tugendhat, *Der Wahrheitsbegriff bei Husserl and Heidegger*, 2nd ed. (Berlin: de Gruyter, 1970).

76 See Fritz K. Ringer, *The Decline of the German Mandarins: the German Academic Community, 1890–1933* (Cambridge, MA: Harvard University Press, 1969).

77 Dreyfus, *Being-in-the-World*, p. 27.

78 Macquarrie and Robinson render the expression "*Weiter- und Nachredens*" as "gossiping and passing the world along." The German does not really connote gossip, however. In German other words are used to suggest gossip, such as "*Klatsch.*" Nonetheless, gossip is a specific form of idle talk.

79 Intrigued? Start here: Bruce B. Savare, *Reforming Sports before the Clock Runs Out: One Man's Journey through our Runaway sports Culture* (Delmar, NY: Bordlice Publishing, Sports Reform Press, 2004).

80 *American Beauty* (Dreamworks SKG, 1999), Sam Mendes (dir.).

81 Hubert L. Dreyfus and Stuart E. Dreyfus, *Mind over Machine* (New York: Free Press, 1986).

82 Fyodor Dostoyevsky, *Notes from Underground, White Nights, The Dream of a Ridiculous Man, and Selections from The House of the Dead*, trans. by Andrew Robert Macandrew (New York: Signet Classics, 1961), p. 103.

83 Fyodor Dostoyevsky, *The Brothers Karamazov*, Vintage Books ed., trans. by Constance Black Garnett (New York: Modern Library, Random House, 1950), p. 289.

84 This is clear both in his remarks on Kierkegaard (see, e.g., p. 494), as well as his consistent dismissal of what he called "world-view philosophy," as for example in the introduction to *Basic Problems*.

85 For example, in Jean-Paul Sartre, *Nausea*, trans. by Lloyd Alexander (New York: New Directions, 1964).

86 Dr. Tonmoy Sharma, of Maudsley Hospital, England, as quoted in Colin Brennan, "Anhedonia," <http://www.netdoctor.co.uk/special_reports/depression/anhedonia.htm>2005. I am grateful to Dr. Patrick

Kilcarr of the Georgetown University Center for Personal Development for drawing my attention to this concept during a presentation to one of my existentialism classes.

87 I am grateful to Charles Guignon for pushing me in this direction, although I do not think he agrees with my reading of §40.

88 Heidegger had first-hand experience with depression, and it is likely that he draws on those personal experiences in §40. See Rüdiger Safranski, *Martin Heidegger: Between Good and Evil*, trans. by Ewald Osers (Cambridge, MA: Harvard University Press, 1998).

89 Dostoyevsky, *Notes from Underground*, p. 104.

90 Taylor, *Ethics of Authenticity*, ch. 10.

91 See, e.g., Ernst Jünger, *The Storm of Steel: From the Diary of a German Storm-troop Officer on the Western Front* (New York: H. Fertig, 1975).

92 Søren Kierkegaard, *Fear and Trembling*, trans. by Alastair Hannay (New York: Penguin Books, 2003), p. 75.

93 James P. Carse, *Finite and Infinite Games* (New York: Free Press, 1986).

94 Indeed, in a footnote to II.1 (pp. 494–495, n. 6) Heidegger praises Jaspers's conception of limit-situations. For a discussion of the connection, see my "Heidegger's Debt to Jaspers's Concept of the Limit-Situation," in Alan M. Olson (ed.), *Heidegger and Jaspers* (Philadelphia: Temple University Press, 1994).

95 According to medicine.net, one in ten people will suffer depression during their lifetime (http://www.medicinenet.com/depression/page7.htm).

96 *Atlantic City* (Parmount Pictures, 1980), Louis Malle (dir.).

97 Delmore Schwartz, "Existentialism: The Inside Story," *The Ego is Always at the Wheel: Bagatelles* (New York: New Directions, 1986), p. 7. The quip is a direct response to Heidegger's ruminations on death. I am grateful to Drew Cross for introducing me to this quip.

98 This is portrayed painfully in *Off the Map*, in the scene in which Arlene (Joan Allen) begs Charley (Sam Elliott), who has barricaded himself in the outhouse, to get help (Manhattan Pictures International, 2003), Campbell Scott (dir.).

99 The word Macquarrie and Robinson render as "nullity," *Nichtigkeit*, could also be translated as "nothingness."

100 Macquarrie and Robinson render "Dasein" as "Dasein," but in this case it sounds better to render it as "existence."

101 Rebecca Kukla has developed a more sympathetic reconstruction of Heidegger's use of "conscience" and the influence that use has had on later thinkers, such as Derrida. See "The Ontology and Temporality of Conscience," *Continental Philosophy Review*, 35/1 (2002).

102 Nietzsche's clearest expression of these views can be found in his *On the Genealogy of Morals*, trans. by Walter Kaufmann (New York: Vintage, 1967).

103 See *Contingency, Irony, Solidarity*.

104 Hubert L. Dreyfus and Jane Rubin, "Kierkegaard, Division II, and Later Heidegger," which is the appendix to Dreyfus's *Being-in-the-World*.

105 For example, in his discussion of punishment in *Genealogy of Morals*.

106 John Stuart Mill, *On Liberty* (New York: Barnes & Noble, 2004).

107 Heidegger's German term is simply *"Augenblick,"* "moment" or "instant." Macquarrie and Robinson expand it to "moment of vision," both because they don't want the component *"Augen,"* "eye," to be lost in translation, and because they don't want the reader to think of moments in the sense of instants of clock-time. The *Augenblick* is the Biblical "twinkling of an eye," the moment of religious transformation.

CHAPTER 4

1 See *Existentialism and Humanism*, trans. by Philip Mairet (London: Methuen, 1948).

2 Kant, *Critique of Pure Reason*, p. A247/B303.

3 The transcript of the debate is translated along with other relevant material in *Kant and the Problem of Metaphysics*, 4th, enlarged ed., trans. by Richard Taft (Bloomington: Indiana University Press, 1990).

4 "What is Metaphysics?" in *Pathmarks*, p. 92.

5 Rudolf Carnap, "The Overcoming of Metaphysics through Logical Analysis of Language," in Michael Murray (ed.), *Heidegger and Modern Philosophy: Critical Essays* (New Haven: Yale University Press, 1978). See Friedman, *A Parting of the Ways*, for more detail on this history.

6 As an example, Paul Edwards, *Heidegger's Confusions* (Amherst, NY: Prometheus Books, 2004).

7 Joseph J. Kockelmans, *Martin Heidegger: A First Introduction to his Philosophy* (Pittsburgh: Duquesne University Press, 1965).

8 *Being and Time* also found its way into the English language through philosophers influenced by Sartre, such as Joseph P. Fell, *Heidegger and Sartre: An Essay on Being and Place* (New York: Columbia University Press, 1979) and later on, Frederick Olafson, *Heidegger and the Philosophy of Mind* (New Haven: Yale University Press, 1987).

9 Most prominently, Friedrich-Wilhelm von Herrmann, *Hermeneutische Phänomenologie des Daseins: eine Erläuterung von "Sein und Zeit"* (Frankfurt am Main: Vittorio Klostermann, 1987) and Otto Pöggeler, *Der Denkweg Martin Heideggers*, 2nd ed. (Pfullingen: Verlag Günther Neske, 1983), first published in 1963. For a more Anglo style of reading Heidegger in Germany, see Carl Friedrich Gethmann, *Dasein: Erkennen und Handeln* (Berlin: de Gruyter, 1993).

10 "Ontology, the *A Priori*, and the Primacy of Practice: An *Aporia* in Heidegger's Early Philosophy," in Steven Galt Crowell and Jeff Malpas (eds), *Heidegger and Transcendental Philosophy* (Palo Alto, CA: Stanford University Press, 2006).

11 Richard Schmitt, *Martin Heidegger on Being Human* (New York: Random House, 1969), arrived independently at Heidegger and drew some of the same lessons for our account of intelligence and the priority of practice.

FURTHER READING

Other Texts of Heidegger's from his Early Period

The Basic Problems of Phenomenology, trans. by Albert Hofstadter (Bloomington: Indiana University Press, 1982).

History of the Concept of Time: Prolegomena, trans. by Theodore Kisiel (Bloomington: Indiana University Press, 1985).

Phenomenological Interpretation of Kant's "Critique of Pure Reason," trans. by Parvis Emad and Kenneth Maly (Bloomington: Indiana University Press, 1997).

Kant and the Problem of Metaphysics, 4th, enlarged ed., trans. by Richard Taft (Bloomington: Indiana University Press, 1990).

The Fundamental Concepts of Metaphysics: World, Finitude, Solitude, trans. by William McNeill and Nicholas Walker (Bloomington: Indiana University Press, 1995).

"What is Metaphysics?" in William McNeill (ed.), *Pathmarks* (Cambridge, UK: Cambridge University Press, 1998), 82–96.

Recommended Secondary Texts on *Being and Time*

Blattner, William, *Heidegger's Temporal Idealism* (Cambridge, UK: Cambridge University Press, 1999).

Carman, Taylor, *Heidegger's Analytic* (Cambridge, UK: Cambridge University Press, 2003).

Dreyfus, Hubert L., *Being-in-the-World* (Cambridge, MA: Massachusetts Institute of Technology Press, 1991).

Gethmann, Carl Friedrich, *Dasein: Erkennen und Handeln* (Berlin: de Gruyter, 1993).

Guignon, Charles B., *Heidegger and the Problem of Knowledge* (Indianapolis: Hackett Publishing Co., 1983).

Haugeland, John, "Heidegger on Being a Person," *Noûs*, 16 (1982), 15–26.

—— "Dasein's Disclosedness," in Hubert L. Dreyfus and Harrison Hall (eds), *Heidegger: A Critical Reader* (Oxford: Basil Blackwell, 1992), 27–44.

Kukla, Rebecca, "The Ontology and Temporality of Conscience," *Continental Philosophy Review*, 35/1 (Mr 2002), 1–34.

Okrent, Mark, *Heidegger's Pragmatism* (Ithaca: Cornell University Press, 1988).

Olafson, Frederick, *Heidegger and the Philosophy of Mind* (New Haven: Yale University Press, 1987).

Rorty, Richard, *Essays on Heidegger and Others: Philosophical Papers, vol. 2* (Cambridge, UK: Cambridge University Press, 1991).

Schmitt, Richard, *Martin Heidegger on Being Human* (New York: Random House, 1969).

Tugendhat, Ernst, *Der Wahrheitsbegriff bei Husserl and Heidegger*, 2nd ed. (Berlin: de Gruyter, 1970).

Two Helpful Biographies of Heidegger

Safranski, Rüdiger, *Martin Heidegger: Between Good and Evil*, trans. by Ewald Osers (Cambridge, MA: Harvard University Press, 1998).

Ott, Hugo, *Martin Heidegger*, trans. by Allan Blunden (New York: Basic Books, 1993).

Further Recommended Literature on Heidegger and the Intellectual Context of *Being and Time*

Friedman, Michael, *A Parting of the Ways: Carnap, Cassirer, and Heidegger* (Chicago: Open Court, 2000).

Herf, Jeffrey, *Reactionary Modernism: Technology, Culture, and Politics in Weimar and the Third Reich* (Cambridge, UK: Cambridge University Press, 1984).

Ringer, Fritz K., *The Decline of the German Mandarins: the German Academic Community*, 1890–1933 (Cambridge, MA: Harvard University Press, 1969).

Sluga, Hans D., *Heidegger's Crisis : Philosophy and Politics in Nazi Germany* (Cambridge, MA: Harvard University Press, 1993).

Thomson, Iain, *Heidegger on Ontotheology: Technology and the Politics of Education* (Cambridge, UK: Cambridge University Press, 2005).

Historically Significant Philosophers Influenced by or Reacting to Heidegger

Carnap, Rudolf, "The Overcoming of Metaphysics through Logical Analysis of Language," in Michael Murray (ed.), *Heidegger and Modern Philosophy: Critical Essays* (New Haven: Yale University Press, 1978), 23–34.

Gadamer, Hans-Georg, *Truth and Method*, trans. by Garrett Barden and John Cumming (New York: Crossroad Publishing, 1975).

Merleau-Ponty, Maurice, *Phenomenology of Perception*, trans. by Colin Smith (London: Routledge & Kegan Paul, 1962).

Sartre, Jean-Paul, *Existentialism and Humanism*, trans. by Philip Mairet (London: Methuen, 1948).
—— *Being and Nothingness*, trans. by Hazel E. Barnes (New York: Washington Square Press, 1953).

Other Important Literature Cited in this Reader's Guide

Dreyfus, Hubert L., *What Computers Can't Do*, revised ed. (New York: Harper & Row, 1979).
Dreyfus, Hubert L. and Stuart E. Dreyfus, *Mind over Machine* (New York: Free Press, 1986).
Kuhn, Thomas, *The Structure of Scientific Revolutions*, 2nd, enlarged ed. (Chicago: University of Chicago Press, 1970).
Rorty, Richard, *Contingency, Irony, and Solidarity* (Cambridge, UK: Cambridge University Press, 1989).
Taylor, Charles, "Interpretation and the Sciences of Man," in *Philosophy and the Human Sciences: Philosophical Papers, vol. 2* (Cambridge, UK: Cambridge University Press, 1985), 15–57.
—— *Sources of the Self: The Making of the Modern Identity* (Cambridge, MA: Harvard University Press, 1989).
—— *The Ethics of Authenticity* (Cambridge, MA: Harvard University Press, 1992).

INDEX

191